MACROECONOMIC CONFLICT AND SOCIAL INSTITUTIONS

MACROECONOMIC CONFLICT AND SOCIAL INSTITUTIONS

Edited by
SHLOMO MAITAL
and
IRWIN LIPNOWSKI

BALLINGER PUBLISHING COMPANY
Cambridge, Massachusetts
A Subsidiary of Harper & Row, Publishers, Inc.

359207

International Standard Book Number: 0-88730-034-0

Library of Congress Catalog Card Number: 84-24376

Printed in the United States of America

Library of Congress Cataloging in Publication Data

Main entry under title:

Macroeconomic conflict and social institutions.

Chiefly papers originating from a session on
"Income policy as a social institution," at the American
Economic Association's 95th Annual Meeting in New York,
Dec. 28-30, 1982.
   Includes bibliographies and index.
   1. Income distribution—Addresses, essays, lectures.
2. Social institutions—Addresses, essays, lectures.
3. Institutional economics—Addresses, essays, lectures.
4. Macroeconomics—Addresses, essays, lectures.
I. Maital, Shlomo. II. Lipnowski, Irwin. III. American
Economic Association. Meeting (95th : 1982 : New York,
N.Y.) IV. Title: Macro-economic conflict and social
institutions.
HC79.I5M225   1985   339.2   84-24376
ISBN 0-88730-034-0

Contents

List of Figures

List of Tables

Acknowledgments

All the chapters in this book are previously unpublished. Five of them, Chapters 2–6, originated as papers or discussants' comments at a session on "Incomes Policy as a Social Institution," chaired by Albert Rees, at the American Economics Association's annual meeting in New York, December 28–30, 1982. Research for Chapters 2, 7 and 9 was partially supported by a grant from the Ford Foundation, through the Israel Foundations Trustees. The editors are indebted to Cynthia Benn for superlative copy editing.

Social Institutions in the Non-Zero-Sum Society

In a serious moment, and with just a touch of hyperbole, James Thurber once wrote that "it is better to ask some of the questions than know all of the answers." Conventional macroeconomics asks, What are the causal relations among money, output, employment, wages, prices, and public spending and revenue? Monetarism, Keynesianism, New Classical Economics, and supply-side economics each supply a full set of answers — but the sets contradict one another. The ten chapters of this book explore a different direction, not solely by challenging old answers, but principally by asking a different question. It is: How can we alter our social institutions in order to mitigate macroeconomic conflict and achieve a more just, stable, and efficient economy?

Social institutions are conventions or rules society evolves to deal with persistent, recurring problems. Some of the most important of these institutions determine the production and distribution of wealth. When economic wealth is wasted and unfairly shared, economists debate the proximate causes: tight money, government regulation, budget deficits, high taxes, or monopoly. But the first stage of the teleology of wealth — social institutions — is not often discussed or pondered. The reason for this is probably the Walrasian language used by modern economics to frame its thinking. General equilibrium models of price-auction markets *assume* particular social institutions from the outset, then go on to examine how utility-maximizing agents function within them. This approach gives economics — the logic of

1

choice — beauty and rigor. Logic, someone said, is the architecture of thought. Thought, like buildings or bridges, needs good architects in order to come out right. But architecture alone never built a happy dwelling, nor logic alone a useful policy. Macroeconomics needs redirection in two ways. First, the logic of choice has to be applied to theorizing about institutions, rather than assuming them, and second, it must be supplemented by close observation of past and present institutions, through history and in other societies. General equilibrium models emphasize the interdependence of *markets*. Institutional macroeconomics emphasizes the interdependence of *people*. As an early social psychologist, James Baldwin, said, "we are all members of one another," and it is this human interrelatedness that makes the national economy soar or stumble. Social institutions channel, regulate and modify these interpersonal links. Institutions, therefore, deserve center stage in macroeconomics.

GAMES AND INSTITUTIONS

How does one theorize about social institutions, particularly those that influence the national economy? Not everyone agrees there is need for such theorizing. Institutional economics, the only indigenous American school of economic thought, has tended to emphasize description. Though interesting and worthwhile, this has a major shortcoming. No descriptive science can aspire to persuasive prescription; in the absence of falsifiable models tested against reality, all prescriptions are dubious and heuristic.

A strong case can be made for using game theory to model social institutions; four chapters in this book do this explicitly. Game theory dissects what Thomas Schelling has called the "structure of behavior," and asks, What conventions are likely to emerge from it? In games, each participant's payoff depends partly on what other people do. This allows direct modeling of interdependence and the norms that regulate it. When the "rules of the game" prove destructive, one can use game theory to theorize about helpful ways to modify them. Concrete examples are found in Chapters 1, 2, and 4, where ways are discussed for extricating society from the social trap of Prisoner's Dilemma games. Another attraction of game theory is its usefulness in bridging the gap between microeconomics and macroeconomics, a gap most economists find intellectually displeasing.

By revealing how people impinge upon one another, game theory shows when, where, and why individually rational behavior leads to collectively disastrous outcomes—a paradox that seems to lie at the heart of macroeconomic failure. Ask of a parable not whether it is true, Robert Solow cautions, but whether it is well told. Game theory's parable of macroeconomic conflict is easy to tell well.

Good social institutions should ultimately drive out bad. Geoffrey Moore's studies reveal the global ubiquity and persistence of business cycles. He notes that since 1933, expansions have been more than four times as long as recessions, and the economy has been in recesson less than one year in five. Even though business cycles, like nostalgia, are not what they used to be, one wonders why institutions have not emerged to improve on that record. Moreover, the depth of the 1981–82 recession, with unemployment touching 1940 peaks, leaves little reason for sanguinity. Macroeconomic conflict seems to resolve itself as destructively today as it did in the late 1920s, when Keynes wrote about England's disastrous return to full convertibility of sterling, at pre–World War I exchange rates.

RETURN TO PAR

There are times when a fall in the price level (England, 1925) or a slowdown in the inflation rate (the United States, 1981) become social objectives. The least destructive way to manage this is for workers to accept lower wages (or lower rates of wage increase) and for businesses to charge lower prices (or lower rates of price increase). As Keynes wrote in 1929,

> If *everyone* was accepting a similar reduction [in wages] at the same time, the cost of living would fall, so that the lower money wage would represent nearly the same real wage as before. But, in fact, there is no machinery for effecting a simultaneous reduction. . . . Those who are attacked first are faced with a depression of their standard of life, because the cost of living will not fall until all the others have been successfully attacked too; and, therefore, they are justified in defending themselves. Nor can the classes which are first subjected to a reduction of money wages be guaranteed that this will be compensated later by a corresponding fall in the cost of living, and will not accrue to the benefit of some other class. Therefore they are bound to resist so long as they can; and it must be war, until those who are economically weakest are beaten to the ground.

"Our problem is to reduce money wages, and, through them, the cost of living," Keynes wrote, "with the idea that, when the circle is complete, real wages will be as high, or nearly as high, as before." In the mid-1920s, as in the mid-1980s, no machinery existed to do this. The main instrument chosen then, as now, was credit restriction. "By what modus operandi does credit restriction attain [its desired] result?" Keynes asked. His answer:

> In no other way than by the deliberate intensification of unemployment. The policy can only attain its end by intensifying unemployment without limit, until the workers are ready to accept the necessary reduction of money wages under the pressure of hard facts.... It is a policy from which any humane or judicious person must shrink. Deflation does not reduce wages "automatically." It reduces them by causing unemployment. The proper object of dear money is to check an incipient boom. Woe to those whose faith leads them to use it to aggravate a depression. ... It is a grave criticism of our way of managing our economic affairs that this should seem to anyone to be a reasonable proposal.

Keynes's words sound prophetic in the aftermath of the 1981–82 U.S. and world recession. The "institutional failure," in Clive Bull and Andrew Schotter's phrase (Chapter 4), that caused deflation and social distress in Keynes's day is still with us. Bad social institutions are as long-lived as the business cycles they aggravate. It appears that not only those who forget the past, but even those who *remember* it, are condemned to repeat it.

ECONOMETRIC EVIDENCE

"Can we not agree, therefore, to have a uniform initial reduction of money wages throughout the whole range of employment, including Government and Municipal employment, of (say) 5 per cent, which reduction shall not hold good unless, after an interval, it has been compensated by a fall in the cost of living?" Keynes asked, anticipating modern work on contingent contracts. Keynes felt this type of social contract might be "too difficult to achieve" and proposed instead a 5 percent devaluation. His proposal suggests a small research project not feasible in Keynes's day but simple in ours: to simulate the effects of a societywide social contract and to determine the payoff matrix in labor-versus-management games.

Ray Fair's quarterly econometric model of the U.S. economy was employed to predict the paths of inflation, unemployment, growth, and real wages for four different scenarios:

1. *Baseline.* Professor Fair's basic extrapolation of current U.S. fiscal and monetary policies to the end of 1986 shows a gradually slowing economic recovery, with inflation climbing from 4 percent in 1984 to 6 percent in 1986, and unemployment rates leveling off at around 7 percent.
2. *Wage Moderation.* Suppose organized labor were to adopt a unilateral policy of wage moderation, so that money wages rise at a constant 3 percent annual rate, instead of the 7–8 percent rate projected in the baseline forecast, while business raised prices at 4–6 percent yearly. How would labor and capital fare under this scenario?
3. *Price Moderation.* Suppose employers and managers agreed to hold price increases to 3 percent annually; at the same time, suppose labor demands and receives money wage increases of 6–7 percent annually. How would the economy perform?
4. *Social Contract.* Let both business and labor adopt moderate behavior, in wage and price decisions, so that both money wages and prices rise 3 percent per annum. Would everyone gain?

"Moderate" policies are assumed to begin in third quarter 1983.

Under scenario 1, wages and prices are determined endogenously. In scenario 2, prices are endogenous, but wages are assumed to be exogenous, rising at a constant 3 percent annual rate. In scenario 3, it is prices that are assumed to be determined exogenously, rising at 3 percent a year while wages are set endogenously. Finally, in scenario 4, both wages and prices are exogenous, increasing 3 percent yearly. Table 1 shows rates of changes for wages and prices, from 1983 fourth quarter through 1986 fourth quarter, for each of the four simulations.

The results of Table 1 can be arranged in the form of a 2×2 game matrix, with labor and business each choosing wage (price) moderation, or declining to do so. This matrix is shown in Table 2.

One way to understand the structure of macroeconomic conflict, as revealed in this econometric exercise, is to express inflation, unemployment, and other variables as functions of labor's and business's behaviors, and estimate the coefficients. Let L or $M = 0$ when labor and business, respectively, behave moderately, and L or $M = 1$ when

Table 1. Econometric Simulation of Wage and Price Behavior, for Four Scenarios, United States, 1983–1986.

Quarter	Baseline		Wage Moderation		Price Moderation		Social Contract	
	Wage Rise	Price Rise	Wage Rise	Price Rise	Wage Rise	Price Rise	Wage Rise	Price Rise
1983 IV	6.7%	4.1%	3.0%	4.0%	6.2%	3.0%	3.0%	3.0%
1984 I	7.0	4.5	3.0	4.3	6.3	3.0	3.0	3.0
II	7.2	4.9	3.0	4.4	6.3	3.0	3.0	3.0
III	7.4	5.2	3.0	4.6	6.4	3.0	3.0	3.0
IV	7.6	5.5	3.0	4.7	6.4	3.0	3.0	3.0
1985 I	7.8	5.7	3.0	4.7	6.4	3.0	3.0	3.0
II	7.9	5.9	3.0	4.7	6.5	3.0	3.0	3.0
III	8.0	6.1	3.0	4.7	6.6	3.0	3.0	3.0
IV	8.1	6.2	3.0	4.6	6.6	3.0	3.0	3.0
1986 I	8.1	6.3	3.0	4.6	6.6	3.0	3.0	3.0
II	8.1	6.3	3.0	4.5	6.7	3.0	3.0	3.0
III	8.1	6.3	3.0	4.4	6.7	3.0	3.0	3.0
IV	8.1	6.3	3.0	4.3	6.7	3.0	3.0	3.0

Note: Constructed with 130-equation econometric model of Fair (1974, 1976). Baseline: Wages and prices are determined endogenously. Wage moderation: Money wages rise at an annual rate of 3 percent (exogenous), while prices are determined endogenously. Price moderation: Prices of final goods rise 3 percent annually, while wage rises are determined endogenously. Social contract: Wages and prices both rise 3 percent annually.

Table 2.   Simulation of Wage and Price Moderation for
U.S. Economy, 1983 Third Quarter to 1986 Fourth Quarter.

		Business		
		No Price Moderation		Price Moderation
No Wage Moderation	π	6.4%	π	4.2%
	u	7.4%	u	5.8%
	$\dot{w}$	1.8%	$\dot{w}$	3.7%
	g	2.5%	g	1.9%
Wage Moderation	π	3.4%	π	3.1%
	u	6.0%	u	5.1%
	$\dot{w}$	−1.3%	$\dot{w}$	0.0%
	g	3.8%	g	2.75%

Note: π is the percentage rise in the gross national product deflator, annual rate, and g is the percentage rise in real GNP, annual rate, averaged for the four quarters of 1986; u is the unemployment rate at 1986 fourth quarter, and $\dot{w}$ is the percentage change in real wages, averaged for the four quarters of 1986.

they do not. Table 2 is consistent, then, with the following equations:

$$\pi = 3.1 + 1.1L + 0.3M + 1.9L \cdot M \qquad (1)$$

$$u = 5.1 + 0.7L + 0.9M + 0.7L \cdot M \qquad (2)$$

$$g = 2.75 + 0.85L + 1.05M - 0.45L \cdot M \qquad (3)$$

$$\dot{w} = 0 + 3.7L - 1.3M - 0.6L \cdot M \qquad (4)$$

where π is the percentage rise in the gross national product (GNP) deflator, annual rate; g is the percentage rise in real GNP, annual rate; and $\dot{w}$ is the percentage change in real wages — all averaged over the four quarters of 1986; and u is the rate of unemployment at 1986 fourth quarter.

All the coefficients have reasonable signs. As one might anticipate, wage and price immoderation has strong nonlinear effects in raising inflation and unemployment and in lowering the growth rate and increase in real wages. (Note that the relatively large constant terms in the first three equations indicate that there are important exogenous forces at work apart from what either labor or business do.)

To make the matrix a payoff matrix, of course, we would need to know the utility functions of labor and business. Experimentation with various types of reasonable functions suggests that Table 2 is not inconsistent with a variety of macroeconomic games described and discussed in this book, including Prisoner's Dilemma and Chicken. Whatever the game, it is apparent that both labor and business could gain if they jointly adopt moderate behavior. This is perhaps the chief lesson embodied by Table 2.

NON-ZERO-SUM INCREMENTS

While the precise type of macroeconomic game we are playing may be unclear, its non-zero-sum nature is not. This raises two fundamental questions:

1. Why has society been unable in the past to realize the large positive increments to jobs and output that accrue to cooperative behavior in these non-zero-sum games?
2. What social institutions would better enable us to do so in the future?

When he observed American democracy two centuries ago, de Tocqueville wrote that "in America, there are not only communal institutions but also a community spirit that supports and enlivens them." Whether communal institutions and community spirit have endured is debatable; but the vital need for them is not. If some agreed upon convention for pro-community behavior in markets could indeed make everyone better off, this suggests a kind of social contract among all parts of society. The most prevalent form of social contract is an incomes policy, where labor, management, and government bargain together in a manner that makes their goals mutually consistent and beneficial. Countries in Scandinavia and Western Europe all implement some form of incomes policy with reasonable success. As Jeffrey Miller and Jerrold Schneider note in Chapter 10, every Democratic administration and even one Republican administration has adopted some form of incomes policy, since World War II. Often, wage and price controls, a policy opposed by a large majority of economists, are a key part of incomes policy. Conservative thinker Irving Kristol has called such controls a "military solution to an economic problem." Several chapters in this book deal with social contracts and incomes policies. A new social contract proposed by the Liberal party in Canada initiated heated debate. Chapter 9 compares attitudes toward such a plan in Canada and the United States. David Colander, in Chapter 3, makes the point that an incomes policy, far from distorting resource allocation, may in fact help markets to work more efficiently. Although incomes policy is one example of a social institution designed to resolve macroeconomic conflict, it is by no means the only one. A wide variety of ways exists to alter macroeconomic games—by changing the rules, the games, or even the perceptions and goals of the players—and all deserve further exploration. As we note in Chapter 2, "the crux of an incomes policy . . . . is not necessarily a statutory freeze of wages and prices, but a mechanism for eliciting (temporary) sacrifices on the part of all players and maintaining pro-social behavior in the face of incentives to act egoistically." Paraphrasing William Baumol, the authors note that "incomes policy is a relation among people, rather than a relation among things."

PLAN OF THE BOOK

This book is divided into four sections. Part I, Macroeconomic Conflict and Market Failure, contains two related but different views on the nature of macroeconomic market failure. David C. Colander and Kenneth J. Koford propose, in Chapter 1, an "alternative new Keynesian general view," in which inflation growth and stabilization are seen as externalities (defined as the effect of one agent's behavior on another's well-being outside the normal workings of the price system). This approach, they believe, is broad enough "to encompass the analysis of all schools of macroeconomics," including the New Classical Economics (rational expectations). In contrast, in Chapter 2 Irwin Lipnowski and Shlomo Maital construct a game-theoretic model of macroeconomic conflict which is viewed as part of a new paradigm, one in which economic outcomes are the result of struggles among groups with varying degrees of power and information. This paradigm, it is argued, rivals, competes with, and contradicts standard Keynesian, monetarist, and New Classical economics. Macroeconomic conflict is interpreted as a series of games, one of which is the social trap known as the Prisoner's Dilemma. A lengthy appendix to the chapter analyzes alternate approaches toward resolving this pernicious form of externalities.

Part II of the book is titled "Incomes Policy: New Approaches." It contains four chapters that tackle an old idea, incomes policy, from new angles. David Colander's essay, Chapter 3, argues that incomes policy makes markets, especially labor markets, work better, not worse. If one believes there are asymmetries between people looking for jobs and those waiting for them, then these people serve society's interest as well as their own in holding down inflation by exerting downward pressure on wages. Colander concludes, in his model, that some proportion of steady-state unemployment serves a "reserve army" function which can "advantageously be reduced by an incomes policy." Clive Bull and Andrew Schotter present, in Chapter 4, a model of what they call "institutional failure," a "failure of the agents in the economy to create a proper type of institutional mechanism to successfully coordinate their activities." They model a contractionary shock, after which governments adopt a higher rate of growth of the money supply, not as a stupid mistake but as a "rational attempt to impose an equilibrium on the resulting contraction-avoidance game." The Shubik Garbage Game, where people dump inflation (garbage) on their neighbors' incomes policy, Bull and Schotter argue, can prove a superior solution. In Chapter 5, Paul Davidson offers a post-Keynesian viewpoint. He agrees that "what game theory does is to emphasize the need for social institutions to encourage cooperative civilized behavior, to protect agents from the terrorism of the laissez faire solution to utility maximization." But he rejects the 2×2 labor-versus-management game model. "In reality," Davidson writes, "the problem exists because there are more than two homogenous, mono-lithic groups. It is workers versus workers versus workers, or people versus people." He concludes by quoting Walt Kelley's paraphrase of Sophocles: "We have met the enemy and they is us!" Davidson sums up: "Rules for civilized behavior are where the answers to our most pressing economic problems lie," a sentence that captures the message of this whole book. The last essay in this part is written by Benjamin Bental. He uses the overlapping generations model to show that in-comes policy can be a result of rational maximization procedures. In his model the government proposes a "package deal" by which it "refrains from raising the inflation rate (through issuance of fiat money)" provided the private sector, made up of two competing groups, refrains from warring over shares of national income. Bental examines the circumstances under which such a package deal might work, and finds that for reasonable parameter values, incomes policy improves well-being, and hence "should be put forward for public debate whenever the occasion arises."

The two chapters in Part III, "Incomes Policy: New Structures," deal with new types of incomes policy. Chapter 7 models the tax-based incomes policy (TIP), in the "carrot" version of the late Arthur Okun, and the "stick" version of Henry Wallich and the late Sidney Weintraub, as the game of Chicken, a two-equilibrium game in which either labor or management acts moderately rather than face the collision course of joint extremism. The authors conclude that "while TIP may well prevent the confluent mutual disaster of immoderately large wage and price increases, neither is likely to achieve the desired goal of both moderate wage increases and moderate price increases." In Chapter 8, Steven Plaut devises a new form of incomes policy which he calls "reverse" incomes policy. In conventional incomes policy, Plaut notes, government "indexes" its revenue to wage and price increases in the private sector. In reverse incomes policy, labor and management index their prices and wages to the size of the government deficit. In effect, Plaut explains, "the producers and unions agree to a rule that will extract a heavier 'toll' from themselves" for inflation, and at the same time will impose a cost on government for monetary expansion. This is consistent with David Lewis's definition of social institution as a convention that is self-policed. "When judiciously formulated," Plaut concludes, "a reverse incomes policy will maintain market clearing, will increase the 'cost' to the government of printing money, and will be self-enforcing for all parties."

The final part is titled "Perceptions and Politics." Shlomo Maital and Noah Meltz report, in Chapter 9, on a comparative survey of Canadian and American labor and corporate leaders' attitudes toward a social-contract incomes policy. They conclude that "there are greater prospects of achieving a social contract in Canada than in the United States," noting that in the United States, management appears to be adamantly opposed. In the concluding chapter, Miller and Schneider focus not on institutional aspects of *implementing* an incomes policy, but on institutional arrangements to *design* an effective one. "For good or for ill," they observe, "politicians, not economists, will ultimately decide which economic policies are put in place." They analyze political obstacles to the proper design of an incomes policy, and express the fear that "the next effort [at implementing an incomes policy] will be an exercise in ad hocery in response to a crisis, because of inadequate policy development prior to the time when the policy must be used."

CONCLUSION

Orangutans live as hermits. Zoologists have theorized this is so because their huge size would make foraging for food in groups, cooperatively, inefficient. Unlike them, human beings choose to live and work in groups, small and large. Given this choice, individualistic "orangutan" behavior is not efficient, and cooperative behavior is necessary. Behaving like orangutans while living in human society is self-defeating, a lesson history repeatedly teaches us, its forgetful and stubborn pupils.

Thomas Schelling once noted that sled dogs cannot function until they establish a clear hierarchy. This is achieved only after each dog fights every other dog. The number of fights required increases approximately as the square of the number of dogs. Human society — both individuals and whole nations — at times seem ready to embrace the sled dog institution. It may be workable for huskies, but is somewhat unsatisfactory for humans. There must be a better way.

Albert Hirschman recently wrote that "love, benevolence and civic spirit...atrophy when not adequately practiced and appealed to by the ruling socioeconomic regime." Yet, cautioned Hirschman, they "will once again make themselves scarce when preached and relied on to excess." His wise words highlight and clarify the challenge facing institutional macroeconomics: to design new conventions that will mine deep veins of community spirit and altruism, and make them into habits, without dangerously depleting them. In a 1973 interview Milton Friedman said, "The problem of social organization is how to set up an arrangement under which greed will do the least harm." Perhaps there is an alternative view of society. Let us define the problem of social organization as designing institutions that make mutual benevolence individually rational (which, at times, it is not) as well as socially optimal (which it always is). A Hebrew adage, suitably modified, says that wise societies avoid tight spots that clever societies can escape from. Cleverness preserves social institutions; wisdom builds and ameliorates them.

REFERENCES

Fair, Ray. 1974, 1976. *A Model of Macroeconomic Activity,* vols. 1, 2. Cambridge, Mass.: Ballinger.

Hirschman, Albert O. 1984. "Against Parsimony: Three Easy Ways of Complicating Some Categories of Economic Discourse." *American Economic Review,* May:89–96.

Keynes, John Maynard. 1929. "The Economic Consequences of Mr. Churchill" (1925). In *Essays in Persuasion.* London: MacMillan.

Moore, Geoffrey H., and Victor Zarnowitz. 1984. "The Development and Role of the National Bureau's Business Cycle Chronologies." National Bureau of Economic Research Working Paper no. 1394, July.

PART I

MACROECONOMIC CONFLICT AND MARKET FAILURE

Chapter 1

Externalities and Macroeconomic Policy

David C. Colander and Kenneth J. Koford

One of the main reasons for the New Classical Economic's great impact on macroeconomics is the strong laissez faire policy conclusions implied by its early models (Lucas 1981, Sargent and Wallace 1976). These strong conclusions have recently been whittled away by a variety of models that include the rational expectations hypothesis (REH), but in place of market-clearing allow for overlapping contracts, multiple equilibria, and true uncertainty. These models, while maintaining the rational expectations assumption, leave room for government stabilization policy by assuming that private markets are less than perfect.[1]

Despite the development of REH models leading to activist policy conclusions, the connection between laissez faire policy and rational expectations remains strong. The reason, we believe, is the rhetorical framework within which the New Classical Economics places the macroeconomic debate. It begins with a framework of perfectly functioning markets and comes to the unsurprising conclusion that, given these perfectly functioning markets, there is no macroeconomic problem.[2] All models that do not come to this conclusion must rely on some type of ad hoc assumption about imperfectly functioning markets.

While advocates of the New Classical Economics agree that their assumption of continuous market-clearing is itself ad hoc, they argue that since it is assumed in almost all neoclassical work, it seems only reasonable to assume it in macroeconomics. Thus, they argue, their assumption, since it is the same ad hoc assumption used in microeconomics, is somehow less ad hoc and provides a microfoundation for its policy conclusions. For example, in an article discussing New Classical Economics in *Fortune* magazine (Guzzardo 1978), Robert Lucas is quoted as saying about Keynesian macroeconomic models: "The flaws are fatal. This condition cannot be remedied by modification." The article goes on to discuss the policies that follow from the new classical models, describing Lucas's view as follows:

> Lucas declares that the profession cannot really assess the consequences of policy unless they are free of surprises, and innocent of all efforts to make those short-term adjustments that people defeat by their intelligent anticipations. Therefore, Lucas prefers the establishment of declared and permanent rules. He says that we should, for example, fix an annual rate of growth for the money supply and stick with it. And we should set tax rates that would on average balance the budget.

The New Classical Economic models stand in marked contrast to the typical Keynesian model, which makes little or no attempt to formulate a microeconomic foundation. Keynesian models, even those framed in a REH framework such as the new Keynesian models of Phelps and Taylor (1977) and Stanley Fischer (1977) or the disequilibrium models of Malinvaud (1977) and Benassy (1982), generally focus on specific assumptions that vary from the standard rational expectations market-clearing model. They rationalize the assumptions that create a potentially activist role as being empirically valid, but they do not really ground them in a full choice-theoretic analysis. This leads New Classical theorists to criticize these models as ad hoc. They question whether the assumptions made by Keynesians are consistent with profit-maximization by all economic agents, particularly the creation of efficient contracts and institutions that would eliminate the "inefficient" rigidities assumed by the new Keynesians. The fixed-price models of Benassy or Malinvaud are possible examples of such "inefficient" rigidities. In defending such a model against a Lucas-type criticism, Peter Neary (1982) responded:

> Whenever I am asked, "Who sets prices?" in such a model, I am tempted to reply facetiously that prices are set by—a little green man! This is no ordinary little green man, however, but the same one who in many other models moves prices costlessly and instantaneously to their Walrasian or market-clearing levels, except that he is on an off day! In other words, I know of no macromodel which provides a satisfactory choice-theoretic basis for its assumptions about price determination.

While Neary's argument is logically correct, there is clearly an historical, artistic, or emotional bias in favor of the Walrasian little green
man even though the process by which a Walrasian economy reaches
equilibrium has never been specified successfully (Fisher 1983). Consistent ad hocery is simply more pleasing that ad hoc adhocery.[3]

Without a general world view that holds the various models
together, the Keynesian models, even those framed in the rational
expectations mold, remain an ad hoc guerilla group, unable to stand
up to the new classical Wehrmacht. Put simply, the New Classical
Economics approach provides a complete world view of the macroeconomy, whereas the new-Keynesian literature has been placed in a
position of making specific arguments against particular assumptions
and models. Each individual model has its adherents, but, for lack of
an organizing world view tying those various models together, that
work does not sum up to a strong alternative; Lucas, Barro, and
other New Classical Economics adherents can reject each of them as
ad hoc.

In this chapter we propose an alternate New Keynesian general
view of the macroeconomy that encompasses a wide range of models
that come to activist policy conclusions. After presenting that general
concept and relating it to the current literature, we examine activist
policy proposals in a historical perspective, suggesting that Keynes
and many Keynesian interpreters had this general conception of the
microfoundations of macroeconomics in mind. Finally, we consider
some new policy proposals that follow from our approach, arguing
that not only is the new approach a useful method of structuring one's
thinking about macroeconomics, but it is also a useful way of formu-
lating new approaches to macroeconomic policy.

The view that we present can be called the "externality" approach to
macroeconomics; it suggests that to the extent that inflation, growth,
and stabilization are problems, they are best viewed as externalities.
The externality approach is sufficiently broad to encompass the analysis of all schools of macroeconomics. We argue that there are few,
if any, fundamental differences between the New Classical and New
Keynesian schools of macroeconomics; the differences are empirical
ones about the relative speeds of market adjustment and the effectiveness of policy in a democratic society, questions about which reasonable people may differ. Opposed modeling strategies have overstated
the theoretical differences. The New Classicals add subtly efficient
market structures and intertemporal optimization while New Keynesians add socially inefficient (but privately efficient) institutional rigidi-

ties or informational problems. But the empirical reality each describes is much the same.

The advantage of the externality approach is its breadth; it transforms the macroeconomic debate from a debate over analytic first principles to a debate over models of specific institutions, making communication between the two schools easier. The need for such a refocus was seen in a recent book of interviews with a variety of top macroeconomists (Klamer 1984). These interviews demonstrated that there were few theoretical differences between Keynesians and proponents of New Classical Economics. Nonetheless, Klamer found a major "failure to communicate" between the two schools, with each ascribing rigidly contrary conceptions to the other camp. By describing these theoretical conceptions in a deeper theoretical structure as externalities, one makes the nature of the policy disputes between new Keynesians and New Classical Economists become clearer.

One's choice of assumptions in turn, reflects one's ideology and one's evaluation of society's ability to devise new ways of adjusting for those externalities. Adherents of New Classical Economics and Keynesianism differ on these judgments, but need not differ in their underlying modeling techniques. Thus, the relevant debate is not about the assumption of rationality. The relevant debate concerns the distinction between individual rationality and collective rationality.

THE CONCEPT OF MACROECONOMIC EXTERNALITIES

An externality may be defined as an effect of a decision which has no private cost or benefit associated with it, so that a utility-maximizing economic agent does not take the effect into account. That definition, while technically correct, is so broad that it transforms almost every action into one involving an externality, since almost all activities have external consequences. For example, if a man wears a bright green suit, it might offend others and hence create an externality. Similarly, if an individual changes his demand for a good, distributional effects may be imposed on others. But as Charles Wolfe (1979) and Carl Dahlman (1979) have argued, in actual use the concept of externality is limited to those external effects that one believes can be advantageously internalized. Used in this manner, the concept of externality presumes that the externality can and should somehow be adjusted for or internalized.

There are numerous methods of internalizing externalities; the question is whether any of these is cost effective. The New Classical Economic's view follows the Chicago school—they have yet to discover an empirically relevant externality, outside of government actions—while the New Keynesians believe macroexternalities are empirically important.

The discussion of externality has always been considered a microeconomic issue, and within microeconomics externalities have been used to justify a diverse range of governmental policies. Externalities have not been used to justify macroeconomic policy. Most Keynesian economists saw no need to establish a choice-theoretic justification for governmental macroeconomic policies. They built the need for the policies into the models' assumptions. The rational expectations revolution has changed that and has thereby necessitated a specific formulation of the choice-theoretic justification for government action—hence the need for a reformulation of the general Keynesian position.

TWO MACROECONOMIC EXTERNALITIES

Macroeconomic externalities can take many different forms, but two are crucial: an inflation or a price level stability externality and a spending externality. Calling something an "externality" implies that some potential market has failed to develop. Thus, to call price level stability and spending an externality, one must be able to specify, at least in theory, precisely how the externality comes about and what market has failed to develop. Moreover, one should be able to explain how the introduction of a market to internalize that externality will improve the workings of the economy. It is to those issues that we now turn.

On the surface, justifying externalities seems easy. There is no market in guarantees of price level stability, so that no individual takes into account the costs to others of the individual's inflation-causing actions. Similarly there is no market in guarantees of stability of aggregate spending, so that no one directly takes into account the effects of one's decisions on aggregate spending and hence on the demand of other individuals. It would seem simple to argue that because these markets do not exist, economies experience greater than optimal fluctuations in income and operate at a lower level of resource utilization than is optimal.

However, such superficial claims are in direct contradiction to the well-known proposition that if there is instantaneous price adjustment and a complete set of markets, an economy will achieve a Pareto-optimal outcome. Since the complete set of markets does not include the markets we are claiming to be missing, there seems to be a contradiction. But there is none. Real world markets do not include — indeed, cannot include — instantaneous price flexibility. The proposition that a perfectly competitive economy is Pareto-efficient holds only for a barter economy, with complete and perfect markets in current and future goods and with costless credit. It does not hold for a monetary economy.

Keynesians emphasize the monetary nature of the economy. Clower (1967) expressed this view nicely when he argued that "Money buys goods and goods buy money but goods do not buy goods." To capture this aspect of the economic system any macroeconomic model must include constraints that require that all purchases be made with money. The use of money and a financial or credit system are themselves public goods that make an economy more efficient. But, as Abba Lerner (1952) argued long ago, instantaneous price flexibility and the resulting distributional fluctuations would destroy the financial system.

The Keynesian position is thus that instantaneous price flexibility imposes a negative externality on an economy. Because it does, societies develop institutions that limit the effect of that negative externality. Thus, while with perfect price flexibility, an economy might have full employment, it would have an extremely low level of output, and real income would be far lower than in a monetary economy, even one with less than full employment.

Money and the financial system make the system far more productive but also introduce the possibility of a less than full employment equilibrium because those social institutions that private individuals create (such as collective bargaining and implicit contracts) are not necessarily the socially optimal ones. The reason is simple: Individuals consider only their private, not the public, benefit. In principle, these externalities could be internalized through private negotiation. But, for these subtle economywide externalities, defining and internalizing the relevant good is very difficult (see Anderson and Hill 1983). Therefore, the government may be the only or at least the most efficient way to provide the public good. What this means is that the assumption of individual profit maximization is insufficient to guarantee the efficient internalization of externalities. High private contracting and transactions costs may well make government the lowest cost provider of both stabilization and price level stability. It is in such a real world economy that macroexternalities exist and can be usefully offset.

Having dealt with why macroexternalities can exist, we now consider them more carefully and relate them to various schools of Keynesian macroeconomic thought.

THE SPENDING EXTERNALITY

The key to the spending externality approach was captured by Abba Lerner back in 1960 when he wrote:

> a small buyer may neglect the effects on income of his decisions to spend or not to spend. Although someone else's income must be reduced by a dollar when he spends a dollar less, he is not concerned with this. It will have no discernible effect on his own income. . . . If the group [comprising a quarter of the economy] wants to increase its saving by a dollar and expects to achieve this by consuming a dollar less, it will be disappointed. Its income will fall by a quarter so that its saving will increase by only 75 cents. If a group consisting of half of the economy tries to save a dollar by consuming a dollar less, it will find itself saving only 50 cents. And finally, if we take the group that is the economy as a whole, we find that when it spends a dollar less, its income falls by the whole dollar and there is no increase in saving at all. The repercussion which could be entirely neglected for a small seller has now, in the other limiting case, become absolute. This is because there is now nobody else to absorb any part of the repercussion.
>
> It is the inability of many to pay attention to the repercussions that leads them to balk at the bridge from "micro" to "macro" and to insist on the "self-evidence" of the proposition that a cut in prices would cure a depression, because a cut in the price charged by a small seller increases his sales.

Price stability is needed not only on an aggregate level; it is also needed on an individual level. Because it is needed, we find that individuals establish implicit and explicit contracts that create the necessary stable environment from their individual level. However, those individual contracts do not necessarily provide the optimal level of aggregate nominal income stability, and to the degree that they do not, stability is an externality. Notice that the issue here is not whether prices are fixed or flexible—at issue is whether there are social by-products of either. Keynesians argue that there are important particular third-party by-products of both flexible and inflexible prices. Society develops institutions to limit the negative effects of the former but in doing so creates a "spending" externality not taken into account by individuals when they make individual contracts.

This income interdependence makes the aggregate supply and demand curves highly unstable. The amount people will rationally decide to produce depends on the amount they expect others to be buying and vice-versa. If people, on average, expect demand to be low, it will be low; if they expect demand to be high, it will be high. Thus, aggregate expectations tend to have a self-fulfilling aspect that can lead to significant fluctuations in income. In such a framework, people's view of the future is a game-theoretic exercise and no single "rational expectation" exists. Formulated in such a game-theoretic framework, the relevant question for macroeconomics is stood on end. The question is not: Why is there instability; the question is: Why is there stability?

An answer to that question can be found in Axel Leijonhufvud's work (1981). Early on, Leijonhufvud recognized this interdependence and provided an explanation of why reasonable income stability exists. Leijonhufvud argued that generally there is a consistent monetary regime, and that within a regime expectations tend to be self-correcting. For instance, if spending falls and the monetary regime is considered stable, most people believe that the cycle will reverse itself and that spending will consequently rise. As they modify their expectations, income rises. Similarly, as a boom continues within a stable monetary regime, more people believe that boom must end, and as they do, it ends. Such self-correcting expectations, however, only operate within what Leijonhufvud calls the "corridor." Outside the corridor, expectations are not self-correcting and the economy can become stuck at an under full employment equilibrium.

Fluctuations themselves are not the externality; the externality is in the excessive amplitude of those fluctuations. The spending externality magnifies any aggregate shock into one that is greater than socially optimal; Keynes's simple multiplier analysis neatly captures this externality. As entrepreneurs' expectations of real demand fall, they reduce real aggregate supply, which further reduces aggregate real demand. Keynes argued that aggregate demand would fall by only a portion (the marginal propensity to consume) of the fall in aggregate supply. But each fall in aggregate demand would bring a further fall in aggregate supply and thus a small random deviation between aggregate supply and demand would cause a large swing in income. The externality is the magnification of the random fluctuation by a multiple of the actual white noise.

The foregoing story is, of course, an old Keynesian story. The externality approach formalizes such outcomes with choice-theoretic foundations. The dynamic disequilibrium approach to macroeconomics proposed by Clower (1965), developed in a preliminary manner in Barro and Grossman (1976) and extended in Grandmont and Younes (1972), Malinvaud (1977), Benassy (1982), and Grandmont (1983), captures this same externality more precisely.

These models still appear somewhat incomplete, but they have established the model as a tractable and general model of market disequilibrium. Benassy (1982) relaxes the neoclassical assumption that market participants can buy or sell all that they want at the market price. When firms face restrictions on the amount that they may buy or sell, market disequilibrium cannot correct itself quickly or evenly. A disequilibrium tends to feed upon itself, for a time, with adjustments to prices being outweighed by adjustments to output. A new disequilibrium in one market tends to affect related markets, placing them in disequilibrium. If one market then gradually returns toward equilibrium, other markets tend to be thrown (further) into disequilibrium by that market's adjustments. The failing in these models was not that they could not demonstrate the multiplier; their problem was in grounding the initial rigidity in a meaningful way. Recent work has grounded it much better. John Bryant (1983) has produced a similar model in which communication among producers is impossible. The resulting incomplete information creates multiple equilibria and an inability to characterize a unique "rational" expectation. Similar models are developed in Frydman and Phelps (1983).

Taking a slightly different tack, Grandmont (1983) develops a financially based disequilibrium model. Money is held to engage in trade. Changes in individual prices affect individual traders' assets and demands. In a temporary general equilibrium framework, it turns out to be difficult to assure a short-run Walrasian equilibrium and, under some conditions, a long-run Walrasian general equilibrium.[4]

The source of the problem in the dynamic disequilibrium models is simple: in markets, prices are the signals that help the market find equilibrium. After firms make price offers, trading occurs until one side has made all of the trades it wants. If both sides make all of the trades they wish, there is equilibrium. If one side has excess supply, or the other side excess demand, that is known. But the magnitude of the excess, and thus the magnitude of the disequilibrium, is not known. The absence of signals of the size of the disequilibrium keeps that market, and other markets, from adjusting quickly to end the disequilibrium.

The models of Phelps and Taylor (1977) and of Stanley Fischer (1977) provide another type of cyclical externality. In these models, workers and/or firms establish contracts that are individually optimal, but are not necessarily collectively optimal. The contracts increase stability for the parties to the contract but in doing so they often increase instability for the rest of the economy. This difference between individually rational and collectively rational price stability leads to cyclical swings that can be greater than optimal. The spending externality magnifies the amplitude of white noise, increasing the severity of fluctuations above the socially desirable level.

Yet another type of externality has been emphasized by Stiglitz (1984), who argues that prices serve as signals of quality for individuals. Firms offer high wages to attract high-quality workers; banks offer low interest rates to attract high-quality borrowers. More generally, agents offer "good deals" to potential contractual partners. Typically, in these models a queue of potential partners develops and the agent chooses the best prospects with whom to make contracts. Alternatively, in George Akerlof's approach (1982), workers believe in an exchange of fair value, and produce more when offered a high wage.

When prices or wages are used to obtain high-quality partners, markets do not clear in any traditional sense. Price or wage adjustment, in response to changing external conditions, disrupts the existing contracts. Since there is no independent external price or wage that agents can observe, it is almost impossible to determine what the appropriate adjustment might be. The spending externality in these models is similar to the previous models of price and wage rigidity: Creating stability within a single contract accentuates the adjustments that others must make in response to demand and cost shocks. Similarly, Martin Weitzman (1984) argues that an externality exists in the nature of the wage-setting institutions. Individuals negotiate for more wage stability than is socially optimal, creating output instability.

A fourth externality occurs in models in which market participants engage in rational search. For example, workers search for jobs and consumers search for desirable products. Such models are developed by Steven Salop (1979) and Christopher Pissarides (1984). Others are reviewed in Jackman, Layard, and Pissarides (1984). In all these models the total amount of search affects the distribution of wages and prices that prevails in the market, as well as the ability of the typical searcher to find a desired job or product. The first effect is a positive externality; one's careful search for a high-wage job forces producers to offer a higher average wage and a narrower distribution of wage offers. Successful search reduces the probability that others' search will be successful. While these externalities tend to offset each other, Pissarides (1984) argues that the negative externality is the largest and that there is too little search effort and that for fairly general assumptions, the equilibrium rate of unemployment is likely to be too high.

The spending externality view and its historical antecedents have recently been discussed by Meir Kohn (1981a,b, 1984). Emphasizing the monetary nature of the economy, Kohn argues that individuals face a finance constraint that can make it impossible for them to buy goods, even if in their long-run wealth maximization decision they would like to do so. The very real cash flow problems of firms and individuals are good examples. Kohn relates this finance constraint to the work of D.H. Robertson. (See also Leijonhufvud 1968, Paul Davidson 1977, and Presley 1983–84, who point out that Keynes was within a neoclassical monetary tradition.) Keynes's contribution, Kohn argues, was to develop a simple model that captured the essence of that work. But the model did so only by taking time out of the analysis. The REH revolution placed the analysis in time once again and, as it did so, necessitated a reintroduction of the finance constraint. Kohn (1981b) demonstrates that the IS/LM model captures one specific type of finance constraint equilibrium and that others are possible. He further demonstrates that the IS/LM model relies on fixed wages but that the source of the externality—the failure of a price to adjust—could also be in the capital market. (See also Leijonhufvud 1981, Ackley 1983, and Kohn 1983.) In such a model interest rate speculation causes fluctuations in the "tightness" of the aggregate finance constraint, fluctuations that have a social, but not a private, cost. Activist monetary policy is called for in such a model, even assuming all individuals have rational expectations.

The spending externality has two components: first, an explanation of why prices do not adjust to market clearing prices; and second, a multiplier aspect that makes the spending fluctuation larger than it would otherwise be. It is this second aspect that can be reduced by government aggregate demand policy.

As we stated previously, an externality can in principle be internalized by creating a new market. One such proposal to do so is the Hazlett–Hart money pump, where whenever a firm fires an individual, it must sell a contract to another firm that guarantees that it will hire an individual (Hazlett 1957, Hart 1957). Under such a proposal employment can be fully stabilized. Alternatively, spending fluctuations could be corrected by a "balance wheel" monetary and fiscal stabilization policy. As long as this stabilization policy is not consistently biased, and is merely a reaction to random shocks, it is itself random and it does not provide information as to future government policy. Thus it can be fully consistent with rational expectations (Colander 1979, Colander and Guthrie 1980–81).

Any stabilization role must follow from the government's comparative advantage in stabilizing. Individuals could contract with one another to achieve optimal "stability" if there existed a complete set of "contingent futures markets" in output or employment guarantees as exists in the Arrow–Debreu model. The government stabilization role derives from the absence of this market. An alternative way of reducing the externality is to increase the price and wage flexibility of present institutions. Weitzman's (1984) proposal for the share economy is one such approach.

PRICE LEVEL AND STABILITY
EXTERNALITIES

Above we argued that there were two macroexternalities that are central to the Keynesian position: the spending externality and a price level stability externality. The spending externality originates with the price being at a non–market-clearing level and it magnifies the resulting income fluctuations, making them greater than optimal. There is, however, no immediate reason why income should be too high or too low. However, if markets were competitive in the long run, income would tend to be too low. This follows from the previously mentioned observation that in capitalist economies the short side of the market prevails.[5] Therefore spending fluctuations are magnified only by downward demand shocks. On the up side, there would be shortages, since suppliers cannot be forced to supply. In a competitive capitalist economy, output above "full employment" is impossible.

In real world economies, output above long-run sustainable rates occurs for significant periods of time. Unless suppliers were continually fooled about the relative price they were receiving, a position neo-Keynesians reject, such would not be the case. It does occur and that suggests that the average level of resource utilization in capitalist economies is below the full-employment level. To explain this, neo-Keynesians need to rely upon a second externality that explains why steady-state levels of resource utilization are below supply-demand equilibrium levels.

Discussion of this externality appropriately abstracts from the "cyclical" externalities and assumes that a unique equilibrium is arrived at. As in the New Classical models, at this equilibrium, buyers and sellers search optimally on an individual basis. But unlike the New Classical models, New Keynesian models question whether that search is socially optimal. There are two reasons why it is not, both of which rely on asymmetries. The two are asymmetric information and asymmetric formation of coalitions.

The informational asymmetry is tied to the producer-set prices that predominate in our economy. Other market organizations react to those prices. The reason is found in the basic technology of the economy. Individuals, including firms, derive their income from just a few sources, while purchasing a much larger number of goods and services. Since auction markets require very high set-up costs, it is cheaper to have many "partial markets" controlled by either the buyer or the seller. Because it is less costly for the seller to fulfill this role, seller-set prices predominate (Stigler 1962).

At a competitive equilibrium, it is irrelevant who sets the price, since supply must equal demand, but when sellers set prices in disequilibrium, they have the power to set prices to benefit themselves. They have temporary monopoly power causing asymmetric price adjustment and causing on average, over several business cycles and over a variety of markets, a steady-state degree of monopoly. This monopoly imparts an upward bias to prices that must be offset with excess supply in order to maintain steady-state equilibrium. Individuals who set prices naturally accumulate information about those prices. As new information becomes available, the seller adjusts prices.

Information about an increase or decrease in demand which is generally available to all sellers will lead each individual seller to raise or lower the offer price to maintain a competitive position. Similarly, seller-specific information about a general increase in demand which is not thought by the seller to be generally available will lead to a rise in price.

The asymmetry occurs because the converse of this is not true. Seller-specific information about a decrease in demand will not lead a seller in a competitive market to lower the price, since all output can still be sold. The seller is better off waiting until others lower prices since he can enjoy monopoly rent in the meantime. Examples of this asymmetry may be found in Scitovsky (1979). Similar arguments of an asymmetry based upon intertemporal substitution are in Reagan and Weitzman (1982) and Colander and Gigliatti (1978). Given inventories, firms avoid cutting prices when demand falls. Since negative inventories are impossible, high demand leads to price increases. If this argument is true, the laws of supply and demand in markets in which sellers set price are likely to be biased, with downward price adjustment slower than upward price adjustment. A common phenomenon provides an analogy to this argument. Supermarkets inevitably find cash shortages at the average check-out counter. The reason is that customers consistently return and correct mistakes made in the store's favor but are less fastidious in correcting mistakes made in their favor. The result is a steady-state loss of receipts; to correct for that expected loss, the posted price must be above the supply-demand price. This dynamic adjustment asymmetry affects the steady-state equilibrium, since in equilibrium the asymmetry must be offset by underutilized resources and unemployment, which impart an offsetting downward pressure on the price level.

Peter Diamond (1983) provides a slightly different perspective on this same theme of information. He argues that the externality results because trading is more costly the thinner the market. As more trading activity develops on one side of the market, costs go down for the other side. Because individuals do not take such costs into account, expectations of low levels of economic activity can lead to low trading, which can fulfill the original expectation. Peter Howitt and R. Preston McAfee (1983) have pointed out that there is also an externality diseconomy associated with search. As one firm recruits more actively, it increases the costs of recruiting for others. Multiple equilibria again result, with the resulting possibilities of nonoptimal fluctuations in income.

A second explanation of why the price level is too high does not involve dynamic monopolies; it involves the formation of coalitions and other noncompetitive market structures to prevent competitive outcomes. The argument as stated in Colander and Olson (1984) is that there is an asymmetric cost of building coalitions so that supplier coalitions predominate in our economy. As suppliers build coalitions, they both raise price and limit entry into their market by blocking mutually advantageous trades between demanders and unemployed suppliers. (Such coalitions are often built into the fabric of society [Akerlof 1982].) An equilibrium finally occurs because the more trades the coalition blocks, the higher the costs of blocking further trades. In this case the creation of coalitions is the externality, because the harm of the barriers to entry on excluded individuals is not taken into account.

The recourse of the demanders and blocked suppliers is through the political process. They can vote for politicians who will expand aggregate output. Colander and Olson (1984) argue that because coalitions can only adjust their price slowly without destroying the coalition, expanding aggregate nominal demand can temporarily reduce the suppliers' monopolies and increase output.

A "political business cycle" then results, because voters pay attention only to the immediate past, judging an incumbent by economic growth over the recent past. Hence incumbents have an incentive to make the economy grow rapidly just before the elections, even though they know that the result is future inflation. The result is both inflation and increased economic turbulence, as the economy must be put into a contraction after the election (Frey 1977, Schneider 1984).

Along these same lines, the "special interests" theory of legislation claims that the overall public benefit, being a "public good," is largely neglected in politics. Instead, small special interest groups largely determine policy, particularly taxing and spending policy. Naturally, these interests assure low taxes for themselves, and high spending, leading to continual budget deficits, which tend to be monetized by the central bank. Moreover, since sellers organize more readily than buyers, we find more government-supported sellers' monopolies than buyers' monopolies, which tends to keep the market price above the equilibrium price. These political externalities cause a continual push for higher prices, a push that must be offset by an offsetting push created by maintaining a lower level of resource utilization than is socially optimal.

The policies to correct these price stability externalities are quite different than those that follow from the stabilization externality. The missing market is in price level stability; individuals in setting their price do not take into account the effect of their decision on the price level. Since price setters do not take all the effects of their actions into account, it is possible to improve the economy by creating a market in "rights to raise prices" or to analog the market with a set of taxes and subsidies. A variety of policies, including a market anti-inflation plan (MAP) (Lerner and Colander 1980), Meade's wage arbitration proposals (Meade 1982), and tax-based incomes policy (TIP) (Seidman 1978 and Wallich and Weintraub 1971), achieve these ends. (See Pissarides 1984, Koford and Miller 1984, and Colander, Chapter 3, this book.)

FORERUNNERS OF THE EXTERNALITY ARGUMENT

The argument by Lerner, quoted earlier, that the correct microeconomic foundation for macroeconomics is the externality approach does not begin with Lerner. For example, Keynes, in *How to Pay for the War* (1940: 70), wrote:

> An individual cannot by saving more protect himself from the consequences of inflation if others do not follow his example; just as he cannot protect himself from accidents by obeying the rule of the road if others disregard it. We have here the perfect opportunity for social action, where everyone can be protected by making a certain rule of behaviour universal.

The externality argument was further developed by William Baumol (1950), who developed the argument in relation to inflation. He argued that individuals did not take into account the aggregate effect of their respective claims and that some type of government coercive action was necessary to internalize the externality. Lerner (1960) argued that externalities were the proper way to think about macroeconomic problems, but the externality approach seems to have dropped from the literature during the golden years of macroeconomics, the 1960s. Macroeconomic policy was working; no one needed a justification.

By the 1970s, that was no longer the case. The rise of inflation combined with the developments of the microeconomic foundations literature and rational expectations necessitated a justification.

If it is true that the externality argument underlies many macroeconomic arguments, why did it not explicitly develop? The reason, we believe, is the strong macro/micro split that occurred; most macroeconomists simply had no concern about a microfoundation for macroeconomic policy. For them the need for macroeconomic policy was so clear-cut that providing an explicit microeconomic argument was unnecessary.

The new microfoundations literature of the late 1960s changed all that. These microeconomists' conception of the aggregate economy was that of a Walrasian economy plus frictions. These frictions would leave some excess demand in equilibrium but otherwise would not change the Walrasian conception of the economy. However, these models were actually partial equilibrium, and assumed the rate of flow out of vacancies or unemployment to be fixed. They did not analyze a fully dynamic general equilibrium; only partial equilibrium effects of policy were considered. Only recently have sufficiently sophisticated search models been developed, as noted above, that allow for the externality argument to be developed. As they have, the 1980s are producing a flood of literature espousing the externality/public goods approach. (See, in addition to the aforementioned literature, Myles Wallace 1983–84.)

A recent paper by Katharine Abraham (1983) provides evidence that the externalities are empirically important. She finds that in the postwar period vacancies have exceeded unemployment by an average ratio of 4 to 1, suggesting a steady-state externality toward excessive unemployment.

MACROECONOMIC POLICY EXTERNALITIES

The existence of externalities does not mean that they can be effectively internalized. It does, however, direct our thinking toward new policy initiatives such as the tax-based incomes policies and poses the question in a framework within which it can be debated. Previously, this was not the case. Thus, Barro writes:

> A typical feature of macro analysis is that government intervention...is recommended without bothering to describe the supposed externality or private market failure that underlies the call for policy activism.... consider the proposal for a tax-based incomes policy...I honestly have no idea what sort of private market sort of externality is supposed to rationalize this sort of government interference with the market process.

Casual arguments about external effects from "price leadership" or the like do not seem helpful (1979: 55).

The external effects described may or may not satisfy Barro, but the externality approach does attempt to answer the question on the same level at which he poses it. Our suspicion is that he will follow the Chicago view of microexternalities: while such externalities may theoretically exist, one has yet to be found that is empirically important. Even that position would be an improvement. It removes the ad hoc bias against government intervention inherent in Barro's new classical approach and returns that bias to the ideological realm where it belongs.

NOTES

1. These include the work of John Bryant (1983), Meir Kohn (1984), Joseph Stiglitz (1984), Edmund Phelps and John Taylor (1977), and Stanley Fischer (1977).
2. Leijonhufvud (1984) emphasizes that it is the assumption of perfect market-clearing that is crucial in obtaining the most striking new classical results. Barro (1984: 11) identifies his approach as the "market-clearing" approach.
3. For a discussion of the importance of such issues see Donald McCloskey (1983). In that article he emphasizes that such factors are often important.
4. General equilibrium theorists have had a difficult time in proving convergence of a Walrasian economy from some point out of equilibrium (Fischer 1982).
5. A digression to the Kornai (1971) model of the socialist economy will emphasize this point. Oversimplifying modestly, under capitalism, everyone has the right to refrain from buying or selling; that is why the short side of the market dominates. Under socialism, the long side of the market dominates; that is, it is always possible to demand goods, or to supply them to unwilling recipients. The result is an economics of "shortage" or "suction," as opposed to the capitalist economy of surplus, or "pressure."

REFERENCES

Abraham, Katherine. 1983. "Structural/Frictional vs Deficient Demand Unemployment: Some New Evidence." *American Economic Review 73* (September):708–24.

Akerlof, George. 1982. "Labor Contracts as Partial Gift Exchange." *Quarterly Journal of Economics* 97:543–69.

Ackley, Gardner. 1983. "Commodities and Capital: Prices and Quantities." *American Economic Review 73* (March):1–16.

Anderson, Terry, and Peter Hill. 1983. "Privatizing the Commons: An Improvement?" *Southern Economic Journal* (October).

Barro, Robert. 1979. "An Appraisal of the Non-Market Clearing Paradigm." *American Economic Review 69* (May):54–59.

———. 1984. *Macroeconomics.* New York: John Wiley.

Barro, Robert, and Hershel Grossman. 1976. *Money, Employment and Inflation.* Cambridge, England: Cambridge Univ. Press.

Baumol, William. 1950. *Welfare Economics and the Theory of the State.* Princeton, N.J.: Princeton Univ. Press.

Benassy, Jean-Pascal. 1982. *The Economics of Market Disequilibrium.* New York: Academic Press.

Bryant, John. 1983. "A Simple Rational Expectations Keynes-Type Model." *Quarterly Journal of Economics* (August):525–528.

Buchanan, James, and Gordon Tullock. 1962. *The Calculus of Consent.* Ann Arbor: Univ. of Michigan Press.

Clower, Robert. 1965. "The Keynesian Counterrevolution: A Theoretical Appraisal." In *The Theory of Interest Rates*, edited by F.H. Hahn and F.P.R. Brechling. London: MacMillan.

———. 1967. "A Reconciliation of the Microfoundation of Monetary Theory." *Western Economic Journal* (December).

Coase, Ronald. 1960. "The Problem of Social Cost." *Journal of Law and Economics 3* (October):1–44.

Colander, David. 1976. Public Finance Stabilization Policy for an Economy with Simultaneous Inflation and Unemployment. Unpublished dissertation, Columbia University, New York.

———. 1979. "Rational Expectations and Functional Finance." In *Essays in Post Keynesian Inflation Theory*, edited by J. Gapinski and C. Rockwell. Cambridge, Mass.: Ballinger.

Colander, David, and Gary Gigliatti. 1978. "On Price Flexibility." *Journal of Economics 4*:78–83.

Colander, David, and Robert Guthrie. 1980–81. "Great Expectations: What the Dickens Do 'Rational Expectations' Mean?" *Journal of Post Keynesian Economics 3* (Winter):219–234.

Colander, David, and Kenneth Koford. 1979. "Realytic and Analytic Syntheses of Micro and Macroeconomics." *Journal of Economics Issues* (September):707–732.

———. 1983. "Tax and Market Incentive Plan to Fight Inflation." In *Economic Perspectives: An Annual Survey of Economics*, edited by Maurice B. Ballabon. New York: Harwood.

Colander, David, and Mancur Olson. 1984. "Coalitions and Macroeconomics." In *Neoclassical Political Economy*, edited by David Colander. Cambridge, Mass.: Ballinger.

Dahlman, Carl. 1978. "The Problem of Externality." *Journal of Law and Economics* (April):141–162.

Davidson, Paul. 1972. *Money and the Real World*. London: MacMillan.

Diamond, Peter. 1984. "Money in Search of Equilibrium." *Econometrica 52* (January):1–20.

Fischer, Stanley. 1977. "Long Term Contracts, Rational Expectations, and the Optimal Money Supply Rule." *Journal of Political Economy 85*: 191–206.

Fisher, Franklin. 1983. *Disequilibrium Foundations of Equilibrium Ecoomics*. Cambridge, England: Cambridge University Press.

Frey, Bruno. 1977. *Modern Political Economy*. New York: John Wiley.

Frydman, Roman, and Edmund Phelps, eds. 1983. *Individual Forecasting and Aggregate Outcomes*. Cambridge, England: Cambridge University Press.

Grandmont, Jean-Michel. 1983. *Money and Value: A Reconsideration of Classical and Neoclassical Monetary Theories*. Cambridge, England: Cambridge Univ. Press.

Grandmont, Jean-Michel, and Y. Younes. 1972. "On the Role of Money and the Existence of a Monetary Equilibrium." *Review of Economic Studies 39*:315–372.

Guzzardo, Walter. 1978. "The New Down-To-Earth Economics." *Fortune*, December 31:72–79.

Hart, Albert. 1957. "Public Management of Private Employment — A Comment." *American Economic Review 47*:148–152.

Hazlett, Richard. 1957. "Public Management of Private Employment Volume — A Proposal." *American Economic Review 47*:136–48.

Howitt, Peter, and R. Preston McAfee. "Search, Recruiting and the Indeterminacy of the Natural Rate of Unemployment." Report 8325. University of Western Ontario. Mimeo.

Jackman, Richard; Richard Layard; and Christopher Pissarides. 1984. "Policies for Reducing the Natural Rate of Unemployment." In James Butkiewicz, ed., *Keynes' Economic Legacy*. New York: Praeger.

Keynes, John Maynard. 1940. *How to Pay for the War*. New York: Harcourt.

Klamer, Arjo. 1984. *Conversations with Economists*. Totowa, N.J.: Rowman and Allenheld.

Koford, Kenneth, and Jeffrey Miller. 1984. "Incentive Anti-Inflation Policies in a Model of Market Disequilibrium." New Ideas in Macroeconomics Conference, Middlebury College. Mimeo.

Kohn, Meir. 1981a. "A Loanable Funds Theory of Unemployment and Monetary Disequilibrium." *American Economic Review 71*:859–879.

————. 1981b. "In Defense of the Finance Constraint." *Economic Inquiry* *19*:177–195.

————. 1984. "The Finance Constraint Comes of Age: A Survey of Some Recent Developments in the Theory of Money." Unpublished paper, Dartmouth College, Hanover, N.H., February.

Kornai, Janos, 1971. *Anti-Equilibrium: On Economic Systems Theory and the Tasks of Research.* Amsterdam: North Holland.

Leijonhufvud, Axel. 1968. *On Keynesian Economics and the Economics of Keynes.* New York: Oxford Univ. Press.

————. 1973. "Effective Demand Failures." *Swedish Economic Journal 75* (March):27–48.

————. 1981. *Information and Coordination.* New York: Oxford Univ. Press.

————. 1983. "What Would Keynes Have Thought of Rational Expectations." Discussion Paper 299. July. Mimeo. University of California at Los Angeles.

Lerner, Abba. 1952. "The Essential Properties of Interest and Money." *Quarterly Journal of Economics 66* (May):172–193.

————. 1960. "On Generalizing the General Theory." *American Economic Review 50* (March):121–43.

Lerner, Abba, and David Colander. 1980. *MAP, A Market Anti-Inflation Plan.* New York: Harcourt Brace Jovanovich.

Lucas, Robert. 1973. "Some International Evidence on Output Inflation Trade-off." *American Economic Reivew 63*:326–334.

————. ed. 1981. *Studies in Business Cycle Theory.* Cambridge, Mass.: MIT Press.

Malinvaud, E. 1977. *The Theory of Unemployment Reconsidered.* Oxford: Blackwell.

McCloskey, Donald. 1983. "The Rhetoric of Economics." *Journal of Economic Literature 21* (June):481–517.

Meade, James. 1982. *Stagflation: Wage Fixing.* London: George Allen and Unwin.

Neary, Peter, 1982. "Comment on Macroeconomic Adjustment under Wage-Price Rigidity." In *Import Competition and Response*, edited by Jagdish Bhagwati. Chicago: Univ. of Chicago Press.

Olson, Mancur. 1982. *The Rise and Decline of Nations.* New Haven, Conn.: Yale Univ. Press.

Phelps, Edmund. 1970. *Microeconomic Foundations of Employment and Inflation Theory.* New York: Norton.

Phelps, Edmund, and John Taylor. 1977. "Stabilizing Properties of Monetary Policy under Rational Expectations." *Journal of Political Economy 85*:163–190.

Pissarides, Christopher. 1984. "Search Intensity, Job Advertising, and Efficiency." *Journal of Labor Economics 2* (January):128–143.

————. 1984. "Equilibrium Effects of Tax-Based Income Policies." New Ideas in Macroeconomics Conference, Middlebury College. Mimeo.

Presley, J.R. 1983–84. "D.H. Robertson: Some Restoration." *Journal of Post Keynesian Economics* 6 (Winter):230–240.

Reagan, Patricia, and Martin Weitzman. 1982. "Asymmetries in Price and Quantity Adjustments by the Competitive Firm." *Journal of Economic Theory* 26:410–420.

Salop, Steven. 1979. "A Model of the Natural Rate of Unemployment." *American Economic Review* 69 (March):117–125.

Sargent, Thomas, and Neil Wallace. 1976. "Rational Expectations and the Theory of Economic Policy." *Journal of Monetary Economics* 2: 167–183.

Schnider, Friedrich. 1984. "Public Attitudes towards Inflation and Unemployment and Their Influence on Government Behavior." Presented at Public Choice Society Annual Meeting (March).

Scitovsky, Tibor, 1979. "Market Power and Inflation." *Economica 45*: 221–233.

Seidman, Lawrence. 1978. "Taxed-Based Income Policies." *Brookings Papers on Economic Activity* 2:301–348.

Stigler, George. 1962. "Information in the Labor Market." *Journal of Political Economy* 70:94–105.

Stiglitz, Joseph. 1984a. "Theories of Wage Rigidity." In James Butkiewicz, ed., *Keynes' Economic Legacy*. New York: Praeger.

————. 1984b. "Price Rigidities and Market Structure." *American Economic Review 74*, no. 2 (May):350–355.

Wallace, Myles. 1983–84. "Economic Stabilization as a Public Good: What Does It Mean?" *Journal of Post Keynesian Economics* 6 (Winter): 295–302.

Wallich, Henry, and Sydney Weintraub. 1971. "A Tax-Based Incomes Policy." *Journal of Economic Issues* 5:1–19.

Weitzman, Martin. 1984. *The Share Economy*. Cambridge, Mass.: Harvard Univ. Press.

Wolf, Charles, Jr. 1979. "A Theory of Nonmarket Failure: Framework for Implementation Analysis." *Journal of Law and Economics* (April).

*   *Chapter 2*

Hanging Together or Separately: A Game-Theoretic Approach to Macroeconomic Conflict

Irwin Lipnowski and Shlomo Maital

> We must all hang together,
> or assuredly we shall all
> hang separately.
> — *Benjamin Franklin*

Stein (1981, 1982) discerns three competing schools of macroeconomic thought. *Keynesians* believe "monetary and fiscal policies affect output and employment relatively quickly through their effects upon aggregate demand" (Stein 1981: 139). Because such policies affect inflation only weakly, many Keynesians support some form of incomes policy. *Monetarists* hold that in the absence of monetary restraint, fiscal policy cannot reduce inflation, and believe there is a short-run Phillips curve. *New Classical Economics* holds that "policymakers cannot systematically change the unemployment rate through monetary policy" (Stein 1981: 139), because rational inflation expectations translate government policy into purely *nominal* effects.

The rivalry of scholars may increase wisdom, as the Talmud says, over the long run; but in the short run, it sows confusion. A random sample of American Economics Association members recently revealed considerable agreement on basic microeconomic propositions, and deep, fundamental disagreement on macroeconomics (Kearl et al. 1979). But even when divided, the house of science still stands, as efforts are made to unite it by reconciling conflicting paradigms, or rebuild it by inventing new ones.[1]

A new macroeconomic paradigm, built on the foundations of a very old one, is emerging. It shares features of all three existing schools of thought — for example, accommodating monetary policy is necessary for persistent inflation; expectations are central to the inflationary process; and demand management in itself is insufficient. But its distinguishing feature is not some proposition about the relation among economic variables, but rather its emphasis on relationships among *people* and *groups*, and its use of game theory to portray the structure of those relations. William Baumol once said that value is a relation between persons, expressed as a relation between things. This is equally true of inflation, unemployment, and growth. Game-theoretic macroeconomics searches for appropriate social institutions. Unlike conventional macroeconomics, which *assumes* particular social institutions, social institutions are seen as the equilibrium *outcome* of games of macroeconomic strategy.[2] Such institutions are defined by David Lewis (1969) and Andrew Schotter (1980) as regularities in behavior agreed to by all, either self-policed or policed by an external authority. They regularize, and optimize, relations among people. A leading example of such an institution is an incomes policy.[3]

Portrayal of unemployment, inflation, and growth as a game-theoretic struggle among competing groups is an old and familiar theme in the literature. Martin Shubik's pioneering *Econometrica* paper (1952) described the business cycle as the result of a two-person (labor versus entrepreneur) non-zero-sum game. Wrong estimations of the opponent's position result in strikes. Mancur Olson (1982) explains differences in growth rates across countries by differences in the extent to which interest groups are dug in. Entrenched interest groups direct effort toward zero-sum redistribution, rather than positive-sum growth. Albert Hirschman (1981) has revealingly dissected "tug-of-war" inflation in Latin America, and Tibor Scitovsky (1978, 1982) describes what he labels "excess claims" inflation, where competition for income causes incompatibility between factor prices and product prices, resulting in inflation.[4]

These and other papers written in a similar vein agree in philosophy but differ in terminology, emphasis, and conclusions. Use of game theory to construct a "theoretical" institutional economics is helping to unify a large literature that views economic outcomes as the result of struggles among groups with varying degrees of power and information.[5]

The purpose of this chapter is mainly to explore game-theoretic ways of resolving social conflict over non-zero-sum increments, and interpret incomes policy in the light of these suggested solutions. Discussion is organized as follows. Simple models are provided of business versus labor and of business versus labor versus government, and the conditions under which Prisoner's Dilemma results are stated. Experimental evidence is then surveyed and proposed solutions to Prisoner's Dilemma reviewed. Finally, implications are drawn for construction of incomes policy. A lengthy technical appendix contains a formal presentation of Prisoner's Dilemma solutions.

BUSINESS VERSUS LABOR: TWO IS COMPANY

The macroeconomics of wages, profits, prices, taxes, and public spending contain the three essential ingredients of a game. First, there are sharp conflicts of interest among the players: labor, business, government. Second, each player can adopt one of several possible courses of action. Third, when choosing a strategy, each player — even government — must carefully take into account how the other players will react.

Initially, we relegate government to the sidelines, and consider only business and labor. Assume these two players are each monolithic and can adopt one of two possible behaviors: moderation or extremism. Moderation, for labor, would involve minimal wage demands, acceptance of labor-displacing technology, abstention from strikes, and work-to-rule, with maximum effort. Moderate behavior on the part of business would be expressed as minimal price increases, modest managerial pay, efforts at cost-cutting and efficiency, and perhaps high retention of earnings. Extreme behavior for labor and business and labor would be the opposite of moderate behavior: excessive wage and price increases, strikes and lock-outs, minimal managerial and labor effort. We seek to learn the answer to the following question: For this simple 2×2 game, under what conditions will society reach a Pareto-efficient equilibrium, in which the social norm is moderate behavior?[6]

Let W and R be the *increments* to real wages and real profits, respectively. Let L and B be the strategy variables of labor and business, and permit them each only two possible values: zero (moderation) and one (extremism). Then, for the simplest possible linear model:

$$W = a_1L + a_2B + J \qquad L, B = \left.\begin{matrix}0\\1\end{matrix}\right\} \qquad (2.1)$$
$$R = b_1L + b_2B + K$$

where J and K are constants, and the a and b parameters reflect the impact of labor's and business's strategies on their own incomes and on those of the opponent.

Assume further that "extreme" behavior ($B, L = 1$) almost by definition imposes losses upon the opponent, so that $a_2 < 0$ and $b_1 < 0$. We will consider only symmetric games, in which the inherent structure of the game is the same for each player.

Four possible configurations emerge from the game described by Eqs. (2.1) and related assumptions (see Tables 2-1). Two of those games, each labeled "Let's Hang Together," are games without conflict. The dominant strategy for both labor and business is moderation, and this behavior leads each player to the maximum possible gain. This occurs when parameters a_1 and b_2 are both negative, meaning that extreme behavior causes loss to the player himself as well as to the opponent. For example, in a small open economy, immoderate price and wage behavior on the part of business and labor could lead to a disastrous erosion in the country's international competitiveness, reflected at once in real wages and profits.

One game, "Extremism Is No Vice," has a structure such that gains to an extremist exceed the loss caused to an opponent. This game has a strongly stable Pareto-efficient equilibrium. Players both attain their second-best outcome by playing $B = 1$ and $L = 1$. Misguided attempts to attain the first-best outcome result in immediate and substantial loss to the players themselves.

Let's Hang Together and Extremism Is No Vice do not pose macroeconomic problems, nor do they suggest the need for any new social institutions. For Let's Hang Together, moderation is its own reward. For Extremism Is No Vice, immoderate behavior imposes little social damage.

The fourth game is quite different. It is "Prisoner's Dilemma," a game characterized by a strongly stable Pareto-inferior equilibrium. In this game, each player would rather suffer the costs of extreme behavior, rather than have moderate behavior exploited by the opponent. When both players reason this way, each gets only the third-best result. It makes no sense for a single player to depart unilaterally

Tables 2–1. Business versus Labor.

$0 > a_1 > a_2 > a_1 + a_2$
$0 > b_2 > b_1 > b_1 + b_2$

Business

		$B=0$	$B=1$
Labor	$L=0$	4, 4	2, 3
	$L=1$	3, 2	1, 1

(a) "Let's Hang Together"

$0 > a_2 > a_1 > a_1 + a_2$
$0 > b_1 > b_2 > b_1 + b_2$

Business

		$B=0$	$B=1$
Labor	$L=0$	4, 4	3, 2
	$L=1$	2, 3	1, 1

(b) "Let's Hang Together"

BUSINESS VS. LABOR

$$W = a_1 L + a_2 B + J$$
$$R = b_1 L + b_2 B + K \qquad L, B = \left.\begin{matrix} 0 \\ 1 \end{matrix}\right\}$$

$a_1 > a_1 + a_2 > 0 > a_2$
$b_2 > b_1 + b_2 > 0 > b_1$

Business

		$B=0$	$B=1$
Labor	$L=0$	2, 2	1, 4
	$L=1$	4, 1	3, 3

(c) "Extremism is No Vice"

$a_1 > 0 > a_1 + a_2 > a_2$
$b_2 > 0 > b_1 + b_2 > b_1$

Business

		$B=0$	$B=1$
Labor	$L=0$	3, 3	1, 4
	$L=1$	4, 1	2, 2

(d) "Prisoner's Dilemma"

Note: Rankings are from Best (4) to Worst (1). The first number in each cell is labor's payoff; the second is business's payoff.

from extreme behavior. It *does* make sense, however, for *both* players to do so.[7] An economy characterized by this type of game structure begs for an incomes policy. Such a policy would formalize "temporary" sacrifices (shifts from extreme to moderate behavior) which would eventually turn into substantial gains, ensuring that no player would betray the other by reverting to extreme behavior.

The Prisoner's Dilemma parable of macroeconomic conflict (Maital and Benjamini 1980, Sutcliffe 1981) is a particular case of market failure owing to externalities. Externalities would pose no problem, were there "markets" for them; an incomes policy, in a sense, provides such a market. James Tobin (1982) reasoned that "were there a full set of simultaneously cleared markets for all commodities, including commodities for future and contingent delivery, there would be no macroeconomic problems, no need for money, and no room for fiscal and monetary policies of stabilization." Prisoner's Dilemma, then, is consistent with both Keynesian and monetarist schools, though its basic assumptions preclude rational expectations, the cornerstone of New Classical Economics.

The game depicted by (2.1) is linear in strategies. Suppose, now, that we introduce a nonlinearity:

$$W = a_1 L + a_2 B + a_3 B \cdot L + J \\ R = b_1 L + b_2 B + b_3 B \cdot L + K \quad \left. L, B = \begin{matrix} 0 \\ 1 \end{matrix} \right\} \quad a_3, b_3 < 0 \quad (2.2)$$

Coefficients a_3 and b_3 allow the assumption that jointly moderate behavior magnifies gains, and jointly extremist behavior compounds losses. As a generalization of (2.1), this game of course permits the four types of games analyzed previously. It does, however, generate a new game, known as "Chicken" (Table 2–2). This is a game with two Pareto-efficient equilibria, neither of which are stable. Each player seeks to "preempt" the other by adopting the extreme strategy. Faced with an extremist opponent, it is in the player's interest to concede and play moderately, rather than be extreme and bring about mutual destruction. But when both players try to preempt, the consequent misunderstanding can be disastrous. This game has also been labeled

Table 2–2. Business versus Labor, Nonlinear Version.

$$a_1 > 0 > a_2 > a_1 + a_2 + a_3$$
$$b_2 > 0 > b_1 > b_1 + b_2 + b_3$$

Business

		B = 0	B = 1
Labor	L = 0	3, 3	2, 4
	L = 1	4, 2	1, 1

"Chicken"

"brinkmanship." A macroeconomic structure of this nature, where misunderstandings are frequent, should call forth some form of "coordination and communication" social institution to forestall catastrophic jointly extreme behavior.

BUSINESS VERSUS LABOR VERSUS GOVERNMENT: THREE'S A CROWD

A long-standing article of faith in economics is that governments try to maximize social welfare, or the median voter's utility function. The resurgence of conservative economics restored respectability to a competing proposition favored by political scientists: Governments maximize *bureaucrats'* welfare functions. In this section, we adopt Leviathan. Government is introduced as a third player, whose aims and interests are at times antithetical to those of business and labor. We show that in such a game, the structure *may be* that of Prisoner's Dilemma, and that achieving consensus on moderate behavior in a three-player Prisoner's Dilemma may be much more difficult even than in a two-player Prisoner's Dilemma. Our case for an incomes policy is therefore not based on the traditional assumption of governmental omniscience and benevolence, but on the opposite: on governmental malevolence, and the need to restrain extreme behavior on the part of government as well as labor and business.[9]

Add government as a third player to the previous business versus labor game, where government controls decision variable G ($=0$ or 1) and seeks to maximize, say, its total expenditures, E, which by assumption bring no benefit to either business or labor:

$$\left.\begin{array}{l} W = a_1 L + a_2 B + a_3 G \\ R = b_1 L + b_2 B + b_3 G \qquad L, B, G = \begin{matrix} 0 \\ 1 \end{matrix} \\ E = c_1 L + c_2 B + c_3 G \end{array}\right\} \qquad (2.3)$$

The game represented by (2.3) can take a great many different forms. Some of these are innocuous—the equivalent of "Let's Hang Together." Others embody bitter social conflict. One example is the three-player version of Prisoner's Dilemma. When each player's gains from extreme behavior fall short of the aggregate losses inflicted by such behavior on the other two players, sharp contradictions arise between individual rationality and collective well-being. The extensive form of such a game is shown in Figure 2-1.[10]

Figure 2–1. Business versus Labor versus Government: Extensive Form. Equilibrium is at $L = 1$, $B = 1$, $G = 1$, and is Pareto-inefficient. The model is

$$W = 0.4L - 0.5B - 0.3G$$
$$R = -0.3L + 0.4B - 0.5G \qquad L, B, G = \left.\begin{matrix} 0 \\ 1 \end{matrix}\right\}$$
$$T = -0.5L - 0.3B + 0.4G$$

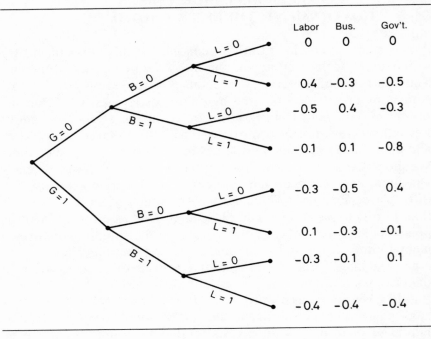

	Labor	Bus.	Gov't.
$L = 0$	0	0	0
$L = 1$	0.4	-0.3	-0.5
$L = 0$	-0.5	0.4	-0.3
$L = 1$	-0.1	0.1	-0.8
$L = 0$	-0.3	-0.5	0.4
$L = 1$	0.1	-0.3	-0.1
$L = 0$	-0.3	-0.1	0.1
$L = 1$	-0.4	-0.4	-0.4

Anatol Rapaport (1970) has argued that the social dilemma inherent in three-player Prisoner's Dilemma is even more severe than in the two-player version. With two players, it is in their best interest to form a grand coalition. With three players, it is not even in the interest of one player to form a coalition with *one* other player, let alone two. In this sense, government is part of the problem, rather than part of the solution. To understand why this is so, consider the game in Figure 2–1, in characteristic form:

$$v(\emptyset) = 0; \qquad v(L) = v(G) = v(B) = -0.1;$$
$$v(LG) = v(LB) = v(GB) = -0.7; \qquad v(LGB) = 0 \tag{2.4}$$

Let us first examine a coalition of government and business against labor. If labor behaves moderately $(L = 0)$, government and business can share a joint payoff of $+0.1$ by playing $G = 0$, $B = 1$; this inflicts a loss of -0.5 on labor. If labor behaves extremely $(L = 1)$, the most government and business can share is -0.7 $(G = 0$, $B = 1)$, while labor gets -0.1. It is therefore in labor's interest to go it alone, and play $L = 1$. But the same reasoning applies to government and business; every two-player coalition will be forced into a joint payoff of -0.7. When all three players behave extremely, each loses 0.4. The outcome $(-0.4, -0.4, -0.4)$ is a saddle point, and is a strongly stable, Pareto-inefficient equilibrium.

GAMES PEOPLE PLAY: EXPERIMENTAL EVIDENCE

An attractive feature of game-theoretic macroeconomics is that the theories based upon it are falsifiable, in Popper's sense, through direct observation of human behavior, rather than through statistical manipulation of aggregate time series. Guyer and Perkel's (1972) survey of experimental games literature lists over 600 articles and books. Since then, the literature has probably doubled. If macroeconomic conflict is indeed some sort of non-zero-sum game, some of this literature can help answer the question: Do people really behave as game theory suggests? For instance, in Prisoner's Dilemma, do people persistently adopt extreme behavior, as game theory suggests? In particular, the experimental studies can help answer the question, Does relaxing the restrictive assumptions of 2×2 and 3×2 noncooperative games — by introducing more players, more strategies, communication, repetitions, and so on — aggravate social conflict or mitigate it?

Conflict among business, labor, and government is not a "one-shot" game, but a repeated one. Does repetition of Prisoner's Dilemma games encourage cooperative behavior, or reinforce extremism? The mathematical answer in unequivocal: When all players know the number of times the game is to be played, the dominant strategy for each is extremism (see Appendix 2A's section titled "The Iterated Prisoner's Dilemma Game"). Experiments reveal behavior that is much more complex.

In their experiments, Oskamp and Perlman (1965) reported "a clear-cut trend toward increasing competition over time, within the span of 30 trials"; by "competition," they mean adoption of extreme behavior. Rapaport and Chammah (1965) found a more complex pattern of behavior. Initially, in more than half of all cases, cooperative (i.e., moderate) strategies were chosen. Then, this initial goodwill decreased and cooperators defected to noncooperative strategies. Eventually, after repeated play—which in some cases amounted to several hundred iterations—a recovery set in, as players understood that mutual distrust inflicts losses on both them and their opponents, and there was a shift toward moderate behavior. Thus, a U-shaped curve was found, where "first the subjects learn not to trust each other, then they learn to trust each other" (p. 201).

The Non-Zero-Sum Society dates, perhaps, from 1973, a decade ago. If mutually destructive macroeconomic conflict persists long enough, players may spontaneously begin to act more moderately. But rather than wait for that millenium to arrive, it makes more sense to *induce* moderate behavior by constructing the appropriate social institutions.

As Baumol (1952) noted long ago, market failure caused by externalities, in the presence of inflation and unemployment, is exacerbated by the large number of persons involved. Does the likelihood of moderate behavior decline, when the number of players increases? Apparently, it does. Studies by Bonacich et al. (1976), Hamburger, Guyer, and Fox (1975), and Fox and Guyer (1978) found substantially more cooperative (moderate) behavior in small groups than in large ones. Fox and Guyer suggest there are two reasons for this. First, "a single uncooperative individual in a group could well cause the whole group to become less cooperative through a contagion of mistrust... (and) it would be more likely for a large group to have such a "bad apple"; second, small groups may be intrinsically less anonymous than large ones, and anonymity may well decrease social responsibility." A phenomenon known as the "risky shift" has long been known to psychologists; risky shift simply says that group decisions tend to be riskier than individual ones (Maital 1982). If extreme strategy is considered daring or risky, then the finding that extremism rises with group size may be a special case of risky shift.

In reality, business, labor, and government can pick from a wide spectrum of behaviors, ranging from very moderate to very extreme. How does relaxing the assumption that only two strategies exist affect the Prisoner's Dilemma outcome? Dolbear et al. (1969) used an oligopoly framework to study this question. They found that "a greater range of choice [of strategies made] joint maximum [i.e., the Pareto-efficient outcome] harder to achieve, and if achieved, harder to maintain." They conclude that "institutional arrangements that limit the number of possible prices firms consider will tend to facilitate cooperation and price stability." Generalized to macroeconomic conflict, this suggests $2 \times n$, or $n \times n$ games, may lock into Pareto-inefficient equilibria even more than 2×2 games.

In business versus labor games, decisions are usually sequential rather than simultaneous. Pricing decisions are usually made after wage negotiations are concluded. Is this type of game more likely to induce moderate behavior than one where wage and price demands are made simultaneously (as implicitly assumed in the previous section)? Evans and Crumbaugh (1966) had players make their moves simultaneously, and then had them play sequentially, one after the other. They concluded that their results "provided no support for the notion that non-simultaneous choices produce more cooperation."

If people are brought to understand the mutually destructive nature of macroeconomic conflict, will they be more likely to behave moderately? In particular, does information on the game matrix help avoid extreme behavior? Rapoport and Chammah (1965) conjectured that display of the Prisoner's Dilemma matrix would serve "as a reminder of the prudence of choosing [the individually rational extreme strategy]." They compared players' strategies under two experimental conditions: with the payoff matrix clearly displayed, and with the payoff matrix left unknown. To their surprise, they found that knowing the matrix "seems to serve as a reminder that tacit collusion is possible" and that "the effect of the displayed matrix is a salutary one from the point of view of achieving tacit cooperation." This suggests that elucidating to the public the costs and benefits inherent in non-zero-sum macroeconomic conflict may lead to more moderation. However, recent research (Maital and Benjamini 1980, Maital 1982) has found that a substantial fraction of ordinary people understand perfectly well that excessive wage or price increases benefit their perpetrators at the expense of other segments of society; so, revealing the structure of the game to the nation may be as effective as peddling sex education to worldly wise sixteen-year-olds.

A criticism often voiced of the business versus labor versus government game is that government is not just another player but possesses sweeping powers to enforce its will and achieve its desired payoff. Though economists often exaggerate governmental power and underestimate its constraints, government should sensibly be assigned greater bargaining power than its two weaker opponents.[11] Game theory (Maschler 1963) suggests weak players will indeed be exploited. But experimental games conducted with a "strong" player and two weak ones (Kahan and Rapoport 1980) revealed the persistent ability of the two weak players to coalesce and make the strong player accede to their demands, especially when interplayer communication was allowed.

PAROLING THE PRISONER

We have thus far described macroeconomic conflict as a situation in which rivalrous attempts to appropriate non-zero-sum increments may convert the latter into individual and collective decrements. This is a particular case of market failure owing to externalities.

Modern economic theory treats external costs and benefits as a problem of missing markets. Creation of a market for externalities — for example, licenses to pollute or refrain from polluting — can often restore efficiency, through the principle that the quantity of something bought and sold in free competitive markets will be Pareto-optimal.[12]

Ever since Princeton mathematician A.W. Tucker spun the tale of Prisoner's Dilemma in 1953, social scientists and mathematicians together have sought ways to resolve it. Every solution proposed can be interpreted as creation of a "market" in "abstention from inflicting damage," where trading is done in kind, often tacitly, under imperfect information. We interpret the social institution known as "incomes policy" as such a "market."

Four types of social behavior can be defined, each capable of shifting society out of the Pareto-inferior equilibrium that Prisoner's Dilemma inflicts.

1. Fundamentally alter the structure of the game by changing the payoff matrix, through, for instance, rewards for moderate behavior and fines for extremism.
2. Play the game repetitively, to permit both retribution and conciliation.
3. Fashion social contracts or covenants, either self-enforced or enforced by third parties.
4. Change the way players perceive the game structure and the way they build their expectations of the opponent's choice of strategy.

Each of these approaches to Prisoner's Dilemma can be depicted as "internalizing" external costs. In this section, we describe each of them briefly. (The lengthy Appendix 2A supplies the necessary mathematical proofs.)

Fines and Rewards

If the structure of the non-zero-sum game business and labor play is problematic, why not alter it? As referee and game-maker, governments have the ability to do so. Consider the following game matrix, where T is the penalty or tax imposed by government upon labor, when labor behaves extremely ($L = 1$):

Business

		$B = 0$	$B = 1$
Labor	$L = 0$	0, 0	$-2, 5$
	$L = 1$	$5 - T, -3$	$-1 - T, -1$

If T is sufficiently large, for *labor* the game shifts from one of Prisoner's Dilemma ($L = 1$ is the dominant strategy) to Chicken. The dominant strategy for business remains $B = 1$ ($B = 1$), as labor well knows. Labor will therefore shift to moderate behavior ($L = 0$). This outcome may not necessarily be to our liking, but it is no longer Pareto-inefficient.

Britain's 1975–76 incomes policy, or "social contract" as it was called, may be an example. Like many incomes policies, it was mainly an instrument for inducing or coercing workers into wage restraint. When asked why he agreed to it, labor leader Hugh Scanlon said, "[Dennis] Healey took us to the edge of the cliff, and we looked over, and didn't like what we saw."[13]

Another, related approach involves altering either ethical norms or utility functions themselves. Burton Weisbrod (1977) suggests that where inefficiencies owing to externalities exist, it may take fewer resources to correct the problem by altering preferences (by making people more thoughtful and altruistic, for example) than by imposing tax-subsidy systems. In this sense, he argues, preference-alteration is Pareto-efficient. As we show in Appendix 2A's section titled "Solutions Based upon Altering Utility Functions and/or Altering Ethical Norms of Conduct," varying degrees of altruism on the part of one or both players can move society away from the extremist equilibrium. (This, however, can be overdone. Schelling (1968) describes an Altruist's Dilemma, where each player seeks to increase the payoff of the other. When *both* act this way, the outcome may be worse for both than if each had acted selfishly!) In one sense, religion is a social institution of this type, seeking to add other people's well-being as arguments to one's own utility function.[14] Welfare economics in general scrupulously avoids "solutions" of this kind, regarding preferences as sacrosanct.

Selten (1978) has proposed a "utility-alteration" solution to Prisoner's Dilemma played repeatedly (see the last pages of Appendix 2A). He posits primary utility linear in money payoffs, and secondary utility that depends on each player's social relations with other players. Selten assumes that players incur secondary *dis*utility from exploiting other players' trust by behaving extremely when others are moderate. This disutility is an increasing function of the total "stock" of trust, measured as the number of rounds in which each player acted moderately (i.e., $L = 0$, $B = 0$). For a finitely iterated game, Selten defines conditions for which moderate behavior on the part of both players is a second Nash equilibrium, in pure strategies. (Extreme behavior is still a Nash equilibrium, because it always pays to fight fire with fire.) A Selten incomes policy involves attaching social stigma to exploitative behavior, and assigning a historian to keep track of all such instances and remind us of them. This is a double-edged sword. Some people may well derive positive utility from exploiting others, apart from the money payoff, and may redouble their efforts when reminded of the option. Experimental studies show that moderate behavior in society cannot be generated through unilateral demonstrations of goodwill by one group alone. When trustworthiness evolves into "martyrdom" (e.g., L plays 0 when B plays 1), that behavior is typically exploited.[15] Generally, political speeches calling for some segment of society to undertake sacrifice, in the battle against inflation, meet little response.

Repeated Play

In reality, business versus labor versus government is not a one-shot game. It is played repeatedly. In principle, extreme behavior is still the dominant strategy for all players when N rounds are played, N

being known to the players (see Appendix 2A). But, under certain circumstances, "response-contingent" strategies—specifically, Tit-for-Tat—can make moderate, cooperative behavior rational for all players.

Some years ago, a Computer Tournament for the Iterated Prisoner's Dilemma was held (Axelrod 1980). Entrants were computer programs that selected "0" or "1" strategies on each move; available to the programs was the history of the game so far. The winner was Anatol Rapoport's Tit-for-Tat algorithm, comprising two rules: (1) Begin with a moderate choice. (2) Thereafter, do what the other player did the previous move. The algorithm piled up the most points. Moreover, Axelrod notes that a single property characterizes the eight top algorithms—they are all "nice," in that none is the first to defect to "extremism" from "moderation." This implies that a major function of an incomes policy is to start the macroeconomic game again from scratch, extricate society from locked-in extremism, and then rely on pure self-interest and a Tit-for-Tat strategy to prevent mutual betrayal.

Markov chains have been used to analyze iterated Prisoner's Dilemma games. A well-known feature of Markov models is that under certain conditions, the long-run steady-state frequency of game outcomes—in this case, the four possible states in Prisoner's Dilemma—depends only on the transition probabilities: the sixteen probabilities of moving from one of the four outcomes to another (see "The Iterated Prisoner's Dilemma Game," in Appendix 2A). Consider a class 1 decision rule, meaning that strategies are based solely on the four possible payoffs and on strategies chosen on the preceding round of play *only*. Define a "probabilistic" Tit-for-Tat as a strategy where a player begins with moderation (L or $B = 0$) and then matches, in round t, the opponent's strategy in $t-1$, with probability p. Suppose, now, that p is labor's subjective *assessment* that on round t, business will match labor's $t-1$ strategy. There exists a threshold value for p, say p^*, such that, for $p < p^*$, labor's best strategy is extremism ($L = 1$), and for $p > p^*$, labor's best strategy is moderation ($L = 0$). The value of p^* is $(a_{10} - a_{01})/(a_{00} + a_{10} - a_{01} - a_{11})$, where a_{ij} is labor's payoff for $L = i$, $B = j$, $i, j = 0, 1$. As we would expect, the greater the gain from betrayal (a_{10}) and the smaller the payoff for martyrdom (a_{01}), the more accuracy is needed in judging the opponent's strategy in order to make moderation an optimal move.

Set into this Markovian framework, an incomes policy would bring labor and business together and help each side better judge what the other side will do. This is close to internalizing externalities; sure knowledge that betrayal will boomerang back on the betrayer is strong incentive for moderation. However, this can only work if players are not already locked into mutual extremism.

For generalized Markov models, players can calculate their average expected long-run payoff: the payoffs implied by the game matrix and steady-state probabilities. A number of proposed solutions to iterated Prisoner's Dilemma are based on such a model. Smale (1980) shows that if both players base strategies conditional upon "history," in Tit-for-Tat fashion, then the game can converge to "moderation" ($L = 0, B = 0$). However, small departures from such strategies quickly move society to the Pareto-inferior stable Nash equilibrum. Those who run incomes policies are familiar with this knife-edge property, with yawning chasms of extremism on either side of a very narrow path.

Some resolutions of iterated Prisoner's Dilemma are based not on *improving* players' mutual understanding but on reducing it. Kreps et al. (1981) show that with informational asymmetry — where one player thinks there is a small chance that the opponent may behave moderately — mutual, moderate behavior may result. This is true as well with two-sided uncertainty, where each player assigns a small probability to his opponent "enjoying" (rather than exploiting) moderation, by matching it. A sequential equilibrium results where each player behaves moderately until the last few plays of the game. (See also Radner n.d., in which a mediator plants an (unfounded) expectation in each plyer that the opponent may be conciliatory; the result may be Pareto-improving for society.)

Social Contracts

In 1762 Rousseau framed the idea that social conflict arises not because of human nature but because of social institutions themselves, specifically, property rights. It follows that social conflict can be mitigated when people agree to give up those rights, through a social contract. In a macroeconomic context, people have "property rights" over the prices they charge for their goods and services, capital and labor, over the skill and effort they exert at work, and over the fraction of their income they choose to spend in each time period. Maintaining those rights rigidly could doom society to prolonged unemployment, stagnation, or inequality, whereas alternate social institutions could make everyone better off. An incomes policy social contract is an agreement in which members of society voluntarily forgo some of their property rights, in pursuit of their own self-interest. (See "Threats, Promises, and Self-penalties" in Appendix 2A.) To prevent mutual promises of pro-social behavior from breaking down, sanctions for anti-social behavior may be required. These may take the form described earlier, with government imposing taxes or paying subsidies; the problem with this is that government is often a key player as well as umpire, with its own interests. Alternately, legal systems may be set up, requiring payment of damages or compensation in the event that one player exploits another by adopting extreme strategies. A major problem with solving macroeconomic conflict in this way is that macroeconomic externalities are difficult to measure and are widely diffused, as Baumol noted in 1952. An interesting variation on damage-compensation systems is agreements in which players restrain *themselves* from the temptation of duplicity. The proposed balanced-budget amendment has been given such an interpretation, as a means of helping government restrain its own appetite.[16]

Incomes Policy as Metagame

In Prisoner's Dilemma, players whose expectations are "rational" may assume that their opponents will pick extremism. Yet, how can an expectation be termed "rational" if it leaves everyone, including the player himself, worse off than under some other type of expectation?

Nigel Howard (1971) tried to resolve Prisoner's Dilemma by defining what he calls a *metagame*: the game that *would* exist if one of the players chose his strategy after the others, knowing of course what other players did. He defines "equilibrium" as a state in which players correctly guess what strategies others will choose. (See the Appendix 2A section titled "Know Thine Adversary.") Suppose business can predict labor's strategy choice. Business has four possible conditional strategies: behave moderately irregardless; behave extremely irregardless; do exactly what labor does; or do the opposite of what labor does. Let labor have some prior conviction about which of these four strategies business will pursue. For *each* of business's four strategies, labor has four possible strategies — the same ones listed for business, giving labor sixteen conditional strategies in all. This creates a 16×4

payoff matrix. Howard shows that $L = 0$, $B = 0$ (joint moderation) is, for this metagame, a stable Nash equilibrium (see Appendix 2A on the 16×4 matrix). How is it that extremism remains the dominant strategy for the original Prisoner's Dilemma game, while moderation becomes the dominant strategy for the metagame? Howard explains that this comes about when the players ask themselves, should they be "rational" (extreme), or might some other policy be rational in view of the fact that the opponents can ask themselves the same question. (Perhaps players could be brought to this view by requiring them to read Kant's *Critique of Pure Reason*.)

Resolving macroeconomic conflict by a metagame incomes policy would do little more than establish a forum in which contestants could bargain, debate, and above all measure more accurately each other's intentions. Communication of this sort does not in itself eliminate the danger of mutual extremism; even in Howard's metagame, the temptation of duplicity and betrayal remains. It simply helps assure that the chance of attaining a Pareto-efficient outcome is not destroyed because the players misunderstand each other.

Austria's successful ongoing incomes policy is perhaps an example. In the postwar period, Austria has had better than average success in moderating inflation and preventing unemployment. Many attribute this to the country's Joint Council on Wages and Prices, composed of representatives from government, labor, and business. Major decisions on wages and prices are taken by the Council; all decisions have to be unanimous. The representatives of government have not exercised their right to vote for over fifteen years. The Council has fostered a firm belief in the mutual benefits of moderation, a belief reinforced by the positive results shown over the past two decades. Some observers suggest this labor–business harmony is in part a product of the post–World War I social conflict in Austria and the recognition that Austria's near-destruction resulted.

SUMMARY AND CONCLUSION

In this chapter, we have interpreted macroeconomics as a non-zero-sum game among business, labor, and perhaps government. Use of a game-theoretic approach to the national economy emphasizes conflict and interaction among *people* and *groups*, and the institutions suitable for resolving that conflict in a just and efficient manner, rather than relations among money, prices, and output.

We described macroeconomic conflict as predominantly a pernicious kind of non-zero-sum game in which each player reasons, "I would rather suffer mutual losses than be exploited," with the result that a situation of mutual losses is the stable Pareto-inferior result. The question "What kinds of social institution can move society to superior equilibria?" was addressed. Incomes policy was interpreted as such an institution. The crux of an incomes policy, in this approach, is not necessarily a statutory freeze of wages and prices, but a mechanism for eliciting (temporary) sacrifices on the part of all players and maintaining pro-social behavior in the face of incentives to act egoistically. Incomes policy, to paraphrase Baumol, is a relation among *people*, expressed as a relation among wages, prices, taxes, etc. Western Europe and Scandinavia have had incomes policies for over two decades, with considerable success. In the United States, severe monetary restraint solved (perhaps temporarily) the problem of inflation, at a dreadful and, to many, unacceptable toll in unemployment and lost output. The time is ripe for a fresh look at incomes policy.

APPENDIX 2A
FOUR APPROACHES TO RESOLVING
PRISONER'S DILEMMA

The following discussion is based on a specific version of Eqs. (2.1):

$$W = 0.09L - 0.09B - 0.085B \cdot L \qquad B, L = \left. \begin{matrix} 0 \\ 1 \end{matrix} \right\} \qquad (2A.1)$$
$$R = -0.18L + 0.09B - 0.010B \cdot L$$

where L is labor's decision variable, B is business's decision variable, W is the change in real wages, and R is the change in real profits.

In this 2×2 game, individually rational behavior results in collectively irrational equilibrium. Game theorists, mathematicians, philosophers, and social scientists have wrestled with the dragon of the Pareto-inefficient noncooperative equilibrium embodied in Prisoner's Dilemma.

The development of "metagame" theory by Nigel Howard (1971) involved a frontal assault on the dragon; his approach entailed recourse to a higher level of decision calculus involving the *mutual prediction of conditional strategies*. An entirely different approach to the dragon could be characterized as a less direct confrontation involving encirclement: the static Prisoner's Dilemma framework was "dynamized" to either an infinite time horizon (i.e., a supergame) or one of finite but unknown length (i.e., an iterated game). Yet another approach endeavored to render the dragon harmless by gingerly stepping around it; this was accomplished by introducing a "deus ex machina" to *transform the Prisoner's Dilemma payoff matrix* so as to render moderation the dominant strategy. The transformation was effected either directly in the static one-shot case or by means of a credible commitment by one party to be bound to a conditional strategy for the iterated framework. We shall describe each of these "solutions" in the context of an incomes policy where there are but two players, business (*B*) and labor (*L*); if the government has any role at all in the ensuing discussion, it will be simply that of neutral referee, arbitrator, and possibly enforcer of commitments by *B* and *L*.

Know Thine Adversary: The Role of Expectations in Inducing Cooperative Behavior in Prisoner's Dilemma Games

The introduction of expectations in the normal form Prisoner's Dilemma game transforms the problem facing a player to a straightforward decision-theoretic problem. Thus, Howard's metagame "solution" introduces the assumption that one of the players in a simultaneous move game can *predict exactly* what his adversary will do. It is as if this player is in a *sequential* move game and has the benefit of observing his adversary's choice of strategy, while the second player is likewise assumed able to predict the conditional strategies of his adversary with the same perfect accuracy as hindsight would afford. A metagame is defined by Howard as "the game that would exist if one of the players chose his strategy after the others, in knowledge of their choices" (1971: 23). Howard's stated purpose in considering metagames is as follows:

> we wish to build a theory of the "equilibrium" state — or rather the state of what we have called *actual stability* — meaning a state in which players guess correctly what strategies the others will choose. If they do not guess this, or guess incorrectly, they are in a "non-equilibrium" state, about which we make no predictions. (1971: 54)

In the 2 × 2 game, the two strategies available to labor or business were each characterized as moderation (*M*) or extremism (*E*). Recall that this yielded the following payoff matrix:

Business

		M	E
Labor	M	0, 0	−.09, .09
	E	.09, −.18	−.085, −.10

Now suppose that B could predict L's strategy in this game. B could then formulate the following four strategies.

1. If B believes that L will play M, then B will play M, whereas if B believes that L will play E, then B will play M; that is, B's first possible strategy is to *be moderate* (select M) *regardless* of B's beliefs about L's strategy. Denote this strategy MM.
2. If B believes that L will play M, then B will play M, whereas if B believes that L will play E, then B will play E. Denote this strategy of matching (i.e., Tit-for-Tat) behavior by ME.
3. If B believes that L will play M, then B will play E, whereas if B believes that L will play E, then B will play M. Denote B's strategy of opposite (i.e., Tat-for-Tit) behavior by EM.
4. If B believes that L will play M, then B will play E, whereas if B believes that L will play E, then B will play E; that is, B's fourth strategy is to *be extreme* (select E) *regardless* of B's beliefs about L's strategy. We denote B's fourth strategy of "extreme behavior regardless" by EE.

Let us further suppose that L has a conviction about which of these four strategies B will adopt. Then L could formulate sixteen possible strategic responses to each of B's four strategies. We denote by $MEEM$, for example, the conditional strategy in which L would respond to a conviction

(i)   that B will adopt strategy (1) (of being moderate regardless) by selecting M;
(ii) that B will adopt strategy (2) (of Tit-for-Tat) by selecting E;
(iii) that B will adopt strategy (3) (of Tat-for-Tit) by selecting E; and
(iv) that B will adopt strategy (4) (of being extreme regardless) by selecting M.

The payoff to L's $MEEM$ strategy is depicted in row 9 of the 16×4 matrix in Figure 2–1.

Having derived this 16 × 4 matrix of conditional strategies, the next step is to search for Nash equilibrium points, regarding *only* such points as a product of the rational choice of strategy. As Rapoport notes,

> it seems rational to choose a strategy that has this equilibrium, since one can assume that the other player, being rational, will also choose a strategy available to him that has the equilibrium. This is so because an equilibrium is an outcome that cannot be improved by either player (and may be impaired) if one player chooses a different strategy while the other player sticks to the strategy that has the equilibrium. (1967: 54–55)

Thus, given the mutual prediction by L and B that the other will consider only equilibrium strategies, and denoting the payoff to L and B in Table 2A–1 by the ordered pair $\langle i, j \rangle$, $i = 1, \ldots, 16$, and $j = 1, \ldots, 4$, we consider three equilibrium points as solution candidates, $\langle 6, 2 \rangle$, $\langle 14, 2 \rangle$ and $\langle 16, 4 \rangle$. Given these three candidates, $\langle 16, 4 \rangle$ may be eliminated from consideration, since by playing ME (Tit-for-Tat), which is B's strategy 2, B could attain payoff 0 (rather than $-.10$ yielded by $\langle 16, 4 \rangle$). L's *dominant* strategy within the choice set of the three equilibria is $EMEE$ (row 14) since Labor does better than row 6 and as well as row 16 against MM, does as well as row 6 and better than row 16 against ME, and does just as well as rows 6 and 16 against EM and EE. Since strategy $\langle 14, 2 \rangle$ yields payoff $(0, 0)$ corresponding to MM ("moderation" by both L and B), recourse to the metagame has resolved the so-called paradox of the Prisoner's Dilemma. It might be noted that this resolution holds even if L and B switch roles as row and column player. This resolution of the Prisoner's Dilemma has been acclaimed by Rapoport (1967) as "the solution" to the Prisoner's Dilemma paradox.

Despite the considerable ingenuity (bordering on mental acrobatics) of Howard's metagame theory, it is important not to lose sight of the underlying assumptions that support the elaborate theoretical edifice. As Howard oberves concerning the process whereby MM emerges as a solution,

> It is of course an irrational solution for each player given the other's choice. But it is a rational solution for each given the other's metachoice. It comes about through [B] asking himself whether he should be rational, or whether some other policy might be rational in view of the fact that [L] can ask himself the same question. (1966: 180)

Although the metagame formalizes each player's imagined calculation process on the assumption that each player can correctly anticipate the other's choice, it is important to stress that the 16 × 4

Table 2A–1. Howard's Metagame Matrix.

	B j			
	1 (M regardless) MM	2 (Tit-for-Tat) ME	3 (Tat-for-Tit) EM	4 (E regardless) EE
i				
1. MMMM	0, 0	0, 0	−.09, .09	−.09, .09
2. MMME	0, 0	0, 0	−.09, .09	−.085, −.10
3. MMEM	0, 0	0, 0	.09, −.18	.09, −.18
4. MEMM	0, 0	−.085, −.10	−.09, .09	−.09, .09
5. EMMM	.09, −.18	0, 0	−.09, .09	−.09, .09
6. MMEE	0, 0	0, 0	.09, −.18	−.085, −.10
7. MEME	0, 0	−.085, −.10	−.09, .09	−.085, −.10
8. EMME	.09, −.18	0, 0	−.09, .09	−.085, −.10
9. MEEM	0, 0	−.085, −.10	.09, −.18	−.09, .09
10. EMEM	.09, −.18	0, 0	.09, −.18	−.09, .09
11. EEMM	.09, −.18	−.085, −.10	−.09, .09	−.09 .09
12. EEEM	.09, −.18	−.085, −.10	.09, −.18	−.09, .09
13. EEME	.09, −.18	−.085, −.10	−.09, .09	−.085, −.10
14. EMEE	.09, −.18	0, 0	.09, −.18	−.085, −.10
15. MEEE	0, 0	−.085, −.10	.09, −.18	−.085, −.10
16. EEEE	.09, −.18	−.085, −.10	.09, −.18	−.085, −.10

L

game is *not* the game actually being played in a one-shot Prisoner's Dilemma game with no communication. Returning to Table 2A–1, *L* realizes that if he plays row 14, *B* will be led to play column 2 and he therefore would proceed, according to Howard, to play row 14. However the *"solution" appears to unravel* for *B* would, in anticipation of *L*'s choice of *M*, respond with *E*. Moreover, anticipating such duplicity on *B*'s part, *L* would opt for *E*. As a consequence, *EE* reemerges as the equilibrium.

Only by imposing the assumption that *L* and *B* can read each other's mind (thereby ruling out *ME* and *EM*) can the temptation to duplicity be removed. Pursuing this line further, it should be noted that mutual predictability need not be infallible (see Brams 1975). For suppose that L realizes that B can correctly predict his choice of strategy (in the 2×2 game) with probability p while B knows that, with probability q, L can correctly predict his choice of strategy ($0 \leq p$, $q \leq 1$). Now suppose each player adopts a conditional Tit-for-Tat strategy, whereby each is moderate if he predicts moderation by the other, and each is extreme if he predicts extremism by the other. Now consider the decision facing L:

Business

		M	E
Labor	M	0, 0	$-.09, .09$
	E	$.09, -.18$	$-.085, -.10$

If L selects M, then with probability p, B will respond with M, and with probability $(1-p)$, B will select E; so L's expected utility from M would be $p(0) + (1-p)(-.09)$. If instead L selects E, then B would counter this by selecting E with probability p, and B would respond by M with probability $(1-p)$; thus L's expected utility from E would be $(1-p)(.09) + p(-.085)$. For M to have a higher expected utility for L than E, it is necessary that

$$p(0) + (1-p)(-.09) > (1-p)(.09) + p(-.085), \quad \text{i.e., } p > 36/53 \tag{2A.2}$$

Likewise a choice by B of strategy M would yield a higher expected utility to B than would strategy E against a conditional Tit-for-Tat strategy for L only if

$$q(0) + (1-q)(-.18) > (1-q)(.09) + q(-.10), \quad \text{i.e., } q > 27/37 \tag{2A.3}$$

Thus where L and B both adopt a choice rule of conditional Tit-for-Tat and each predicts the other's strategy with accuracy of at least 36/53 and 27/37, respectively, an MM equilibrium would emerge in the one-shot Prisoner's Dilemma. To the extent that one player must inform (announce to) the other that he is adopting a strategy of conditional Tit-for-Tat, this resolution of the Prisoner's Dilemma does not strictly preclude communication between the players.

Building on the theory of metagames and on *Newcomb's Paradox*, Brams (1975) assumes that for the one-shot Prisoner's Dilemma game, player j believes that player i ($i, j \in \{1, 2\}$, $i \neq j$) can predict with probability p_i ($0 < p_i < 1$) j's choice of strategy. Assuming that each player believes his opponent to be following a Tit-for-Tat strategy, conditional on the opponent's prediction concerning his own, i.e., j's strategy, a decision-theoretic problem again emerges. Providing p_i and p_j are sufficiently large, MM would represent the jointly optimal strategy.

The *subjective probability* assigned by each player to his opponent's ability to predict his own strategy choice and respond appropriately with Tit-for-Tat becomes the *key determinant of each player's strategy choice*. In the example presented, if L attributed a predictive accuracy to B exceeding 36/53, L would be deterred from playing E in the one-shot Prisoner's Dilemma, while if L believed B's predictive accuracy to fall *short* of 36/53, L would select strategy E. Similarly, B would have to assign a subjective probability that L could correctly predict B's choice of strategy, and accurately reciprocate with Tit-for-Tat, of more than 27/35 in order to be convinced that he should select strategy M; for if B attributed to L a predictive accuracy of less than 27/35, B's expected-utility maximizing strategy would be E.

Identical critical probability values govern the optimal (i.e., the average, expected, utility-maximizing) strategy in a repeated Prisoner's Dilemma where a player confronts a Probabilistic Tit-for-Tat (PTFT) strategy by the other player. Thus, for L facing a PTFT strategy by B in the repeated game, if B plays Tit-for-Tat with probability greater than 36/53, L would find it optimal to play M always; similarly, if L were to play Tit-for-Tat with probability greater than 27/37, B would find it optimal to play M always. Again, the introduction of fixed subjective probabilities creates a game against nature which is a straightforward decision-theoretic problem.

The Iterated Prisoner's Dilemma Game: Resolutions of the "Paradox"

Where both players know in advance the precise number of times that a Prisoner's Dilemma game is to be repeated, a contradiction arises between the result predicted by rigorous mathematical logic and that observed in repeated experiments. By appeal to a rigorous argument based upon backward induction, it is predicted that the two parties will repeatedly play EE. The argument proceeds as follows.

Assuming that L and B know beforehand that the Prisoner's Dilemma game is to be repeated N times, each player recognizes that if he plays E on the final play of the game, his adversary cannot exact retribution so that the Nth repetition is strategically equivalent to a one-shot Prisoner's Dilemma wherein EE is the dominant Pareto-suboptimal result. Consequently, EE would also be played on the $N-1$ trial, which is strategically equivalent to a one-short Prisoner's Dilemma since both players realize that EE on trial N is already a foregone conclusion. This domino effect extends backward *to all trials* so that EE would be the dominant solution for all N trials.

On the other hand, experimental evidence for iterated games with a known number of trials demonstrates conclusively that the establishment of jointly cooperative strategies in finite iterated games (of sufficient length to render effective the retaliatory threat embodied in an observed Tit-for-Tat strategy) can occur for protracted phases of such iterated games.[17]

We shall consider the structure of strategies for inducing cooperation in repeated games. Such structures may be characterized as "solutions" to the iterated Prisoner's Dilemma, because if the players find it individually rational to cooperate, the fundamental incompatibility between individual and collective rationality will have been reconciled.

The essence of greater inducement to cooperation inherent in iterated Prisoner's Dilemma games, in contrast to the one-shot version, resides in their potential for an opponent to adopt a *response-contingent strategy* — for example, for L to make a strategic decision at t depends upon the *history* of previous trials versus B. If, instead, one of the players were to behave as a "stooge," always playing the same strategy on each trial, *independently* of the opponent's strategic choice, the opponent would effectively be confronting a one-shot Prisoner's Dilemma on each trial and, as in the case of a one-shot Prisoner's Dilemma, E would be the opponent's dominant strategy on each trial. The element in iterated games which can render M an individually rational strategy is the *possibility* (or indeed *prospect*) of retaliation by the other player against E; such retaliation could well inflict losses in excess of the fruits wrought in the short run by the choice of E. The reciprocal nature of such response-contingent policies could well render M individually rational to *both* parties. For analytic convenience, we shall adopt a repeated game framework in which we may distinguish the following four main variants of Tit-for-

Tat (TFT), the most common response-contingent strategy in iterated Prisoner's Dilemma; for expository purposes, we shall assume that these are adopted by Column (Business) against Row (Labor).

(i) (Ordinary) Tit-for-Tat. Column plays M initially. Then (for $t > 1$) Row's choice of $M(E)$ at $t-1$ is met by Column's choice of $M(E)$ at t.

(ii) Probabilistic Tit-for-Tat (PTFT). Column plays M initially. Then (for $t > 1$) Row's choice of $M(E)$ at $t-1$ is met, with fixed probability p $(0 < p < 1)$ by Column's choice of $M(E)$ at t. (Note that case (i) corresponds to $p = 1$.)

(iii) Graduated Tit-for-Tat (GTFT). Column plays M initially. Then (for $t > 1$) Row's choice of E at $t-1$ is met by Column's choice of E on the following $f(i)$ $(1 \le i \le t-1)$ trials, where f is a monotonically increasing function and i denotes the total number of trials in which Row has played E. *Unless* Row is being "punished" in trial t for having played E in trial $t-2$ or before (in accordance with the GTFT rule for responding to Row's having played E), Column will match Row's choice of M in $t-1$ by playing M in t.

(iv) Massive Retaliatory Tit-for-Tat (MRTFT). Column plays M initially and thereafter plays M in t whenever Row plays M in $t-1$ and Row has never selected E. Should Row ever select E in $t-1$ $(t > 1)$, Column plays E in t forever after, *regardless* of whether Row "repents" or not for his moment of weakness — i.e., having yielded to temptation, in $t-1$.

If both players were to adopt any of variants (i), (iii), and (iv) of the Tit-for-Tat strategies, a permanent lock-in effect at MM would result. By way of contrast, if one player adopted a MRTFT strategy while the other played PTFT, *eventually* a lock-in effect at EE would occur.

The most sophisticated response-contingent strategies specify a decision rule of strategic choice as a function of the *entire* sequence of outcomes on previous trials. Grofman and Poole (1975) classify various Markovian decision rules in accordance with the number of previous periods taken into account when selecting a strategy in trial t. They consider *only* "homogeneous" decision rules — rules that do not depend upon t. Thus, a *class 0* (or "absolute") decision rule (which could be followed by a "stooge") is a function only of the 2×2 matrix entries; the past has no bearing on the current decision. As already noted, a class 0 decision rule is optimally confronted by always playing E. A *class 1* decision rule is a function of the 2×2 matrix entries and of the state (i.e., the simultaneous strategy choice) on the immediately preceding trial. Examples of homogeneous class 1 Markovian decision rules are TFT and PTFT.

A *class* m *decision* rule $(m < t)$ is a function only of the 2×2 matrix entries and the states that obtained on the preceding m trials, i.e., in periods $t - m$ to $t - 1$ inclusively.

The analytic simplicity of class 1 decision rules rather than their intuitive appeal probably accounts for their frequent appearance in the literature. We shall briefly survey such rules and consider their implications for an incomes policy.

Class 1 Markov Decision Rules

In an iterated game, the system can, at any point in time, be in one of four states; each *state* is described by the ordered pair $\langle x, y \rangle$, where $x, y \in \{M, E\}$, indicating the simultaneous choice of strategy by L and B, respectively, at that point in time. The states are MM, ME, EM, and EE. In the Markov chain model, decisions in period t are governed entirely by the simultaneous strategy decisions reached in $t - 1$, i.e., entirely by the *state* of the system.

Let us denote the *psychological propensities* of L, fixed by assumption, as follows:

$$
\begin{aligned}
e_L &= \Pr(M_L \mid MM); & \bar{e}_L &= 1 - e_L = \Pr(E_L \mid MM) \\
f_L &= \Pr(M_L \mid ME); & \bar{f}_L &= 1 - f_L = \Pr(E_L \mid ME) \\
g_L &= \Pr(M_L \mid EM); & \bar{g}_L &= 1 - g_L = \Pr(E_L \mid EM) \\
h_L &= \Pr(M_L \mid EE); & \bar{h}_L &= 1 - h_L = \Pr(E_L \mid EE)
\end{aligned}
\tag{2A.4}
$$

Similarly, B's psychological propensities are as follows:

$$
\begin{aligned}
e_B &= \Pr(M_B \mid MM); & \bar{e}_B &= \Pr(E_B \mid MM) \\
f_B &= \Pr(M_B \mid ME); & \bar{f}_B &= \Pr(E_B \mid ME) \\
g_B &= \Pr(M_B \mid EM); & \bar{g}_B &= \Pr(E_B \mid EM) \\
h_B &= \Pr(M_B \mid EE); & \bar{h}_B &= \Pr(E_B \mid EE)
\end{aligned}
\tag{2A.5}
$$

From these parameters, the 4×4 Markovian transition matrix, shown in Table 2A–2, is easily derived. Thus, if the system is in state

Table 2A–2. The 4×4 Markov Transition Matrix.

	MM	ME	EM	EE
MM	$e_L e_B$	$e_L \bar{e}_B$	$\bar{e}_L e_B$	$\bar{e}_L \bar{e}_B$
ME	$f_L f_B$	$f_L \bar{f}_B$	$\bar{f}_L f_B$	$\bar{f}_L \bar{f}_B$
EM	$g_L g_B$	$g_L \bar{g}_B$	$\bar{g}_L g_B$	$\bar{g}_L \bar{g}_B$
EE	$h_L h_B$	$h_L \bar{h}_B$	$\bar{h}_L h_B$	$\bar{h}_L \bar{h}_B$

EE on trial $t-1$, since the probability in such a situation of M being chosen on trial t by L is h_L and by B is h_B, the probability of the system moving from EE at $t-1$ to MM at t is $h_L \cdot h_B$.

The essential feature of this model is the irrelevance, with respect to the conditional probability of transition from the system's current state to any other state, *of the system's time path* in reaching its current state. To characterize fully this Markov process, it is sufficient to specify its initial state and the transition matrix. If certain regularity conditions are satisfied by the transition matrix—that is, if for some power of the transition matrix in Table 2A–2, all the entries are positive, which means that *eventually the system can change from some state to any other state*—then the transition matrix converges to a steady-state stochastic matrix of identical rows. Such a row vector would indicate the *asymptotic* probability of being in each of the four states MM, ME, EM, and EE, *regardless* of what the initial probabilities are. Therefore in the long run, the transition probabilities *alone* will determine the frequencies of the states of the system.[18]

Analytic Application of the Class 1 Decision Rule to the Formulation of Optimal Strategy

Grofman and Poole (1975, 1977) considered the optimal strategic response by, say, Row, to Column's adoption of a PTFT. Row wishes to maximize expected long-run average payoffs, and *believes* that Column is playing a PTFT with fixed probability p; that is, p is Row's (subjective) *assessment* of the likelihood that if he plays $M(E)$ at $t-1$, Column will play $M(E)$ at t. Recall Row's payoffs in the Prisoner's Dilemma matrix:

Business

		M	E
	M	0	−.09
Labor	E	.09	−.085

Against Column's PTFT, Row's choice of pure strategy M in preference to pure strategy E requires that

$$p \cdot 0 + (1-p)(-.09) > (1-p)(.09) + p(-.085)$$

In other words, only $p > 36/53$ renders M a superior strategy to E against a PTFT by Column.

Contrast this situation with the one-shot game involving "knowledge" by Row that Column can correctly predict his *current* choice of strategy with probability p and that Column will play Tit-for-Tat according to this prediction about Row's choice of strategy. In both the repeated game and the one-shot game, the critical value of p is 36/53.

Writing the payoff matrix for *Row* as follows:

	M	E
M	a	b
E	c	d

and assuming Column plays PTFT (or alternatively that Row *believes or perceives* that Column will play TFT with fixed probability p), Grofman and Poole formulate the optimal strategy by Row to maximize his long-run average payoff. This entails first deriving the steady-state transition matrix from which the asymptotic payoffs can be calculated. They prove the following interesting result. For $p > (c-b)/(a-b+c-d)$, the pure strategy M is optimal for Row; for $p < (c-b)/(a-b+c-d)$, pure strategy E is optimal for Row; and $(c-b)/(a-b+c-d) > 0.5$.

The Case of Backward Myopia and Infinite Forward Farsightedness

Consider a repeated Prisoner's Dilemma game with an infinite time horizon. As noted, on any trial t, one of four states can obtain:

(i) *MM*, (ii) *ME*, (iii) *EM*, or (iv) *EE*. If the strategy decision on trial $t+1$ depends only on which state prevails at time t, we can construct a 4×4 Markovian transition matrix of order 1. The history of *all* previous strategy choices is *implicit in the recursive structure* of a first order Markovian matrix, since, denoting the simultaneous strategy choices by agents i and j, $(i, j \in \{L, B\})$ on trial t by S_t^{ij}, we have the temporal structure

$$S_t^{ij} = S_t^{ij}(S_{t-1}^{ij}(S_{t-2}^{ij}(S_{t-3}^{ij}\ldots(S_1^{ij})))\ldots) \tag{2A.6}$$

However, the first order Markovian matrix would be identical if both agents could remember only what occurred on the immediately preceding trial and could not, therefore, incorporate history from the more distant (i.e., two or more trials back) past.

A Markovian matrix eventually converges if it is "regular," i.e. if eventually any state can be reached from any other state so that eventually all S_{ij} entries are positive. By convergence to a steady-state matrix is meant the tendency of the probabilities of moving into any given state to approach limiting values. Thus, if the steady-state matrix $S \to S^*$ as $t \to \infty$,

$$S^* = \begin{bmatrix} S_{11}^* & S_{12}^* & S_{13}^* & S_{14}^* \\ S_{11}^* & S_{12}^* & S_{13}^* & S_{14}^* \\ S_{11}^* & S_{12}^* & S_{13}^* & S_{14}^* \\ S_{11}^* & S_{12}^* & S_{13}^* & S_{14}^* \end{bmatrix} \tag{2A.7}$$

That is, each row is identical to the fixed point eigenvector $|S_{11}^*, S_{12}^*, S_{13}^*, S_{14}^*|$, implying that S_{11}^* is the probability in the long run of being in state *MM*; S_{12}^* is the probability in the long run of being in state *ME*; S_{21}^* is the probability in the long run of being in state *EM*; and S_{22}^* is the probability in the long run of being in state *EE*, *regardless* of which of these states was the initial one—that is, which one occurred on the first trial.

It is worthwhile noting that if at least one player adopts a MRTFT, then the transition probability from *ME* or *EM* to *MM* is zero and the Markov matrix would not be regular; that is, the long-run probability of reaching *MM* from *ME* or *EM* would be zero.

The importance of a steady-state Markov matrix is that it enables a player in an infinitely repeated game to calculate his *average expected long-run payoff* (AELRP) resulting from the adoption by his opponent and himself of specified strategic policies. For example, suppose that Column plays PTFT (with probability P_c), that Row adopts

PTFT (with probability P_r), and that the resulting steady-state payoff matrix is given by S^*. Then for payoff matrix

	M	E
M	0, 0	$-.09, 0.09$
E	$0.09, -.18$	$-.085, -0.10$

for example, the expected utility (i.e., the AELRP) would be

$$(0 \cdot S_{11}^* - .09 S_{12}^* + .09 S_{13}^* - .085 S_{14}^*) \quad \text{for Row, and}$$
$$(0 \cdot S_{11}^* + .09 S_{12}^* - .18 S_{13}^* - 0.10 S_{14}^*) \quad \text{for Column.}$$

The AELRP is calculated on the assumption that the *psychological propensities* of each player to play M or E on a particular trial, given that the state *MM*, *ME*, *EM*, or *EE* respectively obtained in the immediately preceding trial, remain *constant*. Alternatively, one could assume that a player who undertakes such an AELRP calculation strictly adheres (or *plans* to adhere) to a strategic policy and, moreoever, *does not anticipate* the revision over time of his subjective probability concerning the psychological propensities of the other player.

The revision of a player's subjective probability assessment of his opponent's psychological propensities would require that whenever such a Bayesian revision of prior distribution occurs, this player would recalculate the AELRP that he expects to realize from pursuing a particular policy.

A player's optimal policy, on this view, would be revised whenever he revises his prior subjective probability assessment of his opponent's strategy. Given a particular prior at trial t for player i ($i \in \{$Row, Column$\}$), player i's "optimal strategy" at t would be that strategy which maximizes his AELRP as calculated at t. In Grofman and Poole (1975), when Row attributes a PTFT policy to Column, Row's optimal counterpolicy is shown to be a *pure* strategy of M or E, and the range of P_c values for which M or E are optimal are delimited, as described previously. Such optimal counterpolicies are predicated on the assumption that the coefficients of the basic Markovian matrix persist indefinitely.

It is important to note that in experimental work in the repeated Prisoner's Dilemma, subjects had a fraction of a minute (according to Rapoport and Dale (1966), 6 seconds) to select M or E on each trial. Clearly, then, the formulation of an optimal policy based on maximization of AELRP, incorporating Bayesian revision of priors, can hardly describe the actual process of subjects in an experimental laboratory.

The Second Order Markov Process Model

Rapoport and Mowshowitz found "a statistically significant improvement in prediction if one knows the responses of the pair of subjects on the previous two trials as against only the preceding trial" (1966: 450). A second order Markov process would be a 16×16 matrix where each row would depict a "state" corresponding to the previous two states which prevailed on the preceding two trials. It would appear as shown in Table 2A–3.

For each row, there are exactly four possible non-zero entries, depicted by a checkmark ($\sqrt{}$). If each checkmark is indeed positive, the matrix is regular and a fixed point eigenvector (of sixteen elements) can be calculated, allowing in turn the calculation of AELRP.

One could proceed, in similar fashion, to determine m-order Markov matrices ($m > 2$) and their corresponding eigenvectors to calculate their AELRP. The motivation in increasing the order of the Markov process is to take the history of interaction between the players into account *more fully* as a determinant of (or at least influence on) their strategy choices.

To this end, Smale (1980) developed an averaging approach to derive a summary statistic of the history of outcomes in a repeated Prisoner's Dilemma game of

	M	E
M	2, 2	0, 3
E	3, 0	1, 1

The average, whether weighted more heavily by more recent past or not, would appear as a point in the convex closure shown as Figure 2A–1.

Smale defines a "good" strategy as one in which a player does not allow himself to be exploited and therefore would select strategy E if the average to date has yielded him an average payoff below 1 (i.e., below the (noncooperative) maximin) or his opponent's payoff is above 2 (which suggests that historically the maximum potential *joint*

Table 2A–3. Second Order Markov Matrix.

	1.	2.	3.	4.	5.	6.	7.	8.	9.	10.	11.	12.	13.	14.	15.	16.
1. MM MM	✓	✓	✓	○	○	✓	○	○	○	○	○	○	○	○	○	○
2. MM ME	○	○	○	✓	○	○	✓	○	✓	○	○	○	○	○	✓	○
3. MM EM	○	○	○	○	✓	○	○	✓	○	✓	○	○	○	✓	○	○
4. ME MM	✓	✓	✓	○	○	✓	○	○	○	○	○	○	○	○	○	○
5. EM MM	✓	✓	✓	○	○	✓	○	○	○	○	○	○	○	○	○	○
6. MM EE	○	○	○	○	○	○	○	○	○	○	✓	✓	✓	○	○	✓
7. ME ME	○	○	○	✓	○	○	✓	○	✓	○	○	○	○	○	✓	○
8. EM ME	○	○	○	✓	○	○	✓	○	✓	○	○	○	○	○	✓	○
9. ME EM	○	○	○	○	✓	○	○	✓	○	✓	○	○	○	✓	○	○
10. EM EM	○	○	○	○	✓	○	○	✓	○	✓	○	○	○	✓	○	○
11. EE MM	✓	✓	✓	○	○	✓	○	○	○	○	○	○	○	○	○	○
12. EE EM	○	○	○	○	✓	○	○	✓	○	✓	○	○	○	✓	○	○
13. EE ME	○	○	○	✓	○	○	✓	○	✓	○	○	○	○	○	✓	○
14. EM EE	○	○	○	○	○	○	○	○	○	○	✓	✓	✓	○	○	✓
15. ME EE	○	○	○	○	○	○	○	○	○	○	✓	✓	✓	○	○	✓
16. EE EE	○	○	○	○	○	○	○	○	○	○	✓	✓	✓	○	○	✓

Figure 2A–1. The Payoff Polygon for Iterated Prisoners Dilemma.

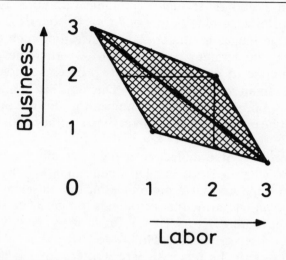

payoff of 4 has been divided unequally, to the detriment of this player and to the advantage of his opponent). The player would select strategy *M* whenever the average indicates that the two players have equal average payoffs and also when the average is in an *open* set containing the equal payoff segment between values of 1 and 2.

Sale proves that if both players adopt a "good" strategy, the payoffs converge to (2, 2) and the strategies constitute Nash equilibria. The *rate* of convergence is positively related to the size of the open set in which moderation prevails.

If these "good" strategies are modified ever so slightly so that *E* is chosen in an open set containing the equal payoff segment between values 1 and 2, the unique Nash equilibrium (which is globally stable) becomes the payoff (1, 1) — the noncooperative outcome wherein the players converge to the trap of a Pareto-inefficient outcome. This illustrates well how the tiniest of epsilons can separate civilization, or cooperation, from the war-of-all-against-all, the noncooperative outcome.

Communication

To this point, we have labored under the self-imposed restriction of *no verbal communication* between the players in order to explore the possibilities for resolving the Prisoner's Dilemma impasse under the most restrictive assumptions.[19] Let us now permit verbal communication between L and B. If such communication consists merely of reciprocal promises to play M in a *one-shot* Prisoner's Dilemma, the communication makes no material difference. For each player, E is *still* the dominant strategy irrespective of whether the other party intends to adhere to or "welch" on his promise; consequently EE would ensue. In an *iterated* Prisoner's Dilemma setting, the *credibility* of one's opponent's verbal communication, his announced strategy, say, can be established with increasing accuracy with the passage of time.

The importance of establishing a high "credibility rating" as a means of resolving the Prisoner's Dilemma can be seen by the following example. Suppose that L announces at the outset of an iterated Prisoner's Dilemma setting that he intends to play M on the first trial and thereafter to adhere to a Tit-for-Tat strategy. Now suppose B — recalling the observation of a Hollywood wag that "verbal agreements aren't worth the paper they're written on" — is a skeptic by nature and suspects that L is up to no good and this announcement is simply a trick designed to induce him (B) to lower his guard and play M; so B plays E and, true to his word, L responds to the ME outcome of the first trial by playing E on the second trial. B now *revises upward his Bayesian prior* probability assumption regarding L's playing Tit-for-Tat, say from $p = 0$ to some *posterior* $p > 0$ (it is as if B regards L as playing a PTFT strategy) and *continues to revise* p *upward* so long as L's play conforms to his announced strategy. Once p exceeds the critical value of $27/37$, the critical "credibility rating," B's utility maximization calculus dictates that he be deterred from choosing E at $t - 1$ by the belief that L will, with probability $p > 27/37$, retaliate with E on trial t. At this stage, the players lock into MM and the Prisoner's Dilemma game is resolved. Perhaps the greatest significance of verbal communication for iterated Prisoner's Dilemma arises from the fact that it can greatly accelerate the process by which each player can discern the (conditional) strategy being followed by the other player. Only once such knowledge is acquired, at least in the probabilistic sense, can the players "coordinate" their strategy choices to their mutual advantage.

In the usual Prisoner's Dilemma setting such coordination expresses itself in the phenomenon of both players locking into the MM pattern in repeated trials. In other variants of Prisoner's Dilemma,

Figure 2A–2.   Quasi–Prisoner's Dilemma.

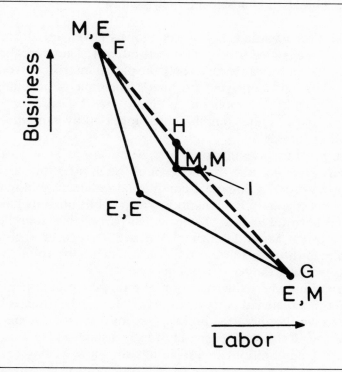

Note: In normal form, this Quasi-Prisoner's Dilemma appears as follows:

		Business	
		M	*E*
Labor	*M*	a, a'	b, c'
	E	c, b'	d, d'

coordination may find other forms. Thus, playing *EM* with probability α and *ME* with probability $1-\alpha$, where $FH/FG < \alpha < FI/FG$ yields correlated strategy payoff mixtures that strictly dominate *MM* in the Quasi–Prisoner's Dilemma game characterized by the relations (i) $c > a > d > b$ and (i)' $c' > a' > d' > b'$ but (*in contrast to the usual Prisoner's Dilemma game*) (ii) $b + c > 2a$ and (ii)' $b' + c' > 2a'$. (See Figure 2A–2.)

Threats, Promises, and Self-penalties

Since the time of Adam Smith, economists have trusted *homo economicus* to be guided by a spirit of self-interest. Thus verbal communication that fails to alter materially the payoff matrix confronting an individual in, say, a one-shot Prisoner's Dilemma, is most unlikely to engender a spirit of moderation. Only *credible* threats, *credible* promises, and genuine commitments supported by *guarantees* could plausibly induce *M*.

For a threat to have any force (i.e., be nonempty or at least probabilistically credible), the threatener must be in a position to carry it out. The nature of a threat is a conditional statement of intent of the form, "Unless you do x, I will do y, which (while possibly harmful to myself) is harmful to you." Since neither party gains from the execution of a threat and at least the threatened party loses, the *rationale* for issuing a threat is to *induce* the threatened party to undertake x, thereby avoiding the nasty consequences of y.

In situations where the execution of a threat would inflict damage on *both* the threatened party *and* the threatener, the threatened party may perceive the threat as hollow (vacuous or empty) and thus be tempted to call the threatener's bluff by refusing to play x (as per the threatener's admonition) *unless* he has somehow visibly committed himself in an irrevocable way to the execution of the threat. Consider, for example, a MRTFT strategy by player I in a repeated Prisoner's Dilemma. Now suppose player II reasons that I would be a fool to execute the threat implicit in this strategy since it would forever *foreclose* the possibility of *MM* and would be harmful to I as well as II. To render such a threat *credible* (albeit implausible), player I builds a "doomsday machine" which is on automatic (and irreversible) control, preprogrammed with a MRTFT to be played on I's behalf. Should II consider calling I's bluff by playing E, he would realize that the execution of the threat is a foregone conclusion, not subject to renunciation due to misgivings on I's part.

A Digression on Threats and Promises in the One-Shot Prisoner's Dilemma Game

In games of threat-vulnerable equilibria where *each* player has a dominating strategy (games 19–2 in the taxonomy of Rapoport and

	A_2	B_2
A_1	3, 4	4, 3
B_1	1, 2	2, 1

	A_2	B_2
A_1	3, 4	4, 3
B_1	2, 2	1, 1

	A_2	B_2
A_1	2, 4	4, 3
B_1	1, 2	3, 1

Guyer 1966), A_1A_2 is a threat vulnerable equilibrium; to induce Column to shift from A_2 to B_2, Row can threaten to play B_1 unless Column acquiesces. While Column would suffer if the threat were executed, so would Row; moreoever if Column called Row's bluff by remaining at A_2, then by carrying out his threat and playing B_1, Row would effect payoff B_1A_2, from which Column would have *no incentive* to move to B_1B_2. If Row irrevocably committed himself to such a threat, not only would it not be empty, but it would appear effective in inducing Column to adopt B_2 so that B_1A_2 would not have to come about.

A combination of *threat and promise* must be provided by Row (in Game 39 in the Rapoport–Guyer taxonomy) if Row is to induce Column to shift from A_2 to B_2.

	A_2	B_2
A_1	2, 4	3, 3
B_1	1, 2	4, 1

Row threatens to upset the initial equilibrium at A_1A_2 by playing B_1 unless Column plays B_2, thereby moving the outcome to A_1B_2. However, such a move would leave Column vulnerable to a shift by Row by B_1, moving the outcome to the worst outcome for Column of B_1B_2. Column would *only* acquiesce to Row's threat *if* this were accompanied by B's promise to permit A_1B_2 to endure by resisting the temptation to shift the situation to B_1B_2.

In the one-shot Prisoner's Dilemma, threats are irrelevant since the players move simultaneously. Only a *joint promise* by both parties, supported by suitable penalties that remove any temptation to renege on such promises, would render outcome MM. Letting a, b, c, d and a', b', c', d' represent u-money

	M	E
M	a, a'	b, c'
E	c, b'	d, d'

only if a fine of $c - a + e$ $(c' - a' + e)$, $e > 0$, were levied on Row (Column) for playing E while the other party played M and a fine of

$d-b+e\ (d'-b'+e)$, $e>0$ were levied on Row (Column) for playing E while the other party played E, would the temptation to play E be removed from both parties. Rendering joint promises credible in this context would require *a third party*—in this case government—to penalize the noncompliance with promises by either party. As Shubik notes:

> In much of everyday political, economic and social life, Prisoner's Dilemma situations are handled by third parties acting as escrow agents, holding bonds that are posted, enforcing outside agreements, or otherwise serving to police agreements. (1970: 193, n. 6)

The above "resolution" of the one-shot Prisoner's Dilemma involves its evasion by *transforming* the payoff matrix to the following:

	M	E
M	a, a'	$b, a'-e$
E	$a-e, b'$	$b-e, b'-e$

The ordinal relationship $c>a>d>b$ (and $c'>a'>d'>b'$) becomes replaced by $a>a-e>b>b-e$; rewritten in ordinal numbers, the matrix appears as

	M	E
M	4, 4	2, 3
E	3, 2	1, 1

(or as the no-conflict game 6 in the Rapoport–Guyer taxonomy of 2×2 games). M thus would become the dominant strategy for both players.

Let us consider next a *sequential* game having a Prisoner's Dilemma payoff structure with, say, Row choosing his strategy first and then Column, being *fully* informed of Row's prior strategy, selecting his strategy. Assume preplay communication with binding agreements. In a one-shot version of this game, Row would only risk playing M if Column could *credibly promise* to respond with M. With payoff matrix

	M	E
M	a, a'	b, c'
E	c, b'	d, d'

Row would risk losing $d - b$ by playing M, since he could have assured himself of payoff d by playing his maximin strategy yet by playing M he would leave himself vulnerable to Column's possible duplicity which would yield Row only b. Column would be tempted to double-cross Row by the prospective gain from duplicity if $c' > a'$. How should a penalty clause be formulated to protect Row against a possible double-cross by Column in the sequential game? *Three* plausible *candidate penalty structures* come into consideration:

I.   Column must pay Row compensation $P_I \geq a - b$
II.   Column must pay Row compensation $P_{II} \geq d - b$
III. Column must pay Row *or a third party* $P_{III} \geq c' - a'$

P_I is *legalistic* in nature (see Shavell 1980); it represents the damage suffered by Row through Column's breach of promise (or "breach of contract" if a formal contract was drawn up) if Row's choice of M is met by Column's countering with E instead of the promised response of M.

P_{II} would render Row's M strategy his *maximin* payoff since it would fully compensate Row for any prospective loss due to Column's duplicity, the loss being measured as the difference between the (precompensation) minimum assured payoff to Row of d and the payoff Row would realize if Column double-crosses him by playing E.

P_{III} would render M an *equilibrium* strategy from Column's point of view by taxing away (at least) all prospective gains to Column from reneging on the promise to match Row's choice of M by M as well.

The structure of the Prisoner's Dilemma payoff matrix (with $a > d$) implies that $P_I > P_{II}$. *Assuming transferable utilities, P_I and P_{II} being* viewed as side payments, we can prove several propositions.

Theorem: P_I induces Pareto-optimal decisions by Column after an *MM* agreement is reached in the sequential Prisoner's Dilemma.
Proof: Case (1). Suppose *ME* is Pareto-superior to *MM*. This implies $b + c' > a + a'$, i.e., $c' - a' > a - b$. Since Column's prospective gain from reneging on his promise to play M is $c' - a'$, which exceeds his penalty of $a - b$, Column plays E and *ME* results.
Case (2). Now suppose *MM* Pareto-superior to *ME*. Then P_I is an effective deterrent to Column, since $a + a' > b + c' \Rightarrow a - b > c' - a'$, so *MM* results. In both cases, the Pareto-optimal outcome occurs under P_I, q.e.d.

Theorem: P_{II} induces Pareto-optimal decisions by Column after an *MM* agreement is struck in the sequential Prisoner's Dilemma if the *ME* is Pareto-superior to *MM*.

Proof: *ME* is Pareto-superior if and only if $a + a' < b + c'$, i.e., $c' - a' > a - b$. But $a - b > d - b$; therefore $c' - a' > d - b$ (i.e., $P_{III} > P_{II}$). Then P_{II} is an effective deterrent in preventing *ME* and Pareto-optimality will result, q.e.d.

Claim: For the case in which *MM* is Pareto-superior to *ME*, it is not clear whether P_{II} induces *MM*; in general it need not do so. For we can only assert that $c' - a' < a - b$ for this case and for P_{II} to induce *MM*, it would have to be the case that $c' - a' < d - b$, an inequality that may or may not hold.

Claim: P_{II} renders *MM* an *un*dominated joint strategy regardless of whether or not *MM* is Pareto-optimal. Where $P_{III} > c' - a'$, *MM* is the dominant joint strategy.

"Solutions" Based upon Altering Utility Functions and/or Altering Ethical Norms of Conduct

If "solutions" to the Prisoner's Dilemma Game are conceived in the broadest sense, the social problem of a socially inferior noncooperative outcome can be overcome in two more ways. First, if the utility functions of the players are appropriately altered — either of their own accord or, à la Weisbrod (1977), through the government's devoting resources to this end — the payoff matrix could conceivably be transformed from one having a Prisoner's Dilemma structure to one having, say, a non-conflict structure.

There are endless possibilities for transforming the payoff matrix by altering the utility function of one or both players. To illustrate this simply, let us first begin with an *outcome* bi-matrix of Prisoner's Dilemma structure in single dimensional *cardinal* units, say dollars, in order to examine its corresponding payoff matrix structure under alternative utility functions for one or both parties (see Table 2A–4). Let U_R and U_c denote the utility functions of Row and Column where $U_i : \langle x, y \rangle \to IR$, $i \in \{\text{Row, Column}\}$ and $\langle x, y \rangle$ is the ordered pair denoting \$ payment to Row and Column, respectively.

Table 2A–4. (Dollar) Outcome Bi-matrix.

		Column	
		M	E
Row	M	3, 3	1, 4
	E	4, 1	2, 2

Case (1). No Interdependence; Utilities Linear in Money. Here the payoff matrix retains the Prisoner's Dilemma structure. If, for simplicity,

$$U_R = 1 \cdot x + 0 \cdot y$$

and

$$U_c = 0 \cdot x + 1 \cdot y$$

the payoff matrix is exactly as above with the difference that the elements in each cell now denote the utility payoffs to each player.

Case (2). Perfect Altruism; Utilities of Each Player (Positively) Linear in Money Payment Accruing Only to the Other Player. Here the payoff structure becomes that of a No-conflict Game. If, for simplicity,

$$U_R = 0 \cdot x + 1 \cdot y$$

and

$$U_c = 1 \cdot x + 0 \cdot y$$

the payoff matrix becomes that shown in Table 2A–5, (Game 9 in Rapoport–Guyer taxonomy), where *MM* is strongly stable equilibrium.

Table 2A–5. (Utility) Payoff Matrix for Two Altruists.

	M	E
M	3, 3	4, 1
E	1, 4	2, 2

Here *MM*, the jointly cooperative strategy, corresponds to the dominant strategy for each player.

Case (3). Imperfect Altruism.   One player, say Row, cares (positively) only about income of Column, while Column cares only about his own income. For simplicity, let

$$U_R = 0 \cdot x + 1 \cdot y$$

and

$$U_c = 0 \cdot x + 1 \cdot y$$

Then the payoff matrix corresponding to Table 2A-4, the (Dollar) Outcome Bi-matrix, has the structure shown in Table 2A-6, for the No-Conflict Game (Game 1 in Rapoport–Guyer taxonomy).

Table 2A-6.   (Utility) Payoff Matrix for Row = Altruist and Column = Purely Selfish Player.

		Column	
		M	*E*
Row	*M*	3, 3	4, 4
	E	1, 1	2, 2

ME is Pareto-optimal equilibrium corresponding to dominant strategies of *M* and *E* for Row and Column, respectively, and entailing a money payment of $1 to Row and $4 to Column.

Case (4). Perfect Invidiousness.   Both players derive utility only from the differential between their income and that of the other player. For simplicity, let

$$U_R = 1 \cdot (x - y)$$

and

$$U_c = 1 \cdot (y - x)$$

Then the (Dollar) Outcome Bi-matrix becomes the matrix shown in Table 2A-7.

Table 2A-7. (Utility) Payoff Matrix for Perfect Invidiousness.

	M	E
M	0, 0	−3, 3
E	3, −3	0, 0

Equilibrium is at *EE* and *E* is the dominant strategy for each player. This corresponds to the egalitarian but Pareto-inferior income distribution of \$2 to Row and to Column.

Case (5). Imperfect Invidiousness. Only one player, say Row, is purely invidious, while the other player is purely selfish. For simplicity, let

$$U_R = 1 \cdot (x - y)$$

and

$$U_c = 0 \cdot x + 1 \cdot y$$

Then the utility payoff bi-matrix corresponding to the (Dollar) Outcome Bi-matrix appears as shown in Table 2A-8.

Table 2A-8. (Utility) Payoff Matrix for Imperfect Invidiousness.

	M	E
M	0, 3	−3, 4
E	3, 1	0, 2

Once again, equilibrium is at *EE* since *E* is the dominant strategy for each player. This equilibrium is Pareto-inferior to *MM*. The Pareto-optimal frontier (in utility space) comprises *MM*, *ME*, and *EM* (as in the Prisoner's Dilemma game) but *EE* is strictly dominated by *MM*.

A taxonomic scheme of various homogeneous linear utility functions, based upon alternative psychological predispositions, is presented by Grofman (1975).[21] These categories may be illustrated (arbitrarily) in terms of U_L as follows (where $a, b, c > 0$):

1. $U_L = a(W + R)$: egalitarian (ethical utilitarian)
2. $U_L = bW + cR$: mixed motive utilitarian
3. $U_L = bW$: pure self-interest utilitarian
4. $U_L = cR$: pure altruistic utilitarian
5. $U_L = a(W - R)$: egalitarian relativist utilitarian
6. $U_L = bW - cR$: relativist utilitarian
7. $U_L = -a(W + R)$: egalitarian sadomasochist
8. $U_L = -bW - cR$: sadomasochistic
9. $U_L = -bW$: pure masochistic
10. $U_L = -cR$: pure sadistic
11. $U_L = -a(W + R)$: egalitarian masochistic-altruistic
12. $U_L = -bW + cR$: masochistic-altruistic

If both players have "pure masochistic" utility functions, a variant of a Prisoner's Dilemma payoff matrix possessing an interesting twist emerges. Thus, using our previous rotation, let

$$U_R = -1 \cdot x \quad \text{and} \quad U_c = -1 \cdot y$$

The (Utility) Payoff Matrix corresponding to the previously shown (Dollar) Outcome Matrix would appear as shown in Table 2A–9.

Table 2A–9. (Utility) Payoff Matrix.

		Column	
		M	E
Row	M	−3, −3	−1, −4
	E	−4, −1	−2, −2

Row and Column each have the dominant strategy M and MM is the equilibrium payoff. The twist is that now, given the "pure masochistic" utility functions of Row and Column, EE would be Pareto-superior to MM, so that moderate behavior leads to a socially undesirable result (judged by the preferences of Row and Column).

Consider finally another twist on the Prisoner's Dilemma theme provided by Grofman (1975) in his "Altruist's Dilemma," wherein the outcome matrix reserves the severest punishment for a lone confessor who assumes the full burden of guilt. Treating time spent outside

Table 2A-10. Outcome Bi-matrix.

		Column	
		Not Confess	Confess
Row	Not Confess	0.9, 0.9	1, 0
	Confess	0, 1	0.1, 0.1

prison as a normal good, the *outcome* matrix appears as shown in Table 2A-10.

A purely altruistic utility function (as in category 4) for both players transforms this outcome matrix into the *ordinal* utility matrix shown in Table 2A-11.

Table 2A-11. Ordinal Utility Payoff Matrix for Pure Altruists, Prisoner's Dilemma Game.

	Not Confess	Confess
Not Confess	3, 3	1, 4
Confess	4, 1	2, 2

The Prisoner's Dilemma game emerges with each player confessing in a vain effort to assume the entire burden of guilt and punishment, bringing about the collectively inferior ordinal utility payoff $\langle 2, 2 \rangle$.

Moving from the one-shot Prisoner's Dilemma game to the finitely iterated Prisoner's Dilemma game in which both players know exactly the number of trials to be played, there remains the task of reconciling the prediction, based on the rigorous logic of backward induction, that only *EE* will be played, with the considerable evidence (and practical common sense) in support of a significant proportion of *MM* strategies occurring, particularly where the number of iterations is large.

Precisely such a task was undertaken by Selten (1978). For definiteness, Selten considers a 100-iteration Prisoner's Dilemma supergame. He grants that the induction argument is extremely compelling for the last periods of the supergame (i.e., from period $100 - r$ to 100), but argues that for the first $100 - r$ periods, an ordinary Tit-for-Tat strategy is recommended. Even if Row, say, *knows* that Column plans to adopt a Tit-for-Tat strategy until iteration 97 (i.e., Column's $r = 3$) and will then adopt an E strategy for the final three iterations, the *best response strategy* of Row would be to also play ordinary Tit-for-Tat for all but the final *four* iterations, exploiting Column only on iteration 96. Each player i using his intuition, would decide upon his own r_i value, that is, would adopt only E strategies from $100 - r_i$ until 100. Of course if each player endeavors too strenuously to second-guess the other and adopt a larger r_i, the situation could slide toward the backward induction trap of an EE lock-in. But as Selten remarks, "for reasonably small r_i it is much more advantageous to be outguessed in the cooperation theory than to use a best reply in the induction theory" (1978: 141).

To formalize his approach, Selten considers a laboratory setting with money payoffs corresponding to the Prisoner's Dilemma matrix structure (see (Dollar) Outcome Bi-matrix presented earlier) and introduces a "benevolence theory." Utility payoffs are assumed to be the *sum* of (1) "primary" utility, linearly dependent on money pay-offs, and (2) "secondary" utility, dependent "on the player's perception of his social relations with the other players."

Let

a = secondary utility to each player whenever MM occurs;

$-b_s$ = (negative) secondary utility to Row from occurrence of EM at t;

$-b_s$ = (negative) secondary utility to Column from occurrence of ME at t;

s = the number of consecutive periods during which MM occurred (i.e., from $t-s$ to $t-1$); thus in $t-s-1$, at least one of the players selected E.

Secondary disutility $-b_s$ results in period t for the player selecting E while the other player selects M, i.e., $-b_s$ is the secondary disutility of betraying the other player's trust. b_s is an *increasing function* of s. This accords with the empirical findings of Rapoport and Mowshowitz, who make the following observation

an examination of our data suggests that so far as "trustworthiness" is concerned, this propensity does not remain constant but increases as a function of the length of a run of jointly cooperative decisions. That is to say, the longer a [MM] run lasts the less likely it is to terminate. This finding corresponds to our intuitive feeling that continued co-operation reinforces the mutual trustworthiness of both players. (1966: 450)

The symmetric bi-matrix of secondary utilities is then

	M	E
M	a, a	$0, -b_s$
E	$-b_s, 0$	$0, 0$

in period t. Combining this with the primary utility matrix

	M	E
M	3, 3	1, 4
E	4, 1	2, 2

yields the payoff matrix

	M	E
M	$3+a, 3+a$	$1, 4-b_s$
E	$4-b_s, 1$	$2, 2$

for period t. In a game of m iterations, player i's payoff is the sum of his primary and secondary payoffs for all m trials; but since $|b_s|$ depends upon the history of the game, the game lacks the structure of a supergame (for which the payoff matrix is invariant with respect to the historical pattern of joint strategy choices). Clearly EE is *always* a Nash equilibrium point; that is, if one's opponent behaves extremely, it is worthwhile to reciprocate with E. But providing $3+a \geq 4-b_s$ (i.e., providing $a+b_s \geq 1$), *a second Nash equilibrium* in pure strategies, namely MM, emerges in period t. Denoting by $\bar{s}$ the smallest integer satisfying $a+b_{\bar{s}} \geq 1$, for sufficiently small $\bar{s}$, an ordinary Tit-for-Tat strategy preserves the equilibrium character of MM. In a 100-iteration game, if $\bar{s} = 99$, then a MRTFT suffices to render MM the perpetual equilibrium strategy.

Thus, by assumptions that appropriately modify the players' utility functions, Selten allows the possibility of escape from the EE trap (via backward induction) in the finitely iterated (a known number of trials) Prisoner's Dilemma game.

A secondary approach to "solving" the Prisoner's Dilemma focuses upon the ethical systems of the players. This approach accepts the Prisoner's Dilemma payoff structure as datum, but *redefines individual rationality* to accord with mutually moderate (*MM*) behavior. Thus, golden rule behavior, or existentialist conduct, or following Kant's "categorical imperative" would, by motivating each player to choose the dominated payoff *M*, result in the "solution" *MM*, which dominates *EE*.

NOTES

1. Stein (1982) sees monetarism as a unifying bridge between Keynesianism and New Classical Economics.
2. "(von Neumann and Morgenstern) saw game theory as, in sum, the theory of the emergence of stable institutional arrangements or "standards of behavior" in a given physical situation or game. . . . the theory tries to predict what stable institutional form will emerge from a given economic background and what the resulting value relationships will be. . . . (social institutions) are an outcome of the theory rather than an input into it." (Schotter and Schwodiauer 1980: 481–482)
3. Institutional economics, the first and perhaps the only purely American school of thought, was of course pioneered by Veblen, Clark, Mitchell and Commons early in this century. It emphasized the influence of the social environment — in particular, the institution of private property — on human behavior. The influence of this approach was limited by its descriptive nature, in an age when economics became formal and analytical. Game-theoretic institutional economics is a direct descendant of Veblen and Commons, but is immensely more powerful and rigorous.
    One of the most basic of all social institutions is money. Tobin (1982) has noted "the difficulty of explaining within the basic paradigms of economic theory why paper that makes no intrinsic contribution to utility or technology is held at all and has positive value in exchange for goods and services" (p. 173). For a game-theoretic explanation of the existence of money, see Schotter (1980: 35–38).
4. For Marxist, class-struggle versions, see Rosenberg and Weisskopf (1981) and Rowthorn (1977).
5. See Schotter (1980), Bull and Schotter (Chapter 4 in this book), Colander (Chapter 3), Maital (1979), Maital and Benjamini (1980), and Sutcliffe (1981).
6. In reality, of course, a great many games are going on simultaneously: within labor unions, among labor unions, within corporations, and so on. Also, there are many strategies between moderation and extrem-

ism. Macroeconomic conflict as a game is of course a parable or allegory. As Solow has said, "you ask of a parable not if it is literally true, but if it is well told" (1970: 1). Even when discussion is limited to 2×2 games, Rapoport and Guyer (1966) have shown that there are 78 conceptually different types of games, when preferences are strongly ordered. When preferences are weakly ordered (i.e., ties are permitted among the four outcomes), there are over 500 different types of games.

7. Of the seventy-eight different 2×2 games, Prisoner's Dilemma is the only one with this property.

8. For a formal analysis of conditions under which it is desirable for government to correct inefficiency stemming from the presence of externalities, by using resources to alter preferences, see Weisbrod (1977).

   In Chapter 7 we interpret tax-based incomes policy (TIP) as a restructuring of the macroeconomic game, turning it into the game of Chicken.

9. W. Arthur Lewis, in his comparison of 1899–1913 and 1950–1979 inflations, notes two major behavioral changes in the economy since 1939: the tying of money wages to the cost of living, and "the ending of the tradition that governments must balance their budgets, which has converted Central Banks into originators of inflation" (Lewis 1980: 436). This is not contradictory to Leviathan.

10. A historical parable of Prisoner's Dilemma is suggested by the analysis of W.A. Lewis (1980). Consider a model with two private goods, B and D, produced and sold by business and government, respectively, using only labor. The consumer price index P_t is a weighted average of $P_{B,t}$ and $P_{D,t}$. P_D is exogenously determined; P_B depends solely on the wage level.

$$P_t = P_{B,t}B + P_{D,t}D, \qquad B + D = 1.0$$

Adopt first the eighteenth-century assumption that money wages are independent of prices. Suppose all prices in $t = 0$ are equal to 1.0. Let there be a 20 percent rise (following Lewis's example) in P_D. There will therefore be a once-and-for-all increase in the consumer price index of $0.2D$. For $D = 0.2$, for example, consumer price index rises by 4 percent.

Now, assume that money wages are indexed, linked 100 percent to consumer prices.

$$W_t = P_{t-1}$$
$$P_{B,t} = W_t$$

A 20 percent rise in the price of D-goods will now cause a 20 percent rise in consumer prices.

$$P_t = 0.8P_{t-1} + (1.2)(0.2)$$
$$\bar{P} = 1.20$$

Finally, assume that money wages are fully indexed, and that government, too, raises D-goods prices in step with the consumer price index P.

$$P_{D,t} = P_{t-1}$$

In this model

$$P_t = 0.8P_{t-1} + (0.2)(1.2)P_{t-1} = 1.04P_{t-1}$$

Prices therefore rise interminably, 4 percent each period, forever. The difference between a once and for all 20 percent rise in the price level, and a perpetually increasing one, has been the behavior of a relatively small sector of the economy. If inflation imposes real costs on labor, business, and government, the attempt of each sector to index its wages or prices will be mutually destructive. Yet no side will unilaterally forfeit such indexation.

11. This has been fashioned into the Catch 22 argument against incomes policy. The former head of Israel's Civil Service Commission, Abraham Friedman, recently wrote that "in order for the package deal (incomes) policy to work and solve the problem, there has to be, among the three sides to the agreement, one side strong enough to ensure that the agreement is kept. But if there *were* one partner strong enough, there wouldn't be any need of a package deal, because that side could "impose" its policy in collective bargaining (Friedman 1980: 231).

12. This is the general spirit of MAP (market anti-inflation plan), proposed by Abba Lerner and David Colander (1982). Under MAP, a new "commodity" is created: "the right to increase value added per unit input." The market for these rights equates supply and demand for them. The price of these rights "provides the appropriate downward counter-pressure against the inflationary upward pressure, and thereby prevents expectational inflation" (pp. 47, 48).

13. Cited by Professor H. Clegg, University of Warwick, in his address on "Incomes Policy, Labor Relations and Inflation," at Tel Aviv University, December 7, 1981.

14. Similarly, Kant's "categorical imperative": Act in such a way that if others also behaved thus, you would benefit thereby. Universal adoption of this norm would permanently resolve Prisoner's Dilemma. The difficulty in implementing it is illustrated by the following passage taken from Joseph Heller's *Catch 22* (cited by Ullmann-Margalit, 1978):

> Yossarian: I don't want to fly milk runs. I don't want to be in the war any more.
> Major Major: Would you like to see our country lose?
> Yossarian: We won't lose.... Some people are getting killed and a lot more are making money and having fun. Let somebody else get killed.

> Major Major: But suppose everybody on our side felt that way.
> Yossarian: Then I'd certainly be a damned fool to feel any other way. Wouldn't I?

15. See Deutsch et al. (1967).

16. Another example of self-enforcement is Israel's 1980–1982 national wage agreement. Prior to this agreement, Finance Ministry officials found their efforts at restraining wages frustrated not solely by labor's wage demands, but by willingness of government ministers to grant excessive wage increases to those employed by their Ministry. High salaries, and the magnitude of total employment and total spending, are viewed by ministers as measures of bureaucratic success. Coalition politics exacerbated competition for such "success."

   To save government from itself, the 1980–1982 wage agreement included a clause whereby *any* departure by a Minister from the wage agreement for some specific group of workers would automatically be granted to *all* public employees (between one-third and one-quarter of Israel's employment), thus making the price of ministerial irresponsibility very expensive (Friedman 1980: 225).

17. See Rapoport and Dale (1966). See also Selten (1978) for an interesting analysis of the *inconsistency* between game theoretical reasoning and "plausible human behavior" in *finite* iterated Prisoner's Dilemma.

18. Rapoport and Dale (1966) determined experimentally a time course of M (in our notation) which reaches its asymptote in 30 days (within two decimal places). The failure of the one-step Markov chain to account for their observed *reversal* of the trend from decreasing to increasing M lead them to discard this one-step model.

19. Shubik has made the following observation: There would be no dilemma if the players were allowed to talk face-to-face before they played and to sign enforceable agreements. The interest in the problem comes about in studying the implications of the relative lack of communication and lack of enforceable agreement between them.

20. Grofman credits Sawyer (1966) with the development of analogous functions.

REFERENCES

Baumol, William. 1952. *Welfare Economics and the Theory of the State.* London: Longmans.

Bental, Benjamin. 1982. Comment on Bull and Schotter, "Garbage Game, Inflation, and Incomes Policy." Technion, Haifa.

Brams, Steven J. 1975. "Newcomb's Problem and Prisoner's Dilemma." *Journal of Conflict Resolution* 19:596–612.

Bonacich, P.; G.H. Shure; J.P. Kaham; and R.J. Meeker. 1976. "Cooperation and Group Size in the N-Person Prisoner's Dilemma." *Journal of
Conflict Resolution 20*:379–387.

Corden, W.M., and P.B. Dixon. 1980. "A Tax-wage Bargain in Australia:
Is a Free Lunch Possible?" *The Economic Record*, September:209–221.

Deutsch, Morton; Y. Epstein; D. Canavan; and P. Gumpert. "Strategies of
Inducing Cooperation: An Experimental Study." *Journal of Conflict
Resolution 11*:345–360.

Dolbear, F.T.; L.B. Lave; G. Bowman; A. Lieberman, E. Prescott; F.
Reuter; and R. Sherman. 1969. "Collusion in the PD: Number of Strategies." *Journal of Conflict Resolution 13*:252–261.

Evans, G.W., and C.M. Crumbaugh. 1966. "Payment Schedule, Sequence
of Choice, and Cooperation in the Prisoner's Dilemma Game." *Psycho-
nomic Science 5*:87–88.

Fox, J., and M. Guyer. 1978. "'Public' Choice and Cooperation in *N*-
Person Prisoner's Dilemma." *Journal of Conflict Resolution 22.*

Friedman, A. 1980. "Collective Bargaining and Wage Policy under Gallop-
ing Inflation." *Economics Quarterly* (Hebrew), September:224–235.

Grofman, B. 1975. "The Prisoner's Dilemma Game and the Problem of
Rational Choice: Paradox Reconsidered." In *Frontiers of Economics*,
edited by G. Tullock. Blackburg, Va.: University Publishing.

Grofman, B., and J. Poole. 1975. "Bayesian Models for Iterated Prisoner's
Dilemma." *General Systems 20*:185–194.

———. 1977. "How to Make Cooperation the Optimizing Strategy in a
Two-Person Game." *Journal of the Mathematical Society 5*:173–186.

Guyer, M., and B. Perkel. 1966. "Experimental Games: A Bibliography
(1945–71)." MS. no. 351. Mental Health Research Institute, University
of Michigan, Ann Arbor, Michigan.

Hamburger, H.; M. Guyer; and J. Fox. 1975. "Group Size and Cooperation." *Journal of Conflict Resolution 19*:503–531.

Howard, N. 1971. *Paradoxes in Rationality*. Cambridge, Mass.: MIT Press.

Hirschman, A. 1981. "The Social and Political Matrix of Inflation: Elabor-
ations on the Latin American Experience." In A.O. Hirschman, *Essays
in Trespassing*. Cambridge, England: Cambridge University Press.

Kahan, J.P., and Amnon Rapoport. 1980. "Coalition Formation in the
Triad When Two Are Weak and One Is Strong." *Mathematical Social
Sciences 1*:11–37.

Kearl, J.L.; C.L. Pope; Gordon C. Whiting; and L.T. Wimmer. 1979. "A
Confusion of Economists?" *American Economic Review 69*:28–37.

Kreps, D.M.; P. Milgrom; J. Roberts; and R. Wilson. 1981. "Rational Cooperation in the Finitely-Repeated Prisoner's Dilemma." Research Paper
#603, Economics Department, Stanford University, June.

Lerner, A., and D. Colander. 1982. "Anti-inflation Incentives." *Kyklos 35*:
39–52.

Lewis, D. 1969. *Convention: A Philosophical Study*. Cambridge, Mass.: Harvard University Press.

Lewis, W.A. 1980. "Rising Prices: 1899-1913 and 1950-1979." *Scandinavian Journal of Economics 82*:425-436.

Maital, S. 1979. "Inflation as Prisoner's Dilemma." *Challenge 22*, July-August:52-54.

———. 1982. *Minds, Markets, and Money: Psychological Foundations of Economic Behavior*. New York: Basic Books.

Maital, S., and Y. Benjamini. 1980. "Inflation as Prisoner's Dilemma." *Journal of Post Keynesian Economics*, Summer:459-481.

Maschler, M. 1963. "The Power of a Coalition." *Management Science 10*: 8-29.

Olson, M. 1982. "The Political Economy of Comparative Growth Rates." In *The Political Economy of Growth*, edited by Dennis C. Mueller. New Haven, Conn.: Yale University Press.

Oskamp, S., and D. Perlman. 1965. "Factors Affecting Cooperation in a Prisoner's Dilemma Game." *Journal of Conflict Resolution 9*:359-374.

Radner, R. "Can Bounded Rationality Resolve the Prisoner's Dilemma?" Bell Laboratories, working paper, n.d.

Rapoport, Anatol. 1967. "Escape from Paradox." *Scientific American*, July: 50-56.

———. 1970. *N-Person Game Theory*. Ann Arbor: University of Michigan Press.

Rapoport, Anatol, and A. Chammah. 1965. *Prisoner's Dilemma: A Study of Conflict and Cooperation*. Ann Arbor: University of Michigan Press.

Rapoport, A., and P.S. Dale, 1966. "Models for Prisoner's Dilamma." *Journal of Mathematical Psychology 3*:269-286.

Rapoport, A., and M. Guyer. 1966. "A Taxonomy of 2×2 games." *General Systems 11*:203-214.

Rapoport, A., and A. Mowshowitz. 1966. "Experimental Studies of Stochastic Models for the Prisoner's Dilemma." *Behavioral Science 2*: 444-458.

Rosenberg, S., and T.E. Weisskopf. 1981. "A Conflict Theory Approach to Inflation in the Postwar U.S. Economy." *American Economic Review 71*:42-47.

Rowthorn, R.E. 1977. "Conflict, Inflation and Money." *Cambridge Journal of Economics 1*:215-239.

Sawyer, J. 1966. "The Altruism Scale: A Measure of Cooperative, Individualistic and Competitive Interpersonal Orientation." *American Journal of Sociology*, 407-416.

Schelling, T. 1969. "Some Thoughts on the Relevance of Game Theory to the Analysis of Ethical Systems" (1968). In *Game Theory in the Behavioral Sciences*, edited by I.R. Buchler and H.G. Nutini. Pittsburgh, Pa.: University of Pittsburgh Press.

Schotter, A. 1981. *The Economic Theory of Social Institutions.* Cambridge, England: Cambridge University Press.

Schotter, A., and G.W. Schwodiauer. 1980. "Economics and the Theory of Games." *Journal of Economic Literature 18*:479–527.

Selten, R. 1978. "The Chain Store Paradox." *Theory and Decision 9*: 127–159.

Shavell, S. 1980. "Damage Measures for Breach of Conduct." *Bell Journal of Economics* 2(2) Autumn:466–490.

Shubik, M. 1952. "A Business Cycle Model with Organized Labor Considered." *Econometrica.*

———. 1970. "Game Theory, Behavior and the Paradox of the Prisoner's Dilemma: Three Solutions." *Journal of Conflict Resolution 14*:181–193.

Smale, S. 1980. "The Prisoner's Dilemma and Dynamical Systems Associated to Non-Cooperative Games." *Econometrica 48*(7), November:1617–1634.

Solow, R. 1970. *Growth Theory: an Exposition.* London: Oxford University Press.

Stein, Jerome L. 1981. "Monetarist, Keynesian and New Classical Economics." *American Economic Review 71*:139–144.

———. 1982. *Monetarist, Keynesian and New Classical Economics.* Oxford: Basil Blackwell.

Sutcliffe, C. 1981. "Inflation and Prisoner's Dilemma." *Journal of Post Keynesian Economics*, 574–585.

Ullmann-Margalit, E. 1977. *The Emergence of Norms.* London: Oxford University Press.

Weisbrod, B. 1977. "Comparing Utility Functions in Efficiency Terms." *American Economic Review 67*:991–995.

✳ PART II

INCOMES POLICY:
NEW APPROACHES

Chapter 3

Why an Incomes Policy Makes an Economy More Efficient

David C. Colander

In a well-known article, James Tobin (1972) argues against what has become known as the Phelps-Friedman theory of the "natural rate" and suggests reasons why the aggregate economy moves toward a nonoptimal steady-state equilibrium. He uses that analysis as a stepping stone into a discussion of the existence of a long-run trade-off between inflation and unemployment. In drawing policy implications from his analysis, he focuses on the long-run trade-off issue and not on the issue of whether or not the steady-state equilibrium of the economy is optimal. Later writers such as Franco Modigliani and Lucas Papademos (1975) and Robert A. Gordon (1979) have christened the nonoptimal unemployment rate the NIRU, for nonaccelerating inflation rate of unemployment (also abbreviated NARU and NAIRU). Thus, there are currently two terms used to characterize aggregate equilibrium in the economy, the NARU and the *natural rate*.

The difference between these two terms has never been totally clear, and often the two have been used interchangeably.[1] Tobin, for example, after discussing his reasons why a nonoptimal steady-state equilibrium is likely, suggests that if there is no long-run trade-off between inflation and unemployment, the economy will move to its "natural rate." Given such past usage, it is not surprising that to many the distinction is more semantic than real.

The purpose of this chapter is to argue that the difference between the two terms is real and that it underlies two different theories about how the economy works and what policies we should use to deal with inflation. In the chapter I expand arguments made earlier (Colander 1981, 1982) and attempt to reorient the NARU/natural state distinction away from the long-run inflation/unemployment trade-off issue and toward a focus on incomes policies in general, and incentive anti-inflation plans in specific.[2] I argue that both the NARU and the natural rate theory are consistent with a vertical long-run Phillips curve. The difference between the two is in the level and causes of unemployment at that equilibrium.

On the one hand, the natural rate theory is consistent with only layoff, search, wait, and other such direct frictional or contractual explanations of unemployment. On the other hand, the NARU incorporates an indirect structural cause of inflation which does not create an inflation/unemployment trade-off but instead generates accelerating inflation before the optimal level of employment is reached. Because accelerating inflation is inconsistent with long-run equilibrium, the economy faces a nonaccelerating price level constraint that feeds back to a constraint on individual price setters in the economy and forces the economy to operate at a resource utilization level less than the "natural" rate. The difference is best seen in the theory's alternative views of the effect of incomes policies. In the NARU theory an administratively feasible incomes policy will improve the efficiency of the economy, while in the natural rate theory it will not.

STATIC REPRESENTATIONS OF DYNAMIC PROCESS

The differences between the NARU and natural rate lie in dynamics, not statics. Most past considerations of these dynamics (which fall under the general heading microfoundations of macroeconomics) have not specifically considered the optimality of the adjustment process nor the effect of an incomes policy on that process. Instead they have begun with a concept of dynamic equilibrium in which the flow of individuals out of the unemployment pool equals the flow of new hires by firms.[3] They have then focused on the resulting quantity flow equilibrium, suppressing the analysis of the price adjustment process.

Just as in linear programming, where every problem has its dual, so too does the steady-state quantity flow equilibrium have a dual in a monetary economy's price adjustment system. The dual equilibrium constraint states that in equilibrium the upward pressure on the price level must equal the downward pressure. Vacancies and excess demand add to the upward pressure; unemployment and excess supply add to the downward pressure. Thus, at some ratio of vacancies to unemployment the opposing pressures will be equal and the aggregate labor market equilibrium will be achieved.

Most microfoundations work has merely taken the equilibrium vacancy/unemployment ratio as given and has analyzed how to improve the efficiency of the dynamic process — by changing the quantity flows in and out of unemployment and vacancy pools. Considering the dual equilibrium condition provides an alternative perspective on the dynamic adjustment process and provides insight into an alternative method of changing the aggregate equilibrium. Exploring this alternative allows one to understand better the distinction between the NARU and the natural rate and the role of incomes policies in changing that equilibrium.

The chapter proceeds as follows: I first describe an "almost competitive" economy, which is the simplest model of an aggregate economy sufficient to incorporate an approximation of a natural rate and NARU equilibrium. I then demonstrate how the normal price adjustment assumptions lead to a "natural rate" equilibrium, and how asymmetrical collusion or a price adjustment asymmetry such as that suggested by Tobin can lead to a nonoptimal aggregate equilibrium with no steady-state trade-off between inflation and unemployment. I then relate my approach to the more traditional microfoundations approach found in Phelps (1970) and Holt (1970), for example, and explain how within their model an alternate aggregate equilibrium can be achieved through the use of an incentive anti-inflation plan, and why within the NARU interpretation of the economy that different equilibrium is preferable.

ALMOST COMPETITIVE ECONOMIES

In order to move from a microeconomic model of individual decisionmakers to a model that incorporates inflation, a certain amount of hand-waving is necessary. Milton Friedman used a bit of hand-waving when he defined the natural rate as

> the level that would be ground-out by the Walrasian system of general equilibrium equations, provided there is imbedded in them the actual

structural characteristics of the labor and commodity markets, including market imperfections, stochastic variability in demands and supplies, the cost of gathering information about job vacancies and labor availabilities, the costs of mobility and so on. (1968: 5)

Numerous objections to Friedman's definition have been raised, and it is so broad that for many it merely says that the natural rate is the actual rate. Nonetheless, it represented a major shift in macroeconomic thinking and focused the analysis of unemployment on market adjustment to random shocks and away from Keynesian fixed wage-price models. The result is the now well-known search, wait, and frictional unemployment explanations of the natural rate.

These microeconomic foundations of unemployment theory have bothered many economists but the "natural rate" explanations of steady-state equilibrium have nonetheless predominated. There have, of course, been modifications of the natural rate explanations such as Okun's (1981) toll model and Salop's (1979) price signaling model, but the natural rate explanation of unemployment has remained central despite the apparent rise in the level of the natural rate without an apparent increase in the number of shocks hitting the economy. Okun's and Salop's models provide part of the answer, but they are more satisfactory in explaining temporary fluctuations in unemployment rather than the steady-state level of unemployment.[4] The explanation of steady-state unemployment in this chapter does not substitute for these other explanations; it complements them and provides a supplementary explanation for the steady-state level of unemployment.

To focus on this particular explanation I attempt to stay as closely as possible to Friedman's Walrasian conception of the natural rate. To do this, I do not differentiate factor and goods markets, but discuss an aggregate trading economy consisting of a large number of semicompetitive markets experiencing continual shocks.[5] I call this economy an "almost competitive economy." In it stochastic variations are added to a general equilibrium trading economy, and "unemployment" (which is represented by excess supply) results from gradual price adjustment. To avoid complexities I make the heroic assumption that this gradual price adjustment is nicely behaved, by which I mean that it moves continually toward a steady-state equilibrium.[6]

This unemployment is not, however, "Keynesian unemployment" and the "excess supply" it represents has a counterpart of "excess demand" in other markets and the aggregate equilibrium is characterized by some prices falling while others are rising. My model is differentiated from Friedman's implicit model because I include one additional aspect to his definition of the natural rate. That is that the economy must be a monetary, or at least a unit of account economy capable of experiencing inflation. Thus, the "almost competitive economy" is the simplest "imperfectly competitive" (less than infinite price adjustment) unit of account aggregate economy that can include inflation and unemployment.

A UNIT-OF-ACCOUNT ECONOMY AND THE NONACCELERATING PRICE LEVEL CONSTRAINT

The aspect of the monetary economy that I focus on is the unit of account function of money. This deviates from the modern standard approach in static macroeconomic theory, which considers the numeraire as a concept without operational significance.[7] To make the model most closely represent our present economy, I assume that the unit-of-account function is served by a token money whose value is the inverse of a composite index of all the trading prices in all markets. The price level is determined by the following equation:

$$\bar{P} = \sum_{i=1}^{n} \alpha_i P_i \tag{3.1}$$

where

P_i = average price at which good i is traded

q_i = quantity of good i traded

$Q = \dfrac{1}{P} \sum_{i=1}^{n} P_i q_i$ = real output

$\alpha_i = \sum_{i=1}^{n} \dfrac{P_i q_i}{PQ}$ = relative importance of price i in price index

This unit of account is used rather than relative price bartering because it makes the economy more efficient by reducing accounting costs, making it so that people need only store nominal prices and the price level, rather than each pair of relative prices.[8] Using such a unit of account also has a cost for society. In order for the unit of account to be useful and for the economy to gain the advantage of money, the price level must be somewhat stable, and in steady-state equilibrium the price level cannot be continually accelerating. Thus while any level of steady-state inflation may be acceptable, steady-state hyperinflation or continually accelerating inflation is not. It follows that, *in order to maintain the advantages of money, a constraint upon individual traders must exist.* This constraint has not heretofore formally been incorporated into an analysis of the role of incomes policies and the macroeconomy. I call it the *nonaccelerating price level constraint* (NONAC) and it merely states that in steady-state equilibrium:

$$\frac{\partial^2 P}{\partial t^2} = 0 \qquad (3.2)$$

PRICE ADJUSTMENT IN THE ALMOST COMPETITIVE ECONOMY

Ideally one would want to develop an analysis of the nonaccelerating price level constraint from individual maximization analysis, considering the search and informational costs of buyers and sellers in each market, determining how actual trading prices in each market respond to shocks, how those trading prices affect the price level and how the price level in turn affects individual traders, all within a general equilibrium context. As a first step it is useful to determine how various price adjustment assumptions affect the aggregate equilibrium, and what the implicit price adjustment assumptions underlying the natural rate and nonaccelating rate are. I take that first step in this chapter.

The problems of specifying a general equilibrium in an almost competitive economy are enormous. Only now are the beginnings of a logical analysis of price adjustment emerging.[9] Instead of starting from first principles, we generally use the following somewhat ad hoc assumptions about price adjustment:

$$(\partial P_i/\partial t) = f_i(D_i - S_i) \qquad (3.3)$$

(i) $f_i(D - S) = f_i(S - D)$
(ii) $f_i' > 0$
(iii) $f_i'' > 0$
(iv) $f_i(0) = 0$

The basic equation merely states that the rate of price adjustment is a function of excess demand in that market. Assumption (i) is usually

Figure 3–1.   Graphic Representation of Normal Price
Adjustment Assumptions.

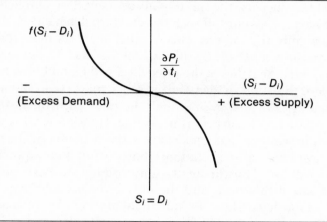

implicit; it states that the functional relation describing excess demand is identical to the one describing excess supply. Assumption (ii) states merely that the price will adjust toward, not away from, equilibrium. Assumption (iii) states that the further from equilibrium the price is, the faster the price will adjust. Assumption (iv) is the equilibrium assumption; it states that a competitive market will be in equilibrium when supply equals demand. Graphically we have Figure 3–1.

Of these assumptions the middle two are grounded in what might be called dynamic profit maximization assumptions, which underlie the search and wait explanations of unemployment. The larger the deviation between supply and demand and hence between supply price and demand price, the larger is the return to search and entry into the market and thus the faster the price adjustment is to equilibrium.[10] By adding these assumptions to a multimarket trading economy, equilibrium is made consistent with unemployment and excess demand in some markets, but not in all markets.

The preceding price adjustment specifications are partial equilibrium; to apply them to an aggregate unit of account economy one must specify them in terms of the price level P and make assumptions about market interdependencies.

The full specification involves the following equation:

$$\partial P_i/\partial t = f(S_1 - D_1, S_2 - D_2, \ldots S_n - D_n) \tag{3.4}$$

In it excess demand and supply in other markets influence price adjustment in a market. Such interrelationships are likely; for example, knowledge that a good in a competing market has excess demand would likely increase the speed of adjustment. For simplicity of analysis, however, I assume all such direct intermarket effects are zero and consider only the indirect effects other markets have through their effect on the price level. By this I mean that each trader makes an estimate of what he believes the price level will be and thus he implicitly considers the state of demand in other markets in determining his nominal price. Thus, even though the price adjustment interrelation among individual markets is negligible, the sum total is not.

I further assume that traders know the structure of the model (i.e., they have rational expectations) but do not know precisely where shocks will hit. Thus in steady-state equilibrium, expected inflation equals actual inflation, and the only error a trader can have made concerns the demand for his individual product. Within such an economy $\dot{P}$ is determined by nominal aggregate demand policy, which, assuming the economy has no real growth in equilibrium, must be increasing at the same rate as aggregate nominal demand. Thus, if there is a generalized upward pressure on prices in all markets, the price level will be rising. But, since all individuals want to raise their relative prices, it will be rising at an accelerating rate and the price level will explode unless that upward pressure is eliminated.

The revised price adjustment equation specified now in nominal terms is

$$dP_i/dt = \dot{P}_e + f'(S_i - D_i) \tag{3.5}$$

where $\dot{P}_e$ = expected rate of inflation. As I stated above, the key to my analysis is the nonaccelerating price level constraint. The constraint implies that for P not to explode or implode and thereby destroy the value of the unit of account to society, the upward pressure placed on the price level by excess demand markets must be countered by an offsetting downward pressure on the price level in excess supply markets. Otherwise the structural dynamics of the price level rise will become expected and will violate the nonaccelerating price level constraint.

The preceding simple description seems to be the basic structure of the "almost competitive economy" that underlies the Walrasian conception of the natural rate that Friedman put forward. We can see that it is a reasonable simplification, given the normal price adjustment assumption by further assuming that all markets are equally important in determining the price level and subdividing all markets

Figure 3–2. The Representative Market with Symmetric Price Adjustment.

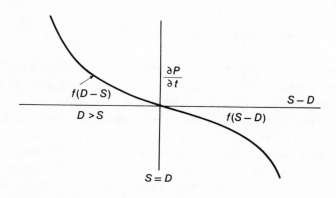

into n excess demand and n excess supply markets. Assuming shocks are randomly distributed, it follows from the symmetry assumption that in steady-state equilibrium:

$$\partial P/\partial t = \tfrac{1}{2}(\dot{P}_e + f(S_i - D_i)) + \tfrac{1}{2}(\dot{P}_e + f(D_j - S_j)) \qquad (3.6)$$

Markets are equally likely to be in excess supply as in excess demand and equilibrium is determined (unless nonrandom shocks are expected to hit the system) by the price level rising at the expected rate. The static representative market for such a stochastic equilibrium would be in equilibrium where $S = D$. Graphically the result can be easily seen in Figure 3–2. The assumption of symmetry makes the composite market, consisting of both excess supply and excess demand markets, located at the midpoint between excess supply and excess demand markets, or at the point where $S = D$.

Put simply, the upward pressure placed on the price level by excess-demand markets just offsets the downward pressure placed on the price level by excess-supply markets, and it is reasonable to speak of such an almost competitive economy as "competitive" in a Walrasian sense.

THE NARU AND PRICE ADJUSTMENT ASSUMPTIONS

The NARU differs from the natural rate because it includes either a different price adjustment assumption or an asymmetric collusion assumption. Either causes a systematic deviation in the equilibrium of the economy.

Asymmetric Collusion

In the NARU view, there is no reason to believe that at a static supply/demand equilibrium in a representative real world market, there will be no accelerating inflation. A real world "equilibrium" is characterized by individuals not accepting competitive markets and doing their best to escape them.[11] This is the view of competition that Adam Smith had in mind when he wrote his famous "Seldom do businessmen gather but that . . ." As long as the costs of collusion or monopolization are less than the gains, individuals will monopolize, which means that they will devise institutional structures to prevent entry. "Equilibrium" occurs only where the costs of collusion equal the gains. Additionally, as soon as one has given up the Walrasian auctioneer assumption and adds a spatial dimension to the analysis, all trades break down to bilateral monopoly. If one or the other of the two monopolists has a lower cost of bargaining, he will likely achieve a better price than he would have in a competitive market. The "market price" is merely the weighted average of all the trades in that commodity in the market.

As long as the weighted average of all trades in the economy has no bias, then the economy could still be represented by a static supply/demand equilibrium and assumption (iv) $f(0) = 0$, which has been called Walras's law, would be reasonable. However, if there are asymmetries between buyers and sellers with sellers' monopolization less expensive than buyers' monopolization at a static supply/demand equilibrium, Walras's law would not be a reasonable assumption and there would be a consistent bias pushing up the price in that market. If one extends that bias to the representative market in the economy, the price level would explode. Thus, to preserve the usefulness of the unit of account, that upward push must be offset. Given our current institutions, the aggregate state of the market performs this role. Weak markets (excess-supply markets) increase the cost of sellers' monopolization or make it more difficult for sellers to collude or take advantage of the bilateral monopoly in other ways.[12]

In some ways the foregoing argument is merely stating that sellers' monopolization causes unemployed resources. Those unemployed resources cannot, however, be transferred to other sectors; they are playing an important role in the monopolization process by preventing further monopolization on the part of existing sellers. The monopolization equilibrium is a probabilistic equilibrium in which the unemployed have a chance of breaking into the monopoly. No one is making monopolistic profits; they are merely being diverted into rent-seeking activities and those rent-seeking activities consume the profit.

For this reason, to assume that $f(0) \neq 0$ is not to assume that the market is not "competitive" in the sense that zero profit is made. It is merely to assume that individuals are not price takers and will compete in raising their incomes by affecting the prices they pay and receive. Thus individuals are seeking rents through affecting the prices they pay and competition in rent seeking will drive the profit from changing price to zero. If there is any asymmetry among buyers and sellers in seeking rents there will be an upward or downward pressure on the price level at a supply/demand equilibrium. Equilibrium is arrived at because excess supply or excess demand changes the cost of further rent seeking and at some level of excess supply or demand, the costs of further rent seeking will equal the expected gains and the economy will arrive at a rent-seeking equilibrium.

To assume equilibrium is not at the point where supply equals demand may seem unusual, but it should not. It would be highly unusual for a supply/demand equilibrium to occur. It would only occur if there were equal costs of monopolization for both buyers and sellers.

Generally one would expect asymmetric monopolization because of differences in costs. Most individuals sell only a few goods, primarily labor; most buy a wide variety of goods. Given that lumpiness exists in finding information about possibilities of monopolization, and of actually monopolizing, we will take a more active role in determining the price of goods we sell than we do in determining the price of the goods we buy. The prevalence of labor unions relative to consumer unions is the obvious example, but even where unions do not exist, an employee's displeasure at not receiving a raise, or at actually receiving a pay cut, can be made quite explicit, increasing the cost to the firm of lowering wages. Given a choice, as long as it can expect other firms to follow suit, the representative firm will choose the path of least resistance and raise prices rather than lowering its profit rate or wage rate. Consumers may complain but they are less likely than seller to take an active role in holding those prices down.

Asymmetric Price Adjustment

A second difference in the NARU and natural rate assumptions is in the assumptions about price adjustment. The NARU view assumes what I call the Schultze/Tobin price adjustment asymmetry. Rather than making the normal price adjustment assumptions that economists have in the back of their minds when they specify an aggregate equilibrium, Tobin (1972) and Schutze (1959) take a different approach and assume an asymmetry that causes prices to respond faster to excess demand than to excess supply.[13] The Schultze/Tobin asymmetry hypothesis only affects assumption (i), changing it to

$$|f'(D-S)| > |f'(S-D)| \tag{3.7}$$

Graphically Figure 3-2 is changed to the price adjustment curve in Figure 3-3. A priori there is no reason to assume the normal symmetry assumption rather than the Schultze/Tobin assumption and many Keynesians have argued that the Schultze/Tobin asymmetry was part of Keynes's analyses.

To determine the effect of the asymmetry on the price level, I specify the following asymmetric price adjustment equations.

Figure 3-3.   Asymmetric Price Adjustment.

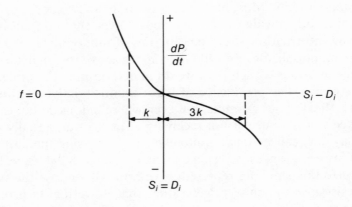

$$(dP_i/dt) = \dot{P}_e + f'(S_i - D_i) = \dot{P}_e + \tfrac{1}{3}(S_i - D_i) \quad \text{where } S_i > D_i$$

$$(3.8)$$

$$(dP_i/dt) = \dot{P}_e + f'(D_j - S_j) = \dot{P}_e + f(D_j - S_j) \quad \text{where } D_j > S_j$$

The asymmetry assumption does nothing to the steady-state equilibrium of an individual market. However, because of the nonaccelerating price level constraint, it *does* affect the sum total of all markets, and that aggregate effect changes the characterization of the representative market in equilibrium.

When the representative market is in equilibrium so that weighted excess supply equals weighted excess demand, the nonaccelerating price level constraint will be violated. In such a case aggregate supply = aggregate demand cannot be an aggregate equilibrium. The issue can be seen by considering the following simple price adjustment equations where weighted markets are equally divided between excess supply and excess demand markets and we consider a representative excess supply and excess demand market. The nonaccelerating price level constraint states that

$$\tfrac{1}{3}f(S_i - D_i) = f(S_j - D_j) \Rightarrow f(S_i - D_i) = 3f(D_j - S_j) \qquad (3.9)$$

In the nonaccelerating price level constrained equilibrium, the economy will never reach the frictional level of unemployment, and in the price adjustment equations stated above there is three times the level of excess supply as there is excess demand.

This can be seen in Figure 3–4. Supply is greater than demand in areas II and III; only in area I is demand greater than supply. In area II, inflation is accelerating even though aggregate supply is greater than aggregate demand. In area II we have dynamic cost push inflation in which the slowly adjusting downward prices do not offset the adjusting upward prices. The resulting rise in the price level becomes expected and causes accelerating inflation.

To offset the dynamic upward pressure on the price level in aggregate steady-state equilibrium, markets on average must be in excess supply; the greater the asymmetry, the greater the necessary "excess supply." This, I argue, is the view of the aggregate economy that is implicit in the NARU conception. Somehow in the adjustment process minute pockets of dynamic monopoly affect the adjustment process, which in turn affects the steady-state aggregate equilibrium. At that steady-state equilibrium some excess supply exists solely to offset the

Figure 3-4. Asymmetric Price Adjustment Function of a Representative Market.

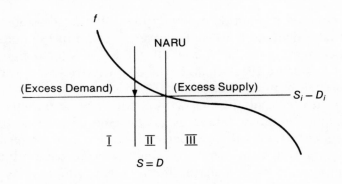

price adjustment asymmetry. That excess supply cannot be eliminated, however, by increasing aggregate demand. It is a necessary steady-state offset to the asymmetry.

MONOPOLY AND UNEMPLOYMENT

The two arguments presented here do not suggest that there is a trade-off between inflation and unemployment. The existence of a trade-off depends on how fully output price inflation is translated into expectations and hence into input prices. At 100 percent throughput, there is no trade-off; at less than 100 percent, there is a trade-off.[14] Instead, the analysis concerns at what level of steady-state "excess supply" or "excess demand" the economy equilibrates under the assumption of 100 percent throughput. Thus I am not making the argument that monopoly in any market causes inflation. Monopoly merely changes relative prices. Since I am considering an equal degree of monopoly in all sectors of the market economy, by definition it cannot change relative prices of market activities relative to each other. The relative price it changes is that of market to nonmarket activity.

The issue concerns how one thinks of monopoly. If monopoly is somehow imposed from outside, an equal degree of monopoly will not affect the market equilibrium. Thus, it has no excess burden. But if entry is allowed, individuals will compete to break into the monopoly. Thus, rather than the unemployed resources merely going into some other market pursuit, individuals spend time and resources figuring out how to enter the market economy. In short, monopoly creates potential profit to entry into market activities and causes people to search and wait longer than they otherwise would. If one can earn $25 per hour in the steel industry, one will wait a long time on the fringe and exert tremendous effort to receive the rent. Prices are slowly adjusting downward and pressure for monopolization exists at zero excess demand because individuals within the market economy have a lower cost of creating or protecting that monopoly than individuals on the outside.

This attempt to break into the monopoly, in turn, forces those with the monopoly to spend time and resources to protect their monopoly. Equilibrium is arrived at when the cost of further monopolization exceeds the gains. Unemployment results when individuals spend their time trying to break into the monopoly and thus are neither engaged in leisure nor engaged in market work. They are unemployed or more precisely, employed in trying to break into the market economy. The higher the degree of monopoly in the market sector, the higher the level of equilibrium unemployment and that equilibrium level of unemployment holds the price level down and limits further monopolization.

THE NONAC AND THE MICROFOUNDATIONS LITERATURE

In some ways my description of the economy is not radically different from Phelps's (1970) or Alchian's (1970) description of the search and wait process. For example, Phelps focuses on wage-setting policies under essentially the same conditions specified above. Some firms find their employment too high and choose a negative wage differential (relative to the expected wage level); other firms find their employment too low (excess demand) and choose a positive wage differential. Equilibrium results where wage differentials of excess supply firms and excess demand firms offset each other. In Phelps's model it is unclear precisely what one would choose to call "optimal" or full employment, although it has sometimes been suggested that vacancies = unemployment would be appropriate. [15]

Phelps (1970: 136) specifically points out the amgibuities surrounding the use of the term *full employment*, and in his initial discussion of the equilibrium condition:

$$\Delta = m(u, v) = 0$$
Δ = average differential set by ith firm
u = unemployment rate
v = vacancy rate
(3.10)

Phelps does not necessarily require that $u = v$, although since much of his focus concerns positions off the steady-state equilibrium, precisely what his position *is* is a bit unclear. The argument he seems to make implicitly is that full employment should be at a level where $u = v$, because at the beginning of his article he asks the questions:

> Why should it be expected that a one unit increase of the vacancy rate always has the same wage effect as a one unit decrease of the unemployment rate? Second, why should it be expected that most of the time in the neighborhood of "equilibrium" (see section 4), vacancies will equal unemployment and that a disequilibrium rise of wage rates requires vacancies to exceed unemployment?

Phelps partially answers that question in his section 4, where he presents the aforesaid macroequilibrium condition for the equilibrium firm, and states that it means "that generalized excess demand for labor as measured by $m(u, v)$ be equal to zero. Any other condition would be disturbing!" Since he does not discuss this question anywhere else in his article (though he does state later that "there is a lot that is hidden in the m function"), this seems to be his answer as to why vacancies and unemployment must be equal in equilibrium. But, translated into the dual, $v = u$ is so only under the normal price adjustment assumptions, which restrict "m" to a certain class of symmetric functions around v and u. Otherwise Phelps's definition of excess demand, as the level of demand at which the wage level begins rising and accelerating, is merely a tautology.[16]

If one interprets excess demand to be proportional to skill-normalized vacancies and excess supply to be proportional to skill-normalized unemployment, with equal adjustment speeds, no labor monopoly, and an equal cost of vacancies and unemployment, one would find $v = u$ in dynamic equilibrium. With either seller's monopolies or unequal adjustment speeds, vacancies and unemployment need not be equal and thus the static representation of the dynamic equilibrium would include excess supply $(v > u)$ in the representative market.[17]

A nontautological definition of aggregate excess demand might be the following: that level of demand at which the representative market has neither excess demand nor excess supply. If the economy includes either sellers' monopolization or dynamic price asymmetries, the price level begins accelerating before equilibrium is reached; thus the static representation of equilibrium would be a market with continual excess supply.

THE ROLE OF INCOMES POLICIES

Having demonstrated how the existence of price adjustment asymmetries or seller's monopoly causes the representative market to operate with excess supply, we are in a position to consider the role of an incomes policy in general and of tax- and market-based incomes policies specifically. If there is an asymmetry or upward pressure at a supply/demand equilibrium, incomes policies work as a type of second best policy allowing the economy to reach a higher level of resource utilization. Whereas incomes policies merely cause shortages in a static model, in a dynamic model they change the equilibrium ratio of shortages to surpluses, reducing supply rationing and increasing demand rationing. The difference between the NARU view and the natural rate view is that, in the natural rate view, the presumption is that the cost of the greater excess demand will exceed the benefit of the lower level of excess supply. In the NARU view, the presumption is the opposite. Since on average excess supply exists in equilibrium, an incomes policy accompanied by an increase in demand will make people on average better off.

Changing the stochastic equilibrium has not been seen as the role of incomes policies because the types of incomes policies that have normally been suggested have not allowed subtle marginal affects on price adjustment decisions but have instead involved nonmarginal effects where it became illegal for sellers to raise their price. This is the equivalent to changing the price adjustment equation to

$$dP_i/dt = 0 \qquad (3.1)$$

It is likely that such a gross change in the price adjustment mechanism will make the economy worse off rather than better off. Thus,

Figure 3-5. Effect of TIP on Price Adjustment for a
Representative Market.

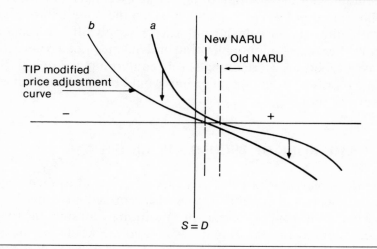

very few economists have been willing even to contemplate a long-
term incomes policy.

Incentive anti-inflation plans such as tax-based incomes policies
(TIPs) provide a quite different view of incomes policies and nicely fit
within the price adjustment analysis. They work through making
marginal adjustments in the price adjustment equations, thereby
changing the equilibrium in the representative market. A generalized
TIP allows one to see their effect best. Under such a TIP, price increases are taxed and price decreases are subsidized, thereby changing the price adjustment curve from one such as *a* to one such as *b*.
(See Figure 3-5.) This lowers the achievable NARU and shifts the
equilibrium of the economy to the left. An incomes policy increases
the cost of seller's search and monopolization while decreasing the
cost of buyer's search and monopolization. In doing so it changes the
equilibrium mix of excess supply and excess demand for the entire
market.

SOME CONCLUDING COMMENTS

The analysis given here clearly does not establish a clear-cut theoretical case for TIPs, but it does establish a framework within which they

can be analyzed. I had initially thought that I could go out and find proxy measures for excess supply and excess demand (such as vacancies and unemployment) and compare the two for the entire economy at a position of nonaccelerating inflation as a test of the two theories. Reasonable vacancy figures did not seem to be available, nor upon reflection did it seem that such a comparison, even if adjusted for skill and costs, would be a reliable measure.[18] There is a subjective element in any interpretation of both vacancies and unemployment. For example, a person might always be able to find a job selling apples on a street corner or in some other individualistic entrepreneurial activity. Thus, the concept of *vacancy* can always be expanded to exceed unemployment. Moreover, what we consider legitimate aspiration levels and appropriate relative wage differentials plays an important role in determining what a vacancy is. Thus, it is unlikely that empirical work will resolve the issue. The issue is more likely to be approached theoretically.

On the theoretical side one must develop the price adjustment equations from individual and firm maximization assumptions and demonstrate precisely how a TIP will affect individual decisions. Finally one must relate the general analysis presented here to the specific institutional structure of the economy, including other possible effects from the institution of a TIP or MAP.

Despite the work to be done, I believe that this chapter helps clarify how asymmetries and monopolies can affect the aggregate steady-state equilibrium, how TIPs can play a role, and what the difference is between the NARU and the natural rate concepts. If one accepts the argument, and believes that asymmetries exist, individuals searching and waiting are not only serving their private interests; they are also serving society's interest by exerting downward pressure and holding down inflation. Thus some proportion of steady-state unemployment serves a "reserve army" function, and that portion can advantageously be reduced by an incomes policy.

NOTES

1.   Economists who have emphasized this distinction include Otto Eckstein (1981), James Meade (1981), and myself (Colander 1981). Each made the distinction but does not explore the theoretical issue in depth. Actually, as discussed in Phelps (1970), the debate goes back much

earlier to the 1950s and the writing of W. Fellner, H. Wallich, and A. Lerner.

2. For readers unfamiliar with incentive anti-inflation plans see Abba Lerner and David Colander (1980) and Colander (1981).

3. Throughout this literature there is a focus on the labor market although the analysis is more general and, as pointed out by Armen Alchian (1970), unemployment can be interpreted as resource underutilization. I shall follow that approach here.

4. They do indirectly provide an explanation since the long run is a collection of short runs, but it is not a direct explanation.

5. Such a treatment is consistent with modern approaches to general equilibrium theory (see, for example, Dreze 1976), where a coalition of producers produces the output and the distribution of the output among the coalition is not considered.

6. The heroic nature of this assumption can be seen by considering some recent papers that attempt to model price adjustment (see, for instance, Benjamin Eden 1981). I can justify my assumption (to myself at least) because my interest is in the interaction between the price level constraint and aggregate price adjustment functions. Even if the individual price adjustment function is not in some sense well behaved, the average price adjustment of many markets may still be as argued by Barro (1972). If that average price adjustment is not well behaved, then not only is the validity of my analysis impugned, so too is much of economic theory.

7. See Jurg Niehans (1978: 119) for a discussion of this issue.

8. The preceding discussion, while not standard in macroeconomic models, is standard monetary theory. The movement of an economy from a barter to a "monetary unit of account" economy makes it more efficient. Niehans (1978) had an excellent discussion of this function. In it he argues that a token money is used because it minimizes price fluctuations and thereby reduces accounting costs. As mentioned in the text of this chapter this nonaccelerating price level constraint is implicit in Phelps et al.'s development of the microfoundations of macroeconomics. However, by focusing on unemployment, vacancies, and flows into and out of the "equilibrium unemployment pool," the constraining nature of this constraint was lost, as was the potential role for an incomes policy.

9. See the work of K. Arrow (1959), B. Eden (1981), R. Barro (1972), and E. Zabel (1979).

10. This discussion is subject to stability conditions that I assume hold true throughout the chapter.

11. For a discussion of this alternative equilibrium, see Colander (forthcoming).

12. See Colander and Olson (1984) for an alternative expression of this same point.
13. The asymmetry assumption has a much longer history than Schultze's or Tobin's work and goes back at least to Keynes's downwardly inflexible wages and prices, which Lerner (1975) called merely a polar assumption of asymmetrical wage and price adjustment. Alchian and Kessel (1969) used it or something similar to it to explain what some people call "money illusion."
14. A variety of stories can and have been told as to why there might be less than 100 percent translation of prices in the short run and the long run. Throughout this chapter I assume 100 percent translation in order to focus on the central issue of a long-term incomes policy.
15. Note, however, that Lord Beveridge suggested the vacancies should exceed unemployment at full employment and other writers have pointed out the ambiguity of the relationship.
16. In a discussion, Phelps said he was probably confused in his earlier writing and now sees no reason why they need be equal.
17. See Abba Lerner (1960) for an equivalent argument that equilibrium in the labor market is at a point off the supply and demand curve.
18. For a discussion of the problems of measuring vacancies, see National Bureau of Economic Research (1967). Recently, Katherine Abraham (1983) has made a first attempt and has concluded that unemployment exceeded vacancies by approximately a 4 to 1 ratio in the postwar period. That ratio has not been adjusted for costs, but it suggests that the NARU view may be the appropriate one.

REFERENCES

Abraham, Katherine. 1983. "Structural/Frictional vs. Deficient Demand Unemployment: Some New Evidence." *American Economic Review* 73 (September).

Alchian, Armen. 1970. "Informational Costs, Pricing, and Resource Unemployment." In *Microeconomic Foundations of Employment and Inflation Theory*, edited by Edmund Phelps. New York: Norton.

Alchian, Armen, and R.A. Kessel. 1960. "The Meaning and Validity of the Inflation-Induced Lag of Wages behind Prices." *American Economic Review 50* (March):43–47.

Arrow, Kenneth. 1959. "Toward a Theory of Price Adjustment." In *The Allocation of Economic Resources*, edited by M. Abromovitz. Stanford, Calif.: Stanford University Press. 41–54.

Barro, Robert. 1972. "A Theory of Monopolistic Price Adjustment." *Review of Economics Studies 39*:17–26.

Colander, David. 1981. *Incentive Anti-Inflation Plans.* Joint Economic Committee. Washington, D.C.: U.S. Government Printing Office.

———. 1982. "Stagflation and Competition." *Journal of Post Keynesian Economics 5*, no. 1 (Fall):17–33.

Colander, David, and Mancur Olson. 1984. "Coalitions and Macroeconomics." In *Neoclassical Political Economy*, edited by David Colander. Cambridge, Mass.: Ballinger. 115–128.

Colander, David. (Forthcoming.) "Some Simple Geometry on Welfare Losses from Monopoly." *Public Choice.*

Dreze, Jacques. 1976. "Some Theory of Labor Management and Participation." *Econometrica 44*:1125–1140.

Eckstein, Otto. 1981. *Core Inflation.* Englewood Cliffs, N.J.: Prentice-Hall.

Eden, Benjamin. 1981. "Toward a Theory of Competitive Price Adjustment." *Review of Economic Studies.*

Friedman, Milton, 1968. "The Role of Monetary Policy." *American Economic Review 58*:1–17.

Gordon, Donald, and A. Hines. 1970. "On the Theory of Price Dynamics." In *Microeconomic Foundations of Employment and Inflation Theory*, edited by Edmund Phelps. New York: Norton.

Gordon, Robert. 1979. "A Skeptical Look at the 'Natural Rate' Hypothesis." In *Theory for Economic Efficiency*, edited by Harry Greenfield et al. Cambridge, Mass.: MIT Press, pp. 369–393.

Holt, Charles. 1970. "How Can the Phillips Curve Be Moved to Reduce Both Inflation and Unemployment?" In *Microeconomic Foundations of Employment and Inflation Theory*, edited by Edmund Phelps. New York: Norton, pp. 224–256.

Lerner, Abba. 1960. "On Generalizing the General Theory." *American Economic Review* (March):121–143.

———. 1977. "From Pre Keynes to Post Keynes." *Social Research* (Autumn): 387–415.

Lerner, Abba, and David Colander. 1980. *MAP: A Market Anti-Inflation Plan.* New York: Harcourt Brace Jovanovich.

Meade, James. 1981. *Wage Fixing.* Boston: George Allen and Unwin.

Modigliani, Franco, and Lucas Papademos. 1975. "Targets for Monetary Policy in the Coming Years." *Brookings Papers*, pp. 141–165.

National Bureau of Economic Research. 1967. *Measurement and Interpretation of Job Vacancies.* New York: NBER.

Niehans, Jurgen. 1978. *A Theory of Money.* Baltimore: Johns Hopkins University Press.

Okun, Arthur. 1981. *Prices and Quantities.* Washington, D.C.: Brookings Institute.

Phelps, Edmund, ed. 1970. *Microfoundations of Employment and Inflation Theory.* New York: Norton.

Salop, Stephen. 1979. "A Model of the Natural Rate of Unemployment." *American Economic Review 69* (March):117–125.

Schultze, Charles. 1959. "Recent Inflation in the U.S.: A Summary." In *Study of Unemployment, Growth and Price Levels.* Joint Economic Committee. Washington, D.C. U.S. Government Publications Office.

Tobin, James. 1972. "Inflation and Unemployment." *American Economic Review 62*:1–18.

Zabel, Edward. 1979. "Competitive Price Adjustment without Market Clearing." University of Rochester (June). Mimeo.

*   *Chapter 4*

The Garbage Game, Inflation, and Incomes Policy

Clive Bull and Andrew Schotter

Incomes policy is an arrangement imposed upon the agents in an economy by the government (wage and price controls) to stabilize prices and mitigate inflationary pressures as they arise. A social or economic institution is a far more elusive concept meaning different things to different people. In this chapter we will use the definition of social institutions presented by Schotter (1981) and define them as conventions of behavior which solve particular recurrent problems faced by economies as they evolve. For instance, when economies first attempt to exchange goods and services, they face the problem of making transactions in the least-cost manner. One solution to this problem is to create a commodity money, which, in short, is a convention in which all agents agree to accept a particular commodity in exchange for any good. This agreed to convention institutionalizes one commodity as money, and the convention of accepting this good in exchange becomes a permanent feature of the economy.

In this chapter we depict incomes policies as the imposed government solution to a particular type of contractionary problem that results in inflations. The solution is imposed because of what we call an "institutions failure," which, like the more commonly known market failures, is a failure of the agents in the economy to create a proper type of institutional mechanism to coordinate their activities successfully. To motivate the problem we present what Shapley and Shubik (1969) call the Garbage Game. Using this game as an analogy for the inflation problem we will then attempt to construct a simplified linear macromodel that captures the salient features of the Garbage Game analogy. Although the analogy formally breaks down here, the model we construct is still instructive in depicting the emergence of incomes policies as solutions to inflationary problems. Furthermore, our discussion casts some light on the controversy existing between monetarists and others concerning the actual causes of inflations by presenting a political theory of an endogenously determined money supply which can be used to explain the statistical correlation between money supply growth and inflationary pressures on prices.

INFLATION, CONTRACTION, AND THE GARBAGE GAME

In this section we present first a somewhat frivolous situation called the Garbage Game by Shapley and Shubik (1969) and then demonstrate the relationship of this problem to the problem of inflation. The institutional arrangements used to solve the Garbage Game will then be presented as well as a stable governmentally imposed solution that will be a direct analogue to the incomes policies we discuss later. A more formal analysis of this analogy will then be presented in the following section.

The Garbage Game

Consider the following situation: N homeowners; indexed $i = 1, \ldots, n$, exist, each having one bag of garbage to be disposed of. There is no city dump so they must either keep the bag or dump it on another homeowner's lawn. It is assumed that each homeowner receives -1 units of utility for each bag of garbage dumped on his or her lawn, that utility is transferable, and that coalitions can form and dump their garbage on the lawns of homeowners outside of the coalition. In the game garbage is obviously an economic "bad," one that all homeowners would like to pass off on others. The question of interest is: Does there exist a stable way to distribute (or redistribute) this garbage and if so, what is it?

To answer such questions, game theorists define a characteristic function stating the amount of utility (or disutility) that each coalition could guarantee itself no matter what the remaining counter-coalition did against it. To be specific, we see that if any homeowner did not form a coalition with anyone else but rather remained alone, then he could not prevent the remaining $N-1$ homeowners from forming a coalition and dumping their garbage on his property. Since each bag of garbage dumped on his lawn creates -1 units of utility, the value of any homeowner i of being alone is $-(N-1)$ or $V(i) = -(N-1)$. Similarly if S homeowners form a coalition, they will not be able to prevent the remaining $N-S$ from dumping on their lawns. Hence, $V(S) = -(N-S)$. If all homeowners form a coalition, then $V(N) = -N$, since the garbage must be dumped somewhere and it cannot be avoided.

This description yields the following characteristic function

$$\begin{aligned} V(i) &= -(N-1) \\ V(S) &= -(N-S) \\ V(N) &= -N \end{aligned} \qquad (4.1)$$

Formally, the Garbage Game is an n-person constant-sum game in characteristic function form.

In trying to decide whether a stable distribution of garbage exists, one might start by thinking that what will happen in the game is that some $N-1$ players or homeowners might get together, form a coalition, and dump their $N-1$ bags on the remaining player's lawn and divide evenly the one bag he dumps on their property. If the player left out of the coalition is player n, this would define the following imputation:

$$x = \left(-\frac{1}{N-1}, -\frac{1}{N-1}, \ldots, \frac{1}{N-1}, -N-1 \right) \qquad (4.2)$$

This imputation is obviously not stable since player n could approach any of the players in the coalition, offer to form a coalition (of two) with them, and accept all of the $N-2$ bags of garbage dumped on them. They would dump their two bags on the $N-2$ players outside of the coalition. If the player approached with this deal is player 1, the following imputation is defined:

$$x' = \left(0, -\frac{1}{N-2}, \ldots, -\frac{1}{N-2}, -N-2 \right) \qquad (4.3)$$

x' obviously dominates x because players 1 and n can enforce this imputation and it makes both of them strictly better off than they were under x.

Following this logic to its natural conclusion shows that there is no stable way to distribute this garbage. Every imputation can be dominated by some coalition and hence the game has an empty core. In this sense the situation is unstable or cyclic.

The fact that this game has an empty core does not mean that we as analysts must throw up our hands and walk away. Game theory provides us with a variety of solution concepts that are capable of making both predictive and descriptive sense out of what we might expect to happen. The solution concept that we will concentrate on here, however, is the Von Neumann and Morgenstern solution since it is this solution concept that we believed comes closest to describing the alternate stable institutional arrangements or as they call them "standards of behavior" (Von Neumann and Morgenstern 1947: 43) that could logically evolve as a solution to our problem.

To define the Von Neumann and Morgenstern solution for this game, we must ask what type of standards or conventions of behavior we would expect to emerge and be stable in this game. One obvious candidate is an equal split standard, in which the players merely remain alone and keep their own garbage. This behavioral standard defines the imputation $x'' = (-1, \ldots, -1)$. Hence we have a standard of behavior in which all people act alone and keep their garbage and an associated imputation x''. As we might imagine, this is not stable because of the domination arguments offered before. Hence the convention of behavor of not forming coalitions and keeping one's own garbage, and its associated imputation is not stable among a set of rational maximizing agents. Now consider the following standard of behavior: $N-1$ homeowners get together, dump their garbage on the remaining lawn and split that lawn's owner's bag equally among themselves. If this is the standard, then the associated set of imputations are defined as follows (depending upon which is left out of the coalition of $N-1$):

$$
V = \left\{
\begin{array}{cccc}
-N-1, & -\dfrac{1}{N-1}, & \cdots, & -\dfrac{1}{N-1} \\[2mm]
-\dfrac{1}{N-1}, & -N-1, & -\dfrac{1}{N-1}, & -\dfrac{1}{N-1} \\[2mm]
-\dfrac{1}{N-1}, & -\dfrac{1}{N-1}, & -N-1, & -\dfrac{1}{N-1} \\[2mm]
\vdots & \vdots & \vdots & \vdots \\[2mm]
-\dfrac{1}{N-1}, & \cdot \ \cdot \ \cdot \ \cdot \ \cdot \ \cdot, & -N-1
\end{array}
\right\}
\qquad (4.4)
$$

This standard of behavior with its associated imputation set is stable in the Von Neumann and Morgenstern sense in that no imputation in V dominates any other and for any imputation not in V there exists one in V which dominates it. What it says is that, although we do not know which $N-1$ homeowners will get together and form a coalition, we do know that only coalitions of $N-1$ will form and that when they do only the imputations in V will be stable.

In addition to this standard of behavior there is also another alternative standard that Von Neumann and Morgenstern call the "discriminatory solution," in which all N players get together, award one player a fixed amount of garbage, and then split the remainder among themselves. Under this standard, all imputations are stable.

What the Von Neumann and Morgenstern solution tells us is that if this garbage problem were a recurrent feature of an economy, we would expect that the agents in the economy would solve it by either forming some coalition with $N-1$ members and dumping their garbage on the remaining homeowner's land (and splitting that person's garbage equally) or forming an N homeowner coalition and agreeing on some split. Coalitions of $N-2$ or $N-3$, etc., and any associated imputations are not stable.

Finally notice that if the agents, for some reason (say transactions costs) fail to establish one of these equilibrium standards of behavior or institutions, the government can always impose one on them by, for instance, taxing each inhabitant $1+\epsilon$ for each bag of garbage dumped. With this tax, all agents would obviously rather keep their garbage than dump it, and we would observe imputation $x'' = (-1, \ldots, -1)$. This imposed solution results because of an "institution-failure" or a failure to establish a stable convention of behavior to deal with this problem on the part of the agents and this, as we will see, will be how we depict incomes policies later.

Inflation as Garbage

The analogy between the Garbage Game and inflation is straightforward. Consider a static economy in equilibrium producing a fixed gross national product using labor and say oil as inputs. Let $P = (P_1, \ldots\ldots, P_n, W, P_o)$ be the equilibrium price vector existing with $P_1, \ldots, P_n$ being the prices for the n manufactured goods in the economy and W and P_o being the wage and price of oil respectively. For simplicity, let us assume that far from being competitive, each sector and factor of production is a monopolist so that they have complete discretion over their price. If this is so, then the equilibrium is not a competitive equilibrium but rather some bargaining equilibrium solution. Finally assume that oil owners are foreigners who take their dollars out of the economy and, who, because they control a factor of production instead of a produced good, are able to negotiate an indexed real price for their oil. All other sectors and labor can only set a nominal price.

At the existing equilibrium vector of prices, let us assume that the share of the final output going to foreign oil suppliers is γ_{oil} while the shares to the domestic sectors and labor are $\gamma_1, \ldots, \gamma_n$, γ_{labor}, with

$$\sum_{j=1}^{n} \gamma_j + \gamma_{labor} + \gamma_{oil} = 1. \tag{4.5}$$

In short, oil is taking a bite of γ_{oil} from a fixed final output pie leaving $1 - \gamma_{oil}$ for the domestic economy.

Now let us assume that oil raises its real price and as a result takes a larger bite $\gamma'_{oil} > \gamma_{oil}$ out of the final output, leaving only $1 - \gamma'_{oil}$ for domestic use. Hence, in real terms, the sectors of the economy plus labor are going to have to consume less and the question is how much less should they consume?

Now the analogy to the Garbage Game should be apparent. In this economy the economic bad that all agents want to avoid is the burden of cutting their real incomes. In short, because of the oil price rise, the domestic economy has contracted in real terms and all sectors want to dump this contractionary garbage onto sectors other than themselves. (See Schotter 1977 for a further analysis of the contraction problem.)

The obvious way to do this is to raise one's price in the hope of being able to turn the real terms of trade in one's own favor and thereby recapture one's old real share of the final output. No one sector can do this, however, since other sectors can retaliate by raising their prices as well so that all that can be expected to follow is a spiral or cycle of price increases equivalent to the dumping cycles seen in the Garbage Game and no clear equilibrium exists. A typical cost-push price spiral results. More precisely we can adopt Machlup's illuminating terminology and say that a defensive cost-push inflation will result which is an increase (in prices) that "merely restores real earnings which the group has long been enjoying; an aggressive increase raises real earnings above that level" (1960: 131). Coalitions of agents, such as government and labor or management and government, may form as well to try to dump the inflation loss onto other sectors.

The solution to this contraction-absorption game is likely to be similar to the solution to the Garbage Game. Each economy over time, as it faces these contractionary problems, will develop its own convention of behavior or institutional arrangements to settle it. In some countries, labor will bear the brunt, in others the brunt will be borne by fixed (nominal) income groups who control no price (see Holtzman 1950), while in others it may be the government's or capital's share of final output that decreases. In any case the different behavioral conventions that are created help explain the differing inflationary experiences of say West Germany and the United States as they faced the 1973 OPEC oil price rise.

Finally, as we will see in the next section, if the economic agents fail to reach an agreed upon convention one possible way out of the instability created by supply shocks is for the government to impose a solution (much as they did in the Garbage Game) by specifying an incomes policy that will dictate how the various sectors and labor will absorb the real loss in the economy. It is this imposition and its political consequences that we will study in our model below.

THE GARBAGE GAME ANALOGY AND INFLATION

Trying to describe a macroeconomic model to formalize the Garbage Game is not an easy task. The most immediate problem is that while in the Garbage Game a coalition can pinpoint who they are going to dump their garbage on by literally throwing the bags on their lawn, coalitions of sectors cannot localize their dumping by raising prices since price rises on specific goods affect all sectors in the economy that use that good whether they are in a coalition or not. Unless special price discounts are offered for coalition members, there is no way for coalitions to form successfully and be beneficial. Hence, we could not formulate a rigorous model that would consistently portray the problem depicted in the Garbage Game. What we have done, however, is to invent two models, one depicting an economy with a fixed real output vector in which an oil shock occurs and another similar economy in which the level of real final output is endogenously determined and influenced, in true monetarist fashion, by the value of real money balances held by economy's agents and the supply of the money. These two models will highlight what we feel are the two opposing schools of thought on the causes of inflation and, by examining both of them, we will be able to investigate the role that incomes policies may play in the economy as well as the role that money supply increases may play in easing the costs of inflations and their political consequences.

Cost-Push Inflations and Incomes Policies

Consider an economy with N sectors indexed $j = 1, \ldots, n$, two factors of production labor and oil, and a Leontief technology defined by an identity output matrix I and an input matrix A. Further assume that there exists a fixed positive vector of final demands d that the economy is asked to produce. d is assumed to be given exogenously and is independent of the prices set in the economy. This assumption will be relaxed later. As we assumed before, prices are not competitively determined but rather set by a bargaining process (explicit or tacit) between the N monopolistic sectors, labor, and foreign owned oil.

As is well known if the economy is viable for any positive vector of final output d, an intensity vector x can be found such that

$$x = (I - A)^{-1} d \qquad (4.6)$$

x is then the intensities with which each sector must be run in order to produce the final consumption vector d.

In value terms let us say that as we enter the analysis a price vector

$$P^* = (P_1^*, \ldots, P_n, W, P_o) \qquad (4.7)$$

exists describing the prices existing in the economy as well as the prices of labor and oil. To find each sector's command over the real resources of the economy, we assume that all agents in the economy (capitalists, workers, and oil shieks) have identical Leontief utility functions

$$U = \min\left(\frac{X_1}{a_1}, \ldots, \frac{X_n}{a_n}\right) \qquad (4.8)$$

This guarantees that all agents desire to consume bundles of manufactured goods in exactly the same proportions independently of prices. As their real incomes grow, they merely expand their demands proportionately. Consequently the vector of final demands reflects this preference and is independent of both relative and nominal prices.

This assumption will be relaxed in our next section. Here we wish only to isolate what we consider to be the cost-push phenomenon in inflation.

Using this assumption we can define each sector's share over final outputs as follows:

First define the value added of each sector as

$$VA_j = P_j X_j - \sum_i a_{ij} P_i X_j - a_{jL} W X_j - a_{oj} P_o X_j \qquad (4.9)$$

Consequently, the total value added for the all n sectors is

$$\sum_j VA_j = \sum_j P_j X_j - \sum_i \sum_j a_{ij} P_i X_j - \sum_j a_{jL} W X_j - \sum_j a_{oj} P_o X_j \qquad (4.10)$$

We will then define the share of final outputs d going to each sector and to each factor of production as follows:

$$\gamma_j \equiv \frac{VA_j}{\sum_j VA_j + WL + P_o O}, \qquad j = 1, \ldots, n \qquad (4.11)$$

(where L and O are the total labor and oil required to produce d),

$$\gamma_{\text{labor}} \equiv \frac{WL}{\sum_j VA_j + WL + P_o O} \qquad (4.12)$$

$$\gamma_{\text{oil}} \equiv \frac{P_o O}{\sum_j VA_j + WL + P_o O} \qquad (4.13)$$

It is obvious that

$$\sum_j \gamma_j + \gamma_{\text{oil}} + \gamma_{\text{labor}} = 1. \qquad (4.14)$$

Hence, at the initial price vector each sector's and each factor's share of the final vector d is given by identities (4.11)–(4.13).

Finally, we will assume that oil is special in the model in that it alone has the ability to negotiate a "real" price for its product, whereas all other sectors can set only nominal prices. This is achieved by specifying an indexed oil price as follows:

First, oil specifies a share of the final output vector d that it desires, say $\bar{\gamma}_{\text{oil}}$. Given (4.11) we then see that

$$\bar{\gamma}_{\text{oil}} = \frac{P_o O}{\sum_j VA_j + WL + P_o O} \qquad (4.15)$$

$$\bar{\gamma}_{\text{oil}} = \frac{P_o O}{\sum_j (P_j X_j - \sum_j a_{ij} X_j P_j - P_o a_{oj} X_j - WL_j) + WL + P_o O} \qquad (4.16)$$

$$\bar{\gamma}_{\text{oil}} = \frac{P_o O}{\sum_j (P_j X_j - \sum_j a_{ij} X_j P_j)} \qquad (4.17)$$

Hence, given any γ_{oil}, the real price of oil is a linear function of sector prices defined as

$$P_o = \bar{\gamma}_{\text{oil}} \frac{\sum_j (P_j X_j - \sum_j a_{ij} X_j P_j)}{O} \qquad (4.18)$$

If price vector P^* starts our analysis, the observed shares are $\gamma^* = (\gamma_1^*, \ldots, \gamma_n^*, \gamma_{\text{labor}}^*, \gamma_{\text{oil}}^*)$ with real consumptions $\gamma_j^*(d)$ for each sector. Assume that these are equilibrium outcomes of the bargaining game that $n+2$ agents play. Next let us say that oil decides to raise its real price from γ_{oil}^* to γ_{oil}' with $\gamma_{\text{oil}}' > \gamma_{\text{oil}}^*$ by increasing its nominal price appropriately as defined by (4.18). This oil price rise will alter the original share vectors differentially depending on how oil intensive each sector is. Let $\gamma' = (\gamma_1', \ldots, \gamma_r', \gamma_{\text{labor}}', \gamma_{\text{oil}}')$ be this new vector. As a result of the higher price of oil, the amount of final output available for domestic consumption has decreased from $(1 - \gamma_{\text{oil}}^*) \sum_j P_j d_j$ to $(1 - \gamma_{\text{oil}}') \sum_j P_j d_j$.

Now each sector can be expected to try to preserve its pre-oil-shock real income $\gamma_j^*(\sum_j P_j d_j)$ by raising its price. From (4.11) to (4.13) we can see that, *ceteris paribus*, if any sector raises its price its share of final output will increase. However, from (4.18) it is also clear that this increase must come from other sectors of the domestic economy or labor and not from oil.

The resulting question is exactly the question asked in the Garbage Game: Who (which sector) is going to absorb the contraction of final output $(\gamma_{\text{oil}}' - \gamma_{\text{oil}}^*) \sum_j P_j d_j$ and who is going to be able to dump it on other sectors by raising its price? The difference between this situation and the Garbage Game is that in this model the advantageousness and feasibility of coalitions are very limited. Hence, we can think of a noncooperative game in which in each period, after the oil shock, sectors are allowed to raise their price by any percentage between 0 and 100. Hence, the strategy set for any sector and labor is the closed interval [0, 100] and their payoffs are defined as the fraction of final output available to them as specified by (4.11) to (4.13). If the resulting game is played only once, it is obvious that the only Nash equilibrium is one in which all sectors raise their price 100 percent. This is obviously mutually destructive although in our model, with d fixed, there are no real effects of the inflation (this will be modified in the next section). If this simple game is repeated period after period, then a supergame is defined in which the payoff to any sector is the (either discounted or undiscounted) stream of future consumptions available to them. As is well known (see Aumann 1959), the equilibrium of these supergames can be interpreted as outcomes of a static cooperative bargaining game; in our context we can interpret what ultimately happens in the domestic economy as depending upon the equilibrium convention of behavior or norm established by the agents in these economies. For instance, as was stated before, some economies may solve this contractionary problem by forcing agents who live on fixed nominal incomes and who control no price (the dependent poor or the retired) to absorb the contraction. Others will force labor to absorb the loss while still others will split it up among themselves in some agreed upon way. For those economies who cannot agree upon a solution, protracted inflations or hyperinflations are the only solution. It is for these economies that incomes policies are required. These policies, like the government-imposed solution to the Garbage Game, are necessary solutions to contraction—avoidance situations where the domestic sectors of the economy seem unable to settle this problem for themselves. In the context of this model, (where inflation is costless since the d vector is exogenously fixed and unaffected by the inflation and there are no sectors living in fixed nominal incomes), incomes policies are mechanisms that impose a bargaining solution on agents that cannot solve these problems by themselves. They result from a form of what we may call "institutions failure" just as other government interventions result from market failures. In our context, if the agents can create an acceptable standard of behavior with which to deal with the contraction problem no imposed incomes policy would be needed. The policies are needed only if either no contraction split is settled upon or if the split settled upon is unacceptable to the government for some reason of equity.

EMPIRICAL VALIDITY OF THE MODEL

The model of the previous section, though crude, has all the major characteristics of the family of cost-push models of inflation which dominated the inflation literature in the 1960s and provided the economic rationalization for the use of wage and price controls as the key, or indeed the only, element in the anti-inflation policies adopted by many countries.[1] As is well known, these cost-push models came under fire increasingly on both empirical and theoretical grounds from the late sixties onward. At the empirical level the two stumbling blocks for these models were how to explain the dramatic acceleration of inflation rates in, say, the United States and the United Kingdom, during the late sixties and seventies, and how to explain why such acceleration did not exist in all countries? For instance, why did West German and Italian inflation experiences differ so much over this period?[2] Because of the lack of a systematic reply by supporters of cost-push models to such questions, these models began to fall out of favor with empirically minded economists.

At the same time as cost-push theories were running into trouble explaining the data, economists were also becoming more critical of them on theoretical grounds. On this level the major criticism was the omission of asset effects in general and any consideration of real money demand and supply in particular. This latter objection was central to the monetarist criticism led by Milton Friedman. Moreover, Friedman could point to a consistent correlation, over time and across country, between the rate of growth of the nominal money supply, suitably defined, and the rate of growth of prices. Interpreting the correlation as indicating a chain of causation running from an exogenous money supply to an endogenous price level, the data enabled Friedman to "explain" divergent inflation experiences, over time and across countries, precisely the empirical events that stripped the cost-push theories of their credibility. As a result of these theoretical criticisms of the cost-push theories and the superior empirical performance of the monetarist approach, the cost-push models have dropped from the literature and a consensus has formed around the view that the rate of growth of the money supply is the key determinant of the rate of inflation.

For the purposes of this section, we will accept Friedman's view that "Every major inflation has been produced by monetary expansion" (Friedman 1968). In the context of anti-inflation policies, this raises two difficult questions. The first concerns wage and price controls. Over the last two decades, governments both here and abroad have viewed wage and price controls as a crucial part of their anti-inflation programs. Yet if cost-push models of inflation are wrong, then wage and price controls are useless. The question arises then as to why such a dysfunctional policy has apparently thrived in the political marketplaces of so many countries? Any kind of policy Darwinism, akin to the competitive Darwinism we use in economics (see

Alchian 1950), would suggest that such policies would drop out of favor with the electorate. Of course, one may argue that sufficient time has not elapsed for this to happen. Alternatively, one could equally well argue that this indicates that cost-push models of inflation do capture some relevant aspects of the operation of the economy that are overlooked in monetarist analysis.

The second question involves monetary policy. As Friedman has recently admitted (1982: 115), while his empirical work showed that the rate of growth of the money supply has a strong influence on the rate of inflation, his work did not consider why such apparently malevolent monetary policies have been implemented both here and abroad. Again we face the question of why such a dysfunctional policy as a rapid and accelerating rate of growth of the money supply has remained a viable commodity in the political marketplace.

Naturally, a complete answer to these two questions is far too complex to be answered in this chapter even if the authors had the appropriate interdisciplinary skills to be able to tackle them in their entirety. However, below we will reformulate the cost-push model of the previous section to allow for monetary effects and the possibility of deviations of GNP from its natural level. In this setting, we will show that, to the extent there is a strategic reaction, analogous to that of the Garbage Game, in response to a downward real shock to the economy, monetary expansion and wage and price controls are substitute policies for reducing the costs associated with the gaming behavior within the economy. Thus, at least in an economy subject to periodic downward real shocks, the repeated use of what are, on monetarist grounds, dysfunctional macroeconomic policies can be readily explained and may be an efficient response on the part of the government.

To adopt the model of the previous section to encompass both monetary policy and positive (output) costs of inflation we introduce both an interaction between real money demand and goods demand, and a "natural rate of output" in each sector. This latter notion, due to Friedman (1968), represents an optimal rate of output in each sector which we denote by X^*.[3] Corresponding to this vector X^*, there is a vector of optimal final outputs d^*. Thus the cost of inflation in this model will be some positive function of the Euclidean distance between d^* and the vector of actual final outputs. In more familiar macroterminology this translates into measuring the cost of inflation as a positive function of the deviation of actual unemployment from its natural rate. This is, of course, somewhat crude as much of the current discussion of these costs deal with either movements in the natural rate itself (Friedman 1977 and Leijonhufud 1980), or with the distribution of deviations of actual output from its natural level (Barro 1976). However, as we are concentrating on inflation as a response to a transient contractionary shock to real GNP rather than as a prolonged process, it seems legitimate to treat the natural rate of output as an exogenous constant.

Turning to the monetary side of the model we treat the stock of money M as being determined solely by the monetary authorities. Denoting a suitable weighted average of the sectoral prices by P, the price level, we adopt a simple Cambridge demand for money function

$$\left(\frac{M}{P}\right) = k \sum_{j=1}^{n} \frac{P_j X_j}{P}, \qquad k > 0 \qquad (4.19)$$

A particular instance of this demand function, which we call the natural demand for money and denote by $(M/P)^*$, occurs when (4.19) is evaluated at the natural rate of output.

$$\left(\frac{M}{P}\right)^* = k \sum_{j=1}^{n} \frac{P_j X_j^*}{P} \qquad (4.20)$$

We then say that the economy is in monetary equilibrium when, given the level of M, P, and X are such that (4.19) is satisfied. Moreover, we require the economy to be in a monetary equilibrium each period.

It is important to notice that by virtue of the fact that the prices in each sector are set monopolistically, it is quantities that will adjust in the short run to ensure monetary equilibrium. Thus for a given M and vector of P_j's, the imposition of monetary equilibrium results in equation (4.19) determining the vector of outputs X; i.e., (4.19) is an output equation.[4] This interpretation does not hold for the natural money demand equation (4.20). As X is fixed at X^*, the imposition of monetary equilibrium on (4.20), given a level of M, results in a natural price level, P^*. Of course, the economy need not have chosen prices such that $P = P^*$. This natural price level is introduced here simply as a benchmark in the sense that it is the price level that would be generated in the economy if the economy followed the classical quantity theory of money.

Consider an economy that is initially in a full equilibrium in the sense that the agents in the economy have chosen a vector of prices such that each sector is satisfied with its share of final output and so does not wish to change its price and, given the money supply, those prices satisfy (4.20). Now the oil producers exercise their monopoly power and commit themselves to a higher relative price of oil, thereby forcing the domestic economy to consume a smaller share of the vector final outputs d^*. That is, real GNP drops because of the adverse movement in the terms of trade. This upsets the equilibrium or standard of behavior to the distributional game and so the players, the sectors, reconsider their price strategies. In order to recapture their lost real income, each sector will readjust their price. As in the last section we assume that the final demand for each product is invariant with respect to relative prices between the goods. However, unlike the equations in the last section, the present equations include an asset or real balance effect on goods demand. More specifically we assume that the final demand for good j, d_j, is given by

$$d_j^d = d_j^* - \beta\left[\left(\frac{M}{P}\right)^* - \left(\frac{M}{P}\right)\right], \qquad \beta > 0 \qquad (4.21)$$

This form of real balance effect, which is currently popular in the rational expectations literature (see Barro 1976), can be rationalized as the result of an infinite horizon individual's maximization in which the desired, long-run level of real balances is given by $(M/P)^*$. Thus when actual real balances fall below this level, expenditure on goods is reduced in an attempt to accumulate further real balances.

With this specification for final goods demand, our system (4.6) can now be written as

$$(I - A)X = \left[d^* - \beta\left(\left(\frac{M}{P}\right)^* - \left(\frac{M}{P}\right)\right)e\right] \qquad (4.22)$$

where e is a unit vector consisting of ones. For a given M and P, if we invert $(I - A)$ we find that the final amount of good j produced, X_j, can be expressed in a form similar to (4.15) and represented as follows:

$$X_j = X_j^* = \delta\left(\left(\frac{M}{P}\right)^* - \left(\frac{M}{P}\right)\right), \qquad \delta > 0 \qquad (4.23)$$

where δ is a linear function of β with coefficients constructed from the A matrix.

If we assume that δ is small, as is each goods weight in the price index, then it is straightforward to show that each sector can increase its share of final goods by increasing its price.[5] Thus in order to recoup their real income, given the prices of the other goods, each sector will raise its price. Again, as in the last section it is obvious that if this game is played once the only Nash equilibrium is one in which all sellers raise their prices by 100 percent, the maximum allowed. But in this game, such a "defensive inflation" is destructive because, in contrast with the game of the previous section, the sum of this game is not constant. From (4.19) we see that raising all prices by 100 percent, and so P by 100 percent, will result in a fall in output of each sector by one-half. Moreover, as the oil producers have pegged the relative price of oil, this domestic inflation will not even improve the terms of trade and so real GNP will drop by the full 50 percent. In response to this further drop in their real incomes each sector will in turn raise its price, thereby engendering an ongoing process of defensive inflation and a cumulating recession as a result of the initial contractionary shock.

When viewed in a game-theoretic light, this modified Garbage Game is simply a Prisoner's Dilemma with a cooperative, Pareto-optimal outcome and a suboptimal equilibrium noncooperative outcome. If a cooperative solution is attainable by the economy's agents — that is, if they can reach an implicit agreement to accept lower real incomes by keeping prices constant — no incomes policies are needed. In fact, in West Germany where there is a highly centralized wage bargaining against the background of an econometric assessment of the state of the economy over the coming year, a social convention has been developed in which the cooperative solution is chosen and, for example, the oil shock is absorbed rapidly and with a minimum of price level adjustment. The government may aid such a solution by adhering to a monetary constitution, to borrow Leijonhufud's term (1980), which binds them to a very low rate of growth of the money supply.

West Germany notwithstanding, it is true that in most countries the noncooperative solution to the game has been adopted: there has been an institutions failure. As with analogous market failures, such an institutions failure may suggest a role for government policies to fill the gap. In the model of this section the government will be assumed to have two policy tools at its disposal, wage and price controls and the money supply, and we will consider which configurations of these policy instruments may enable the government to make up for the institutions failure.

The most obvious policy to follow would be to impose a cooperative solution — no price rises — by fiat in the form of a wage and price control policy. The monetary side of this policy would be a constant money supply. For the moment let us skate over various very serious real world problems with the implementation of this policy (we will turn to them later on) and simply ask if there are any alternative policies that will achieve the same end.

If we consider the price impact of the defensive inflation we see that, because of the price increases in the economy, the actual price level P, which used to be equal to P^*, goes above P^* and continues to diverge from it. Moreover, there is a one-to-one mapping from $(P-P^*)$ to (X^*-X), so as the price level rises above P^* the real output of the economy falls below X^*. P^*, however, is, from (4.20), a linear homogenous function of M and so $(P-P^*)$, and consequently (X^*-X), can always be set equal to zero by an appropriate increase in the money supply. In other words, the monetary authorities can simply finance or validate the price increases and restore real output to its natural level. At the game-theoretic level, by choosing this monetary policy the authorities are behaving like a "fictitious player" (see Von Neumann and Morgenstern 1947) converting the n-person variable sum game played by the economy's agents into an $n+1$ constant sum game by absorbing the economy's losses in real output by inflating its currency. Such a policy cannot go on indefinitely for a variety of reasons (the international balance of payments problems not being the least). However, in the short run a government official may find it politically expedient to do this and disguise the real costs of inflation rather than intervene directly in the economy and control prices—a politically undesirable alternative.

These two policies, wage and price controls with no growth in the money supply and no wage and price controls with a growing money supply, are alternative ways in which the government can make up for the institution failure in the economy. It is our hypothesis that, after a contractionary shock has occurred, the adoption by various governments of either an incomes policy or a higher growth rate of the money supply, apparently dysfunctional economic policies, does not represent mistakes on the part of the governments but rational attempts to impose an equilibrium on the resulting contraction-avoidance game. Thus, at least in postcontractionary periods, the repeated use of these policies may not pose a problem for policy Darwinism but rather may indicate that the models used to interpret the rationality of these policies are at fault.

While the model proposed is suggestive of why incomes policies and inflationary policies are followed in some periods and is consistent with the high correlation between the growth rates of the money supply and the price level in non–price control years, it is obviously highly simplified and may miss some of the relevant features of the economy that should impinge on policy choice. For instance, on the monetary side we assumed that the inflation rate has no impact on the natural rate of output, which is incorrect, though the magnitude of the effect is still open to debate. Perhaps of more importance are the problems involved in the imposition of wage and price controls. Clearly the choice of the "correct" relative prices to freeze, especially after a change in the terms of trade, is no easy task and practical experience with wage and price controls is not encouraging in this respect. In some sense though this is a technical, but nonetheless major, difficulty. A more fundamental objection to this policy would be that it assumes that the government can *impose* a cooperative solution on the economy. This, however, begs the question of why there was an institutions failure in the first place. If this failure was due to the lack of a way for the various sectors of the economy to make a commitment, then it seems probable that the government can impose the cooperative solution. But British experience, for example, suggests that the reasons for the institutions failure may go much deeper, to the question of what a cooperative solution should look like. In this case, given a democratic political system, it is not clear that the government can impose a cooperative solution on the game, since the rivalries that made it impossible to choose this solution without government intervention will also limit the powers of the government.

While these problems may cast doubt on these policy choices, the fact still remains that the defensive inflationary game will be played out after a contractionary shock and so must be dealt with. Simply to point to the impossibility of an economically clean or politically acceptable wage and price control policy is no reply to the question of what the optimal government response should be. The closer one is to a classical view of the economy (e.g., Barro 1976: 26), the more one can propound a fixed money supply as the policy response and allow the competitive price system to work itself out. But even if the market system is competitive in the classical sense, the political system is *not* in the sense that it relies on bargaining rather than impersonal market forces to allocate resources. Thus a competitive market system may just result in the defensive inflation game being played in the political, rather than economic, system. Certainly, to return to the main theme of this section, a classical economist must face the empirical question of why, if he or she is right about the efficacy of a constant money supply role, governments repeatedly choose one of the two alternative policies described in this chapter.

NOTES

1. The alternative recent argument in favor of wage and price controls is that they enable the government to lower abruptly the public's inflation expectations, thereby reducing the costs of a disinflationary monetary policy. Note that here it is the monetary policy that reduces inflation.
2. See Spinelli (1980) for a recent test of the cost-push approach to Italian inflation.
3. The elements of X^* we assumed to be consistent with each other given the B matrix.
4. As there are many nonnegative vectors X that will satisfy (4.13), we will restrict ourselves to those that are scalar multiples of X^*.
5. From (4.20)

$$\frac{\partial VA_j}{\partial P_j} = \left[P_j - \sum_{i=1}^{n} a_{ij} P_i - a_{j1} W - a_{oj} P_o \right] \frac{\partial X_j}{\partial P_j} + X_j$$

and from (4.21)

$$\frac{\partial X_j}{\partial P_j} = -\delta \frac{M}{P^2} \frac{\partial P}{\partial P_j}.$$

Thus by making δ small and assuming $\partial P/\partial P_j$ small for all j, and noting that

$$\left[P_j - \sum_{i=1}^{n} a_{ij} P_i - a_{j1} W - a_{oj} P_o \right] > 0,$$

given $\partial VA_j/\partial P_j > 0$, then $\partial VA_j/\partial P_j > 0$.

REFERENCES

Alchian, Armen A. 1950. "Uncertainty, Evolution, and Economic Theory." *Journal of Political Economy* 58(3), June:211–221.

Aumann, Robert. 1959. "Acceptable Points in General Cooperative *n*-Person Games." In *Contributions to the Theory of Games*, vol. 4, edited by A. Tucker and R.D. Luce. Annals of Mathematics Studies, No. 40. Princeton, N.J. pp. 287–324.

Barro, Robert J. 1976. "Rational Expectations and the Role of Monetary Policy." *Journal of Monetary Economics* 2(1), January:1–32.

Friedman, Milton. 1968. "The Role of Monetary Policy." *American Economic Review* 58(1), March:3–17.

———. 1977. "Nobel Lecture: Inflation and Unemployment." *Journal of Political Economy* 85(3), June:451–472.

———. 1982. "Monetary Policy: Theory and Practice." *Journal of Money, Credit and Banking* 14(1), February:98–118.

Holtzman, F.D. 1950. "Income Determination in Open Inflation." *Review of Economics and Statistics* 32:150–158.

Leijonhuvd, Axel. 1980. "Theories of Stagflation." Department of Economics, University of California, Los Angles. Working Paper No. 176.

Machlup, Fritz. 1960. "Another View of Cost-Push and Demand-Pull inflation." *Review of Economics and Statistics* 42:125–139.

Von Neumann, John, and Oskar Morgenstern. 1947. *The Theory of Games and Economic Behavior.* Princeton, N.J.: Princeton University Press.

Shapley, Lloyd, and Martin Shubik. 1969. "On the Core of an Economic System with Externalities." *American Economic Review* 59:678–684.

Schotter, Andrew. 1977. "Economically Efficient and Politically Sustainable Economic Contractions." In *Mathematical Economics and Game Theory*, edited by R. Henn and O. Moeschlin. Berlin: Springer-Verlag.

Spinelli, Franco. 1980. "The Wage-Push Hypothesis: The Italian Case." *Journal of Monetary Economics* 6(4), October:493–508.

✳ *Chapter 5*

Incomes Policy as a Social Institution

Paul Davidson

Both Bull and Schotter (Chapter 4) and Lipnowski and Maital (Chapter 2) suggest in this book that game theory rather than neoclassical theory provides a better analytical framework for discussing the persistent problem of all modern economies: inflation.

I am very sympathetic to these views and hence found much to agree with in both these chapters. But my function here is to provide some critical discussion rather than merely words of praise.

ASSUMPTIONS INHERENT IN THE USE OF GAME THEORY

The use of game theory requires the belief of the analyst that inflation is a symptom of a struggle over the distribution of income in which agents "believe" they can and do affect the outcome by certain actions. In contrast, neoclassical theory, as Samuelson pointed out, requires an assumption that he called the "Ergodic Hypothesis" (1969: 184). It is "a belief in unique long-run equilibrium independent of initial conditions." Samuelson indicates that the Ergodic Hypothesis implies that "If the state redivided income each morning, by night the rich would again be sleeping in their beds and the poor under the bridges." (This view, Samuelson notes, "makes economics out of fairy tales.")

Thus, in opposition to neoclassical theory, the use of an analytical tool such as game theory already predisposes the user to the belief that agents can affect the distribution of income in a meaningful way — even if the equilibrium outcome (in the absence of a socially derived incomes policy) is not what any of the game participants desired. Neoclassicists, on the other hand, are trapped, by the logic of their assumption, into the belief that the ultimate or long-run distribution of income is determined by the parameters of the system provided by a divine providence under an Ergodic Hypthesis.

"IRREFUTABLE" NATURAL BEHAVIOR

The neoclassical belief in the immutability of the market-determined distribution of income involves the Lakatsosian hard core (irrefutable) propositions that agents optimize while pursuing their self-interests (Weintraub 1982–83: 301). This "irrefutable" natural behavior, it is asserted, will result in the stable neoclassical contract curve solution, which maximizes total welfare given any initial distribution of resources. Thus, left to their own devices, economic agents will "naturally" and inevitably find the long-run, blissful welfare-maximizing solution.

In his presidential address to the American Economics Association, Kenneth Boulding noted the fairy tale aspect of orthodox Pareto-oriented theory when he noted that the Pareto-optimality required an assumption about the existence of Snow White and the Seven Marginal Conditions! The Snow White analogy suggests the fairy tale aspect of assumed behavior and the Seven Marginal Conditions represents the mathology of this mythology.

As an empirical fact the neoclassical optimizing behavior resulting in the contract curve is far from the one actually found in nature. For example, suppose we put two dogs in an Edgeworth Box, one possessing some lamb bones and one beef bones. Neoclassical theory tells us these two agents should exchange portions of each's initial endowment of bones to arrive at a Pareto-optimal solution on the contract curve. The solution actually worked out by the dogs under a laissez faire environment, however, is far from Pareto-efficient — as any dog owner can verify.

Thus my first conclusion is that what game theory does is to emphasize the need for social institutions to encourage cooperative civilized behavior to protect agents from the terrorism of the laissez faire solution to utility maximization. Neoclassical theory denies this requirement for a civilized solution to the economic problem. Until economists understand that there is nothing natural or civilized about the neoclassical solutions to economic problems, we will continue to pursue a theory that is precise—but wrong (Samuelson's economics as a fairy tale)—rather than roughly right.

To understand production and exchange in a civilized society, one must realize that it is *the social institutions which create that civilization*. Economic theory without any institutional content is theory without meaning for real world economies. Good neoclassical theory is strictly axiomatic logic—it does not contain any institutions, not even the market, despite the continual cavalier use of that term by neoclassicists.

I define *social institutions* slightly differently from Bull and Schotter. My definition of social institutions is *rules of behavior imposed by the community which have been developed to help resolve particular persistent problems*. Until the problem becomes persistent, therefore, the social institution to deal with it may not exist.

The recent persistent high rates of inflation suffered by modern economies have not been a persistent problem historically. The great Spanish inflation left a price level 500 percent higher at the end of the sixteenth century than it was at the beginning; the spillover to France left prices 250 percent higher in 100 years and England only 300 percent in 100 years (Keynes 1930: 136–137)—this despite the huge inflow of precious metals to Europe. If we could only have a 2.5 to 5 percent inflation for the next 100 years, we would call it the great era of price stability. The great German inflation lasted less than sixteen months and was ended with the adoption of a new money—a fiat social institution to settle production contracts that were not indexed to a price level as the old money had been (Davidson 1978: 393–394).

In contrast, in the last fifteen years, the U.S. Consumer Price Index has risen almost 300 percent (or the equivalent of 2,000 percent for 100 years). Since persistent 2000 percent century rates of inflation are a recent problem, it is no wonder we need a new knd of social institution to deal with it.

UNDERSTANDING SOCIAL INSTITUTIONS

Civilization is nothing more or less than a set of social institutions. An understanding of civilized (law-obeying) behavior in modern society requires an analysis of such institutions as part of the economic system. If we doff these institutions and allow laissez faire behavior, we do not get rational behavior or even rational expectations. Instead we get war, crime, and the dogs in the Edgeworth Box as the solution of utility maximization of agents constrained only by their initial strength or resources.

Accordingly, any analysis of inflation in modern economies requires the explicit recognition of the following existing *social institutions*, which have been developed by society to organize its production and exchange activities and to study why they have been futile in recent decades in resolving the inflation problem.

1. *Time-related organized markets.* Time is a device that prevents everything from happening at once. Production and consumption take time, and hence payment and delivery must be *contractually* specified with specific dates in historical time.
2. *The law of contracts.* This law prevents "recontracting" without income costs whenever an agent enters into a "false trade."
3. *Money.* Primarily a social institution for the discharge of contractual obligations, money is not just a numeraire!

INFLATION AND INCOME DISTRIBUTON

Why should the struggle over the distribution of national and international income result in inflation? Why not in war, crime, or even trashing-vandalism (Bull and Schotter's Garbage Game)? After all, game theory has had its most successful applications in war games and the like. It is not a theory in which the use of money plays a significant, unique, role!

Here I think that game theory has failed to build into it the aforementioned institutions before attacking the inflation problem. Hence, game theorists have instituted an empirically obvious but ad hoc aspect to their analysis — namely, that the players fight via the contract prices for the things they sell rather than turn to war or crime to gain income and wealth from the other players. Game theorists should explain why the former behavior and not the latter behavior predominates. And here Keynes's *General Theory* and post-Keynesian monetary theory provides the necessary explanation via the explicit discussion of the institution of the law of contracts for commitments spanning long periods of calendar time (forward contracts).

Since production takes time, the hiring of factor inputs and the purchase of materials to be used in any production activity must precede in time the date when the finished product will be at hand. These hiring and material purchase transactions will therefore require forward contracting (and no recontracting permitted) if the production process is to be *efficiently planned*. These forward contracts are the way a free market economy institutes wage and price controls, which are necessary for entrepreneurs to limit their liabilities if they are to undertake their financing of positions in working capital goods. As long as the duration of these forward hiring and material purchase contracts exceeds the gestation period of production, entrepreneurs can limit their liabilities when undertaking any production activity.

Accordingly, contrary to the modern neoclassical contract theory, where the existence of contractual arrangements obstructs the Pareto-efficient solution, it is the existence of long-term fixed nominal contracts which is a necessary institution for the efficient organization of long-term production processes (Davidson 1982: ch. 1). If, however, the social institution of long-term hiring contracts begins to break down, the entrepreneur's liabilities may become prohibitively uncertain. Then a "social contract" to limit wage and price movements over calendar time must be developed to buttress the institution of lengthy private forward contracts, if production activities requiring long periods of time are to be maintained. Thus, with the growth in importance of contractually organized, lengthy production activities, the civilized battlefield for struggle over the distribution of income has been the money terms of settling forward hire and material purchase contracts. In fact, the definition of income in *The General Theory* (Keynes 1936: ch. 6) and in the national income accounts is derived from the contractual relations among entrepreneurs, their sales contracts, and their input hire forward contracts. Income, in a modern society, cannot be defined independently of these contractual relations, and hence income distribution is determined via the social institution of contracts. Thus the civilized battlefield for a struggle over the income shares is the recontracting of contractual arrangements. Such continual recontracting, which provides almost erotic pleasure to neoclassical economists, is sheer hell to real world economies.

POST WORLD WAR II INFLATION

Why has the inflationary struggle become such a persistent problem only since World War II? What has happened to our institutions that the magnitude of inflation we have experienced for over a decade worldwide has become so dramatic? We have become too civilized — at least B.R. (before Reagan)! In the period since World War II, the community has explicitly recognized that one's place in the income distribution is not made via the Ergodic Hypothesis or, as in earlier centuries, divinely determined. (God must have loved the poor, he made so many of them — and so has Reagan!) People were educated to the belief that they were masters of their own fate, that one could and should control one's Kismet and do one's own thing. To control one's destiny, one must first control one's income. Hence our education since World War II set not labor against capital as in the traditional game theory of Lipnowski and Maital, but labor against labor, all against all to promote the welfare of numero uno, as in the Garbage Game of Bull and Schotter. And in that kind of Garbage Game, as Bull and Schotter show, a stable solution is possible only when the community — or at least all but one member of the community — gets together and communally agree on a social rule about how to distribute the income.

REAL WORLD EXAMPLES

Initially, Lipnowski and Maital assume two monolithic group players, labor and management. Labor moderation in conjunction with business moderation can result in a Pareto-efficient solution; Let's-Hang-Together-type games pose no macroeconomic problems, because it is assumed that immoderate behavior by either player "causes losses to the player himself as well as the opponent." *Are there real world examples of such games?* Lipnowski and Maital use a small open economy as an example where extreme behavior of both business and labor could lead to a disastrous erosion in international competitiveness and hence encourage the Let's Hang Together game. Yet is is just such banana republic economies — and recently oil-producing nations as well — which have engaged in extreme behavior! These real world counterexamples raise doubts as to whether the Let's Hang Together game solution can occur voluntarily in a "free market" environment with great differences in the distribution of income within any group and between the groups. (The Extremism Is No Vice game—which results in the same thing—is not shown to have any real world equivalent).

KEYNES AND FRIEDMAN

When they restrict their analysis to two-player games, Lipnowski and Maital indicate that it is only in the Prisoner's Dilemma game that each player is willing to suffer the costs of extreme behavior rather than have moderate behavior exploited by his opponent. In the multi-player Garbage Game, on the other hand, moderate behavior is always threatened by any single other agent or coalition of agents dumping on the moderate. Thus here we need a social institution to get cooperation. In the absence of organized cooperation, individuals will find it in their own self-interest to follow a new Golden Rule: "Dump on your neighbor before he dumps onto you."

Lipnowski and Maital argue that the Prisoner's Dilemma is consistent with both monetarist and Keynesian schools. In a similar manner Bull and Schotter provide a model involving the natural rate hypothesis and other neoclassical apparatus to demonstrate how inflation and the Garbage Game operate. I believe that both sets of authors are involved in logical error here, for the microfoundations of both monetarism and neoclassical Keynesianism are, as Samuelson indicated, the "Ergodic Hypothesis" and long-run equilibrium, where a unique distribution depends on the divine parameters and not on any incomes policy.

It is true that some Keynesians such as Tobin or Samuelson have recommended incomes policies as a cure for inflation—but Friedman, to his credit, has always argued that the logic of his position is against incomes policies. Friedman, unlike the neoclassical synthesis Keynesians, offers us the supreme intellectual achievement, unattainable by the weaker-spirited Keynesians, of adopting a hypothetical world remote from reality as though it were the world of experience and then living in it consistently. Most neoclassical synthesis Keynesians, on the other hand, cannot help but let their common sense break in—with injury to their logical consistency.

COORDINATING CLAIMS

Lipnowski and Maital suggest that it is a lack of "coordination and communication" that cause the Prisoner's Dilemma game in the Keynesian macrotheory. To some extent that is true, since inflation is people trying to exercise claims for more than 100 percent of the existing national or international income. But such incoordination and lack of communication is not logically possible in any macroeconomic world that has a general equilibrium system as its foundation. That such a general equilibrium world could generate unemployment was due to the ad hoc assumption of Keynesians of a *rigid* money wage, so that the labor market need not clear. But in the inflationary processes we are talking about, money wages are far from rigid or inflexible — they are in each round of the "defensive inflation" and cumulating recessionary process of Bull and Schotter, only too flexible.

Moreover, once we have expanded the game to more than two players, better communications alone is not sufficient to resolve the problem, as Bull and Schotter's Garbage Game indicates. Even if we communicate to all groups that their relative income demands exceed 100 percent of the gross national product, there is no reason to believe that they will voluntrily coordinate claims to just exhaust the GNP pie — that is, to resolve the "adding-up" problem without attempting to dump inflation on others.

GOVERNMENT AS PLAYER

Lipnowski and Maital introduce government as a third malevolent player in this Prisoner's Dilemma game. They find, in the words of Bull and Schotter, that "The situation is unstable or cyclic" and hence there is a need for a social institution to institute standards of behavior that provide at least stable solutions either by the community of $N-1$ agents dumping on the Nth; or by a convention awarding one player a fixed amount and splitting the remainder among all other players.

NO MONOLITHIC PLAYERS

Here, I believe, we come to the essence of the inflationary Prisoner's Dilemma game. I believe that Lipnowski and Maital are wrong in thinking that the players are a "monolithic" labor and a "monolithic" business. This may make interesting literature for the Marxists among us who like to think in terms of the class struggle. But, in reality, the problem exists because there are more than two homogeneous, monolithic groups. It is not Workers versus Capitalists, or Us versus Them. It is workers versus workers versus workers or people versus people. (We have met the enemy and they is us!) Loose coalitions form, dissolve, reform, etc. as we join and rejoin various groups to get better pieces of the action. We are, each one of us, nonmonolithic. As professors we want higher salaries; as taxpayers, lower taxes; as savers higher interest payments; as home buyers, lower mortgage rates; as humanitarians higher wages for workers, as patrons of the arts, lower theatre ticket prices. We move from group to group supporting each of these measures in turn, based on the highest moral and selfish principles, without ever concerning ourselves that the groups may have incompatible objectives in terms of claims on the distribution of income.

Lipnowski and Maital indicate that empirical studies have shown that the larger the number of players, the less likely they are to achieve moderate behavior, since mistrust and anonymity decrease social responsibility. And is that not true for consistent behavior in democratic nations where one is free to choose, and time is not suspended, by the Walrasian auctioneer, until he assures us that all cries are consistent with each other?

PAYOFF MATRIX AND PRICES

Lipnowski and Maital note that displaying the payoff matrix, in empirical game studies, tends to encourage cooperation. Thus education and an incomes policy go hand in hand. But in neoclassical theory, this would be wasteful because the prices players call out in a laissez faire environment are supposed to be the educating process; but prices are the resource allocation informing devices, not the income distributing information device. Yet, as Hahn has shown, in a world of calendar time and uncertainty, Arrow–Debreu equilibrium shows the conditions that are necessary to provide a proper allocation and the theory shows "why the economy cannot be in that state. . . . Practical men and ill-trained theorists everywhere in the world do not understand what they are claiming to be the case when they claim a beneficent and coherent role for the invisible hand" (Hahn 1973: 14–15). Once we recognize that the conditions necessary for prices to provide a Pareto-efficient resource allocation cannot exist in the real world, it is possible for economists to realize that prices are largely an income distributive device. Every price is someone's income, and rising prices are the symptom of people trying to raise their incomes.

RULES FOR CIVILIZED BEHAVIOR

What social institutions can reduce the Prisoner's Dilemma to a co-operative game? Lipnowski and Maital suggest four types of social institutions: (1) alter the payoff matrix; (2) repeat the game permitting retribution and conciliation; (3) employ social contracts; and (4) change the players' perception of the game.

Tax-based incomes policy is an obvious solution for (1), (3), and (4). I am not sure what the authors had in mind in terms of (2), but if it is to play the game in the hopes of utility alteration, I fear this has not much going for it.

In the last chapter of *The General Theory*, Keynes noted, "The outstanding faults of the economic society in which we live are its failure to provide for full employment and its arbitrary and inequitable distribution of wealth and income" (Keynes 1936: 372). Nevertheless Keynes believed that there are

> Social and psychological justifications for significant inequalities.... Dangerous human proclivities can be canalised into comparatively harmless channels by the existence of opportunities for money making... which if they can not be satisfied in this way may find their outlet in cruelty....It is better for a man to tyrannise over his bank balance than over his fellow citizens....But it is not necessary for the stimulation of these activities...that *the game* should be played for such high stakes as at present. Much lower stakes serve the purpose equally well, as soon as the players become accustomed to them. The task of transmuting human nature must not be confused with the task of managing it. Though in the ideal commonwealth men may have been taught or inspired or bred to take no interest in the stakes, it may be still wise and prudent statesmanship to allow *the game* to be played subject to rules and limitations. (Keynes 1936: 374, emphasis added)

Rules for civilized behavior is where the answers to our most pressing economic problems lie.

REFERENCES

Davidson, P. 1978. *Money and the Real World,* 2nd ed. London: Mac-Millan.

———. 1982. *International Money and the Real World.* London: Mac-Millan.

Hahn, F.H. 1973. *On the Notion of Equilibrium in Economics.* Cambridge, England: Cambridge University Press.

Keynes, J.M. 1930. *A Treatise on Money,* vol. 2. London: Macmillan.

———. 1936. *The General Theory of Employment, Interest, and Money.* New York: Harcourt, Brace.

Samuelson, P.A. 1969. "Classical and Neo-Classical Monetary Theory." In *Monetary Theory,* edited by R.W. Clower. Harmondsworth, England: Penguin.

Weintraub, E.R. 1982. "Substantive Mountains and Methodological Mole-hills." *Journal of Post Keynesian Economics 5.*

Chapter 6

Welfare Analysis of Income Distributions: A Neoclassical Approach

Benjamin Bental

Walrasian general equilibrium models fail to rationalize the existence of most economic institutions. In particular these models fail to explain social arrangements that regulate the distribution of income. This failure ensues from the fact that usually different distributions of income are Pareto noncomparable. Therefore, there is no rationale to favor one particular distribution, and there is no room for intervention that aims to change any given initial income distribution.[1]

Incomes policies have been linked with anti-inflationary measures (see Bull and Schotter, Chapter 4, and Lipnowski and Maital, Chapter 2, in this book). However, inflation is another phenomenon that is inexplicable by Walrasian general equilibrium models, because the social institution of fiat money cannot be rationalized by such models. Accordingly, if incomes policies are indeed related to an inflationary environment, a model in which such an environment can be described is called for. The framework suggested below gives rise to valued fiat money, and hence to inflationary paths, which are caused by the existence of government deficits. Therefore, this framework is also potentially capable of connecting incomes policies to the rate of inflation. Since the model describes explicitly the technology in the economy and the tastes of the agents who populate it, any policy measure can be defended if it brings about a Pareto improvement. Thus, if a redistribution of incomes improves matters for *everybody* involved, it is likely that such a redistribution will indeed occur.

The specific model used here is Samuelson's (1958) overlapping generations model. As Wallace (1980) and Cass and Shell (1980) claim, this is the only available framework in which equilibria with valued fiat money exist. Therefore, if one is to discuss inflation explicitly in a general equilibrium framework, there is little choice in models. Further, the overlapping generations model enables an explicit welfare analysis, since all agents are characterized by well-specified preference orderings.

In the version used below, there are two groups in the economy, who share a given endowment of a perishable consumption good. In addition the government extracts a certain amount of this good by issuing new fiat money. As it turns out, the inflation needed to extract that amount of the good may depend on the distribution of the total endowment between the two groups. Since the rate of inflation has an impact on utility, the distribution of income matters in a welfare analysis. In particular, a lower inflation rate is clearly welfare-enhancing. The government may therefore be able to propose a "package deal," by which it refrains from raising the inflation rate if the private sector reaches an appropriate arrangement concerning the distribution of income in which one group (workers, for example) agrees to refrain from raising its share. This proposal is acceptable to everybody if it is Pareto-superior to the initial situation. I show below the circumstances under which such a proposal might work. An example demonstrating that these circumstances could arise for parameter values in line with accepted economic theory is developed, and some concluding remarks close this chapter.

THE MODEL

Time is discrete. At each point in time, a continuum of agents is born. The agents are indexed on a closed interval of the real line of total length N. Each agent lives two periods.

There is a single good in the economy, Y units of which appear each period. This good is nonstorable.

Preferences of all agents born at $t = 1$ and later are identical, and defined over their lifetime consumption. Let $U(c_1(t), c_2(t))$ denote the utility of an agent born at t who consumes c_i units of the good at age i, $i = 1, 2$. I assume $U_1 > 0$, $U_2 > 0$, $U_{11} < 0$, $U_{22} < 0$. Further, let

$$v(c_1, c_2) = \frac{U_1(c_1, c_2)}{U_2(c_1, c_2)}. \tag{6.1}$$

(Subscripts denote partial derivatives.) I assume

$$\lim_{c_1 \to 0} v \to \infty, \qquad \lim_{c_2 \to 0} v \to 0, \qquad v_1 < 0, \qquad v_2 > 0. \tag{6.2}$$

The last two relations imply that c_1 and c_2 are both normal goods.

In the economy discussed here, only young agents are endowed with some amount of the good. Let each generation be split into two groups, of sizes αN and $(1 - \alpha)N$, respectively. Let βY be the amount of the good given to the first group and $(1 - \beta)Y$ to the second. Further, suppose that within each group income is evenly distributed. Hence we have

$$y^1 = \frac{\beta}{\alpha} y \tag{6.3}$$

$$y^2 = \frac{1 - \beta}{1 - \alpha} y \tag{6.4}$$

where y^i is income of a member of group i, and $y = Y/N$ is average income.

In addition, the old persons of time 1 are endowed with $M(0)$ units of fiat money. Their utility depends solely on their consumption (in a direct relation, of course). Hence, their supply of money is perfectly inelastic.

The young of time 1 and onward have the following maximization problem:

$$\text{MAX } U(c_1^i(t), c_2^i(t)) \tag{6.5}$$

$$\text{S.T. } c_1(t) + p(t) m^i(t) \leq y^i \tag{6.6}$$

$$c_2(t) \leq p(t + 1) m^i(t) \tag{6.7}$$

where $m^i(t)$ is the amount of money purchased at time t, and $p(t)$ is the price of money in terms of the consumption good at time t. The superscript i indicates the group to which the agent belongs.

The government in this model consumes each period G units of the good. It purchases the good by creation of new money, rather than by taxation.[2] Hence, its budget takes the following form:

$$p(t)[M(t) - M(t - 1)] = G \tag{6.8}$$

Normalizing by N, and using individual money holdings, this expression becomes

$$p(t)[\alpha m^1(t)+(1-\alpha)m^2(t)-(\alpha m^1(t-1)+(1-\alpha)m^2(t-1))]=g$$
(6.9)

An equilibrium in this model is defined as follows:

Definition 1. An *equilibirum* consists of sequences:

$$\{c_1(t),c_2(t-1),m^i(t),p(t)\}_{t=1}^{\infty} \qquad i=1,2,$$

such that
(a) all agents maximize utility;
(b) all markets clear; and
(c) perfect foresight prevails.

Definition 2. An equilibrium is *stationary* if

$$c_1^i(t)=c_1^i, \quad c_2^i(t)=c_2, \qquad t=1,2,\ldots$$
(6.11)

The fact that many equilibria exist in this model is well known (see Wallace 1980). I concentrate on stationary equilibria, due to the stationary nature of the environment in this model. Since nothing changes over time in endowments or tastes, time should not play any role in agents' information sets. They should not care if they are born at date t_0 or t_1, since the world is identical at either date.

The sequence $p(t)$ may be identically zero, if g is too large. In such a case, the government is unable to finance its deficit through money creation. In the following discussion, I assume that g is such that there exists a monetary equilibrium; that is, money has value at every t. In the next section, the equilibrium conditions are derived and analyzed.

SOLUTION

The first order conditions for the young agents' problem yield

$$v(c_1^i(t),c_2^i(t))=\frac{p(t+1)}{p(t)}\equiv R(t+1)$$
(6.12)

where R is the reciprocal of unity plus the inflation rate.

Let $s^i(t) = p(t)m^i(t)$. Then we can rewrite (6.12) as

$$v(y^i - s^i(t), R(t+1)s^i(t)) = R(t+1) \qquad (6.13)$$

In a stationary equilibrium, $s^i(t) = s^i$, and hence also, $R(t) = R$. Accordingly, the government budget becomes

$$s(1-R) \equiv (\alpha s^1 + (1-\alpha)s^2)(1-R) = g \qquad (6.14)$$

Thus, we have three equations in three "unknowns": s^1, s^2, and R, consisting of the maximizing conditions of the agents of types 1 and 2, and the government budget.

We can write the solution as

$$s^1 = F^1(\beta, \alpha, g) \qquad (6.15)$$

$$s^2 = F^2(\beta, \alpha, g) \qquad (6.16)$$

$$R = H(\beta, \alpha, g) \qquad (6.17)$$

The utility level of an agent of type i is given by

$$U^i = U(y^i - F^i(\beta, \alpha, g), H(\beta, \alpha, g) \cdot F^i(\beta, \alpha, g)) \qquad (6.18)$$

The utility of the old increases as $S \equiv \alpha S' + (1-\alpha)s^2$ increases. The problem can now be stated precisely: Does there exist a case such that

$$\text{sign} \frac{\partial U^1}{\partial \beta} = \text{sign} \frac{\partial U^2}{\partial \beta} = \text{sign} \frac{\partial S}{\partial \beta} \qquad (6.19)$$

I concentrate on the conditions under which changing β in the appropriate direction increases *both* U^1 and U^2. To find these conditions, I calculate

$$\frac{\partial U^1}{\partial \beta} = U_1\left[\frac{1}{\alpha}y - F_1^1\right] + U_2[H \cdot F_1^1 + F^1 \cdot H_1] \qquad (6.20)$$

Using the fact that $v = R$, I obtain

$$\frac{\partial U^1}{\partial \beta} = \frac{1}{\alpha}yU_1^1 + s^1 U_2^1 H_1 \qquad (6.21)$$

Similarly,

$$\frac{\partial U^2}{\partial \beta} = -\frac{1}{1-\alpha}yU_1^2 + s^2 U_2^2 H_1 \qquad (6.22)$$

The next step is to find H_1. I now use the implicit function theorem on the solution of the model. The Jacobian of the system is given by

$$J = \begin{bmatrix} -v_1^1 + Rv_2^1 & 0 & s^1 v_2^1 - 1 \\ 0 & -v_1^2 + Rv_2^2 & s^2 v_2^2 - 1 \\ \alpha(1-R) & (1-\alpha)(1-R) & -(\alpha s^2 + (1-\alpha)s^2) \end{bmatrix} \quad (6.23)$$

$$|J| = -(-v^1 + Rv_2^1)[(-v_1^2 + Rv_2^2)(\alpha s^1 + (1-\alpha)s^2)$$
$$+ (s^2 v_2^2 - 1)(1-\alpha)(1-R)] - (s^1 v_2^1 - 1)[(-v_1^2 + Rv_2^2)\alpha(1-R)]$$
$$(6.24)$$

If $(s^i v_2^i - 1) > 0$, then $|J| < 0$. This condition implies that c_1 and c_2 are not gross substitutes. If c_1 and c_2 are gross substitutes, then $(s^i v_2^i - 1) < 0$, and the sign of $|J|$ is ambiguous.

H_1 takes the form:

$$H_1 = \frac{1}{|J|}\left[\alpha(1-R)(-v_1^2 + Rv_2^2) \cdot \frac{1}{\alpha} y v_1^1\right.$$

$$\left. - (1-\alpha)(1-R)(-v_1^1 + Rv_2^1)\frac{1}{1-\alpha} y v_1^2\right]$$

$$= \frac{1}{|J|}(1-R)Ry[v_2^2 v_1^1 - v_2^1 v_1^2] \quad (6.25)$$

Claim 1. If U is homothetic, $H_1 = 0$.

Proof: In the case of homothetic utility functions, v depends only c_1/c_2. Since all agents face the same R, c_1/c_2 is the same for everybody, and then $v_2^2/v_1^2 = v_2^1/v_2^1$.

Clearly, then, for homothetic utility functions, the inflation rate is independent of income distribution. The static result obtains: The sign of $\partial U^1/\partial \beta$ is opposite to that of $\partial U^2/\partial \beta$, and any initial income distribution cannot be improved upon in the Pareto sense.

Suppose now that the first group (αN) consist of "workers," and the incomes policy calls upon them to reduce their share in total income, or to refrain from increasing it. If it is to be optimal for that group to agree, then $\partial U^1/\partial \beta < 0$. Hence, necessarily $H_1 < 0$. In other words, a necessary condition for a reduction in β to be utility-enhancing is that the inflation rate be inversely related to β. If it is, then reduced inflation may offset the reduction of utility brought about by the reduction of income. Note also that $H_1 < 0$ implies, from (6.14), $\partial S/\partial \beta < 0$. Therefore, the initial money holders (the initial old) also benefit from a reduction of the share of the "workers" in total income.

AN EXAMPLE

Let $U(c_1, c_2) = Ac_1^\gamma + Bc_2^\delta$, $0 < \delta < 1$, $0 < \gamma < 1$, $\gamma \neq \delta$. The first order conditions imply

$$v = \frac{\delta A c_2^{1-\delta}}{\gamma B c_1^{1-\gamma}} = R \tag{6.26}$$

Suppose that $|J| < 0$. If $H_1 < 0$, $|J| < 0$ implies

$$v_2^2/v_1^2 - v_2^1/v_1^1 < 0 \tag{6.27}$$

The latter holds if $c_1^1/c_2^1 > c_1^2/c_2^2$.

Let $c_1^1/c_2^1 = 2$ and $c_1^2/c_2^2 = 1$. Then

$$s^1 = (\beta y)/(\alpha(1+2R)), \quad s^2 = (1-\beta) y/(1-\alpha)(1+R) \tag{6.28}$$

I now set $\beta = 0.7$, $\alpha = 0.95$. In other words, the "workers" constitute 95 percent of the population and get 70 percent of total income. Further, I set $R = 0.8$; that is, the inflation rate is 25 percent.

The first order conditions imply

$$\left(\frac{c_2^1}{c_2^2}\right)^{1-\delta} = \left(\frac{c_2^1}{c_1^2}\right)^{1-\gamma} \tag{6.29}$$

By substituting these values, γ and δ have to satisfy the following linear relation:

$$\delta = 0.279 + 0.721\gamma \tag{6.30}$$

The last step is to evaluate $\partial U^1/\partial \beta$. In this example we get

$$\partial U^1/\partial \beta = \left[R + \frac{1}{D} \frac{(1-R)(1-\gamma)(1+2R)(1+R)}{2\beta(1-\beta)R}\right] \cdot M \tag{6.31}$$

where M is an expression that includes v_1^1, v_2^2, and other parameters, and D is proportional to $|J|$. In particular,

$$D = -\frac{1+2R}{\beta}\left(\frac{1-\gamma}{2R} + 1 - \delta\right)\left[\frac{1+R}{1-\beta}\left(\frac{1-\gamma}{R} + 1 - \delta\right)\left(\frac{\beta}{1+2R} + \frac{1-\beta}{1+R}\right)\right.$$

$$\left. - \frac{\delta}{R}(1-R)\right]$$

$$+ \frac{\delta}{R}\frac{(1-R)(1+R)}{(1-\beta)}\left(\frac{1-\gamma}{R} + 1 - \delta\right) \tag{6.32}$$

Clearly, we need $D < 0$. But D should also be small enough in absolute value, so that $\partial U^1/\partial \beta < 0$. For $\delta = 0.89$ and $\gamma = 0.847$, such a situation arises, and $\partial U^1/\partial \beta = -0.786$. This indicates that it is in the interest of the workers to reduce their share of national income, in return for a reduction in the rate of inflation. We can also calculate g, which turns out to be $0.087y$. In other words, the deficit in the government budget is 8.7 percent of national income.

Although there is no pretense here that this model is realistic, the parameters chosen do not seem to be extreme or unreasonable. Still, it should be noted that the range of γ and δ for which $\partial U^1/\partial \beta < 0$ is very small.[3] Indeed, getting $\partial U^1/\partial \beta < 0$ should not be "easy," if the model captures, in my sense, some aspects of reality. After all, incomes policies are always subject to prolonged negotiations, and more often than not, fail to be implemented even if an agreement is reached.

CONCLUSION

The example contained in this chapter is of an economy in which income distribution may affect intertemporal rates of substitution through its effect on inflation. Therefore, it is possible to justify a redistribution of income that seems to hurt a certain group as being a Pareto-improvement. The group that gives up some of its income gains by the fact that as a result of its concurrence, it (and the rest of the economy) faces a lower inflation rate, and hence an improved intertemporal rate of substitution. In this way, the model presented here, which contains no elements of growth, can circumvent the unavoidable conclusions of static zero-sum-game models. In such models, a change in income distribution can never be a Pareto improvement; there are always some who are worse off.

It is still true that the set of parameters for which a redistribution of income is Pareto-improving seems to be small. This result should be expected. Social contracts pertaining to a redistribution of income are hard to achieve and even harder to implement. Yet, if the theory presented here is at all relevant, incomes policies can be a result of rational maximization procedures, and should be put forward for public debate whenever the occasion arises.

NOTES

1. Redistribution of incomes was rationalized in static models that deviated from the strict Walrasian paradigm. For example, the existence of externalities in tastes serves as a rationale for intervention (see Nakayama 1980 for references of earlier work that followed this line of reasoning).

2. The fact that taxation is not used has to be explained. As shown in Wallace (1980), deficit financing through money creation is nonoptimal. However, this result depends on the costlessness of direct taxation. Clearly, direct taxation is much more costly than money creation. Hence, it may well be optimal, if not necessary, to use inflation as a means of taxation. I assume here that there is no taxation at all, in order to simplify the analysis. The results will not change, in principle, as long as there is some amount of taxation by inflation.

3. The exact range has not been calculated, but it seems that $0.88 < \delta < 0.9$ is approximately the space in which, for this example, $\partial U^1 / \partial \beta < 0$.

REFERENCES

Cass, D., and K. Shell. 1980. "In Defense of a Basic Approach." In *Models of Monetary Economies*, edited by J.H. Kareken and N. Wallace. Minneapolis: Federal Reserve Bank, pp. 251–260.

Nakayama, N. 1980. "Nash Equilibria and Pareto Optimal Income Redistribution." *Econometrica*, July.

Samuelson, P.A. 1958. "An Exact Consumption-Loan Model of Interest with or without the Social Contrivance of Money." *Journal of Political Economy 66*:467–482.

Wallace, N. 1980. "The Overlapping Generations Model of Fiat Money." In *Models of Monetary Economies*, edited by J.H. Kareken and N. Wallace. Minneapolis: Federal Reserve Bank, pp. 49–82.

* *PART III*

**INCOMES POLICY:
NEW STRUCTURES**

Chapter 7

Tax-Based Incomes Policy as the Game of "Chicken"

Irwin Lipnowski and Shlomo Maital

Undoubtedly, even the most wisely conceived tax-based incomes policies are likely to be subject to considerable leakages and significant administrative costs. But I would expect them to shine as a paragon of efficiency in comparison to the social costs of unemployment and slack as a cure for chronic inflation.

— *Arthur Okun* (1981: 253)

I remain to be convinced that any form of tax-based incomes policy has yet been devised that meets even minimum standards of workability, equity, or reliability in achieving the results desired from it.

— *George Freeman, Deputy Governor of the Bank of Canada* (1981: 7)

Wallich and Weintraub (1971) supported their tax-based incomes policy (TIP) with "the historical evidence (that) the average markup of prices over unit labor costs has been remarkably constant" so that "restraint of wage increases implies restraint of price increases." We propose to examine the viability of the Wallich and Weintraub version of TIP, and the relation between wage and price increases, in the framework of a 2×2 labor-business game that turns out to be "Chicken," with government tipping the scale in favor of business.

We shall also examine Okun's (1981) variant of TIP, where labor is rewarded with tax concessions if the wage settlement falls within the government's guideposts. We show that both the "carrot" (Okun) and "stick" (Wallich-Weintraub) versions of TIP result in a game of Chicken. In Chicken, there are two Nash equilibria in pure strategies; in each, one player exploits the other. (When strategies are chosen simultaneously by all players, a Nash equilibrium occurs when no player finds it advantageous to deviate unilaterally from the strategy he picked.) According to our analysis, while Wallich-Weintraub TIP and Okun TIP may well prevent the confluent mutual disaster of immoderately large wage and price increases, neither is likely to achieve the desired goal of both moderate wage increases and moderate price increases.

TIP AS CHICKEN

Under Wallich-Weintraub's TIP, government establishes a wage guidepost, or standard, which if exceeded by a firm in its wage settlement by some percentage — say, x — would require the firm to pay a surcharge on its basic corporate profit tax rate equal to some specified multiple of x. The Wallich-Weintraub TIP is designed to "stiffen the company's back in wage negotiations" and by lowering the general rate of wage settlements, to effect a lower rate of inflation.

Given this strategy of government, we depict the subgame between labor and business as simply as possible by assuming each player has only two strategies, characterized as "easy" (E) and "tough" (T). There is a function that maps strategies chosen by labor and business into outcome space. Outcome space is a vector of economic indicators, such as the rate of unemployment, rate of inflation, real wage, real profits. All three players — labor, business, government — have a preference ordering with respect to all possible outcomes. In a 2×2 game, there are four possible outcomes from simultaneous choice of strategy by labor and business. We assign ordinal utility indicators to each of these four outcomes to indicate their ranking by each player. Table 7-1 shows one possible set of outcomes. Though these outcomes are given here impressionistically, they can be derived formally from a conventional macroeconomic model (Lipnowski and Maital 1981).

When we recast this game into a two-player non-constant-sum game in normal form, between labor (row player) and business (column player), we have the following payoff matrix:

Table 7-1. Outcomes for Three-Player Non-Constant-Sum Game.

Labor's Strategy[a]	Business's Strategy	Unemployment Rate	Inflation Rate	Real Wage	Real Profits	Ordinal Utility Indicator for Labor, Business, and Government
T	T	High	High	Low	Low	$\langle 1, 1, 1 \rangle$
T	E	Low	High	Medium	Low to medium	$\langle 4, 2, 2 \rangle$
E	T	Low to medium	Low	Low to medium	Medium to high	$\langle 2, 4, 4 \rangle$
E	E	Low	Low	Low to medium	Medium	$\langle 3, 3, 3 \rangle$

[a] T is "tough" (immoderate wage and price increases); E is "easy" (moderate wage and price rises). The triplet $\langle i, j, k \rangle$ indicates the order of preference for labor (i), business (j), and government (k), with 1 indicating worst and 4 indicating best.

Business

		E	T
Labor	E	3, 3	2, 4
	T	4, 2	1, 1

This game is Chicken; each player would rather be exploited than endure mutual destruction, but each would rather exploit the other than be exploited. For labor, the necessary condition for this, maintained in the above matrix, is

$$(T, E) > (E, E) > (E, T) > (T, T)$$

For business, there is a comparable condition.[1]

There are two Nash equilibria in pure strategies: (E, T) and (T, E). Government attaches greater utility to (E, T) than (T, E) (see Table 7-1). How can government intervene most effectively to bring about (E, T)?

In order to win at Chicken each player must persuade his opponent that he is irrevocably committed to an uncomprising (T) strategy. The following passage by Herman Kahn illuminates this strategy:

> Some teenagers utilize interesting tactics in playing "chicken." The "skillful" player may get into the car quite drunk, throwing whiskey bottles out the window to make it clear to everybody just how drunk he is. He wears very dark glasses so that it is obvious that he cannot see much, if anything. As soon as the car reaches high speed, he takes the steering wheel and throws it out the window. If his opponent is watching, he has won. If his opponent is not watching, he has a problem; likewise, if both players try this strategy. (1965: 11)

In the context of the Wallich-Weintraub TIP, government would endeavor to persuade labor that business is committed firmly to a strategy choice of T, because of the tax penalty facing business should it instead choose E. If labor then is convinced businesses will play T, labor then sees itself facing the following payoff matrix:

Business

		T
Labor	E	2, 4
	T	1, 1

Labor will, of course, play E. By publicly threatening business with a penalty should it fail to play T, government's role is not only to induce business to play T, but no less importantly, to convince labor that business will play T so that labor will feel obliged to play E. If labor were to play T, the concomitance of (T, T) would lead to strikes, layoffs, unemployment, and leave labor worse off than if E were played: labor opts to be exploited rather than court disaster.

Strategies can lead to an "infinite regress." Labor knows business incurs tax penalties for playing E; business knows labor knows, and so on. This strengthens the likelihood of the Nash (E, T) equilibrium.

Is there a dual, "carrot" approach to TIP that achieves the same result as the "stick" version? Recently Okun (1981) proposed a wage-incentive version of TIP to counter alleged anti-labor bias in the Wallich-Weintraub TIP, and designed to soften the spine of labor in wage negotiations. Okun's TIP, too, leads to an (E, T) outcome, as the following argument shows.

Suppose government undertakes publicly to reward labor with tax concessions should it play E. Now, with business convinced labor will play E, business sees itself facing the following reduced payoff matrix:

Business

		E	T
Labor	E	3, 3	2, 4

Business will clearly choose T. Tax concessions to labor may well be large enough to cause labor to rank the (E, T) outcome above that of (E, E) — but this simply strengthens the likelihood of (E, T) and makes the socially first-best outcome (E, E) even *less* likely.

BEHAVIORAL EVIDENCE

Faced with economic and social dilemmas that Chicken depicts, how do people really behave? Rapoport and Chammah (1966) conducted a series of game-experiments with University of Michigan undergraduates. Game theory suggests equilibrium should fluctuate between (E, T) and (T, E), with each player choosing E about half the time. In fact, players chose E significantly *less* than half the time. Moreover, the trend to shift from T to E over time, after a series of mutual annihilations, was less pronounced than expected. The authors surmise that there may be a belief that as the punishment for double defection (from E to T) grows, each player thinks the other will be reluctant to take the punishment associated with retaliation.

Maital and Benjamini (1980) compared the labor-business game to Prisoner's Dilemma, where each player chose T. Rapoport and Chammah note that in Chicken, "preemptors" (a player who moves from an EE equilibrium first, by playing T, is a preemptor) tend to "repent" more readily than in Prisoner's Dilemma, even though in Chicken, retaliation is *less* certain than in Prisoner's Dilemma. They conclude that the greater severity of the punishment for extremism in Chicken must counteract the smaller likelihood that extremism will meet retaliation.

From this, they draw an interesting conclusion. Penologists often claim that certainty of conviction is a more powerful deterrent to crime than severity of punishment. Rapoport and Chammah's results with Chicken suggest the opposite: Severe punishment seems to be a more effective deterrent than more *certain* punishment. (A game-simulation study of tax evasion by Friedland, Maital, and Rutenberg 1978 confirmed this result.) This suggests that a stick-stick version of TIP, with tax penalties on both labor and business for playing T, may be more effective than the Wallich-Weintraub or Okun versions alone.

CONCLUSION

Both the Wallich-Weintraub and Okun versions of TIP face labor and business with macroeconomic conflicts characterized by the game of Chicken, likely to lead to moderate behavior on the part of labor and tough behavior on the part of business. While this is preferable to immoderate behavior on the part of both labor and business, it still does not lead us to the goal incomes policy is supposed to achieve: moderate behavior on the part of both.

NOTES

1.   We assume that the only arguments in labor's utility function are the unemployment rate and real wage. It follows that (T, E) strictly dominates (E, E), because in both the employment rate is low but the real

wage is higher for (T, E). By the same reasoning, (E, E) strictly dominates (E, T), and (E, T) dominates (T, T). If inflation and real profits affect labor's utility as well — for instance, when labor is envious of business, or disturbed by inflation *per se* — this ordering may well change.

REFERENCES

Barber, C.L., and J.P.C. McCallum. 1982. "Incomes Policies: A Three Year Program to Control Inflation." U. of Manitoba, Unpublished paper.

Colander, D. 1979. "Incomes Policies: MIP, WIPP and TIP." *Journal of Post Keynesian Economics 1*(3), Spring:91–100.

Freeman, George, et al. 1981. *Policies for Stagflation: Focus on Supply.* Toronto: Ontario Economic Council.

Friedland, N.; S. Maital; and A. Rutenberg. 1978. "A Simulation Study of Tax Evasion." *Journal of Public Economics 10*:107–116.

Kahn, Herman. 1965. *On Escalation, Metaphors and Scenarios.* New York: Praeger.

Lipnowski, I., and S. Maital. 1981. "Hanging Together, or Separately: A Game-Theoretic Model of Incomes Policy." Faculty of Industrial Engineering and Management, Technion-Israel Institute of Technology, Haifa, Israel.

Maital, S., and Y. Benjamini. 1980. "Inflation as Prisoner's Dilemma." *Journal of Post Keynesian Economics 2*(4), Summer:459–481.

Okun, A. 1981. *Prices and Quantities: A Macroeconomic Analysis.* Washington, D.C.: Brookings Institution.

Rapoport, A., and A.M. Chammah. 1966. "The Game of Chicken." *American Behavioral Scientist 10*(3), November:10–28.

Seidman, L.S. 1981. "Equity and Trade-offs in a Tax-Based Incomes Policy." *American Economic Review, Papers and Proceedings 71*(2).

Wallich, H., and S. Weintraub. 1971. "A Tax-Based Incomes Policy." *Journal of Economic Issues 5*:1–19.

Chapter 8

The Reverse Incomes Policy:
An Institutional Cure for Inflation

Steven E. Plaut

One problem in economics that has been the subject of institutional analyses of various forms is inflation and its remedies. Among the institutional innovations that have been proposed to stop inflation are tax-based incomes policies (TIPs) and various forms of price and wage indexation. These institutional remedies do not reduce inflation, at least not in the sort of economy modeled in this chapter, although they may be useful as remedies for other problems besides inflation. Instead, the institution I will describe as a reverse incomes policy is capable of reducing inflation. Reverse incomes policies will be defined shortly.

A social institution, as defined by Lewis (1969), is a regularity in behavior that is agreed to by all members of a society and that specifies behavior in specific recurrent situations. Schotter (1981) modifies that definition: "A social institution is a regularity in social behavior that is agreed to by all members of society, specifies behavior in specific recurrent situations, and is either self-policed or policed by some external authority."

Most approaches to inflation treat government fiscal and monetary policy either from a positivist approach, taking the government behavior as given, or from a normative approach, asking what policy *should* be followed. In contrast, an institutional approach is useful because its starting point is the institutional structure of the economy that makes inflation possible. Even if we knew how inflation occurred and how it could be stopped, it would still be useful to ask *why* it is created. Someone must be creating inflation. But why?

The largest body of institutional literature on inflation deals with TIPs in their various forms. Advocates of TIP have included Scott (1961), Wallich and Weintraub (1971), Lerner (1977a, b, 1978, 1980), Okun (1975), and Seidman (1976, 1978a, b, 1979). Critics and other analysts who have discussed them would include Boyes and Schlagenhauf (1981a, b), Dildine and Sunley (1978), and Rees (1978).[1]

The TIP literature generally suffers from the weakness of seldom specifying formally how it views the inflationary process and its causes. It often seems to view inflation as a process where prices are set haphazardly with no determinate equilibrium, where inflation is a sort of inertia that can be stopped through temporary braking. Without a specific model, it is difficult to judge TIP on the basis of theoretical consistency, let alone practical applicability.

This chapter formally specifies an economy and clearly identifies the source of the inflationary process. Inflation is due to monetary expansion, the rate of which is determined by a governmental utility function that depends on household utility, the level of public spending, and the tax burden.

I will discuss the impact of several institutional "remedies" to inflation including the "social contract," indexation, incomes policies, and reverse incomes policies. The economy being modeled is a small economy with highly distorted commodity markets, universal unionization, and with inflation—possibly very high inflation—resulting ultimately from monetary expansion. I do not insist that the economy being modeled is to be accepted as a realistic representation of any given economy, although it is my unsubstantiated opinion that it captures a number of features of the economy of Israel, and possibly of other hyperinflated economies.

THE MODEL

The economy in this model consists of households, producers, and the government. Households choose quantities of n consumer goods, hold money, and supply labor. Producers purchase labor and supply consumer goods with very simple production functions that depend on only one input, labor. The government provides public services, which are financed through taxation and through monetary expansion.

The economy is characterized by a number of distortions. No market is characterized by perfect competition. In markets for commodities, consumers behave as price takers. Each commodity is produced by a single producer with unrestrained monopolistic power. In order to make our accounting easier, we will assume that all producers operate with zero profits.[2] This might be due to monopolistic competition[3] or due to profits being expropriated by a firm-specific non-distorting Pigovian tax.

Firms have market power as sellers, but behave as price takers in the labor market. Households are united in a labor supply monopoly or union that fixes a uniform wage (but may not price discriminate). No labor is supplied except through the union.

Finally the government has an objective function that depends on consumer utility and also on its budget revenue and expenditure. The government's objective function may be thought of as a proxy for some sort of reelection probability function.

Formally, the economy is composed of a large number of identical consumers with homothetic utility functions. Since consumers are identical, we may represent total household utility in any time period as a single utility function. We assume it is of the following form:

$$\bar{U} = U(C_1, C_2, \ldots, C_n, L, G, M/P) \cdot V(\dot{P}) \tag{8.1}$$

Here C_i is consumption of good i, L is total labor supply by the household sector, and G is the consumption of public goods and services. M/P is the real balance of money held by the households, where $P = \sum_i C_i P_i$, where P_i is the price of good i. $\dot{P}$ is inflation or $P/P^{-1} - 1$, where P^{-1} is P one period earlier; that is, inflation as measured by a Paasche price index.

The utility function is separable. Inflation is intentionally included as an argument in the function; its inclusion means that the consumer is assumed to be "inflation averse"; that is, consumers lose utility from inflation even if their real income remains constant.[4] Representing utility in a separable form means, in effect, assuming that consumer demand and labor supply will not depend on inflation (as long as real balances stay constant), even though the total level of utility does.

$\bar{U}$ is a continuous, differentiable, concave function. The first partial differentials of U with respect to C_i, G, and M/P are positive, while the second partials are negative. The first partials with respect to L and $\dot{P}$ are negative, and the second partials are negative. All other differentials are not restricted.

In any given period, consumers must select C_i ($i = 1, 2, \ldots, n$), L, and M in order to maximize (8.1) subject to the consumer budget constraint:

$$\sum_i P_i C_i + (M - M^{-1}) = wL - T \tag{8.2}$$

where w is the wage, T is the amount of taxes paid. Unless stated otherwise, T is a nondistorting Pigovian tax.

The first order conditions for a maximum are (8.2) and (8.3)–(8.5).

$$U_i' = \lambda P_i; \qquad i = 1, 2, \ldots, n \tag{8.3}$$

$$U_L' = -\lambda \frac{d(wL)}{dL} \tag{8.4}$$

$$U_m' = \lambda \tag{8.5}$$

where U_i', U_L', and U_m' are the first partial differentials of $\bar{U}$ with respect to the ith good, labor and real balances, respectively. λ is the Lagrangian multiplier representing the marginal utility of an additional dollar of current income. Equation (8.4) is a simplified representation of a somewhat more complex relationship (see below).

Firms produce goods from labor alone and sell them in monopolistic markets. We assume that the utility function shown in (8.1) is of a specific form that is consistent with Cobb-Douglas demand functions of zero degree homogeneity. That is, the demand for good i may be represented by

$$C_j = a_j (T^{-\eta_{jt}}) \prod_{i=1}^{n} (P_i^{-\eta_{ji}}) w^{\eta_j} M^{\eta_{jm}} \tag{8.6}$$

where $-\eta_{jt} + \eta_j + \eta_{jm} - \sum_i \eta_{ji} = 0$, for all $j = 1, 2, 3, \ldots, n$.[5] Note that $\eta_{jj} > 0$ for all j; all other elasticities are unrestricted. The demand functions in (8.6) are characterized by constant price and income elasticities.

Producers have continuous, quasiconcave differentiable production functions

$$X_i = X_i(L_i) \qquad (i = 1, 2, \ldots, n) \tag{8.7}$$

where L_i is the labor input in sector i. Producers are price takers in the labor market, and treat the wage rate w as exogenous. Producers seek to maximize profits subject to (8.7). The first-order condition for profit maximization is

$$P_i\left(1-\frac{1}{\eta_{ii}}\right)X_i' = w; \qquad i = 1, 2, \ldots, n \qquad (8.8)$$

where X_i' is the marginal product of labor.

Now labor supply, as noted above, is monopolized or unionized. To find the specific form of Eq. (8.4), we must totally differentiate (8.8) and (8.6) and aggregate into a total labor demand function. This is done formally in the appendix. The new first order condition may then be written as

$$\frac{-U_L'}{\lambda} = w\left(1+\frac{1}{\psi}\right) \qquad (8.4')$$

where ψ is defined in the appendix.

The government has the following objective function in each time period:

$$W = W(\bar{U}, G, T) \qquad (8.9)$$

G, T, and M are chosen to maximize W, subject to the constraint,

$$G = T + M - M^{-1} \qquad (8.10)$$

W may be thought to be some sort of reelection probability function. The first partial differentials of W with respect to $\bar{U}$ and G are positive, and that with respect to T is negative. All second partial differentials are negative.

It should be noted that we list G and T as separate arguments. That is, changes in G and T have a direct effect on W going beyond their indirect effect through $\bar{U}$. This may be because government policymakers simply enjoy spending money or lowering taxes, or because the election rules are such that election results are not simply direct mappings of $\bar{U}$, or because voters do not select their votes on the basis of $\bar{U}$ alone.

In any case, the government chooses fiscal and monetary policy to maximize W. The first order conditions are

$$W_G' + W_U'U_G' = \lambda^* \qquad (8.11)$$

$$-W_T' - \lambda W_U' = \lambda^* \qquad (8.12)$$

$$W_U'\left(-U_P'\frac{1}{M^{-1}}\frac{\dot{P}}{M} + \frac{U_M'}{M^{-1}}\left(1-\frac{\dot{P}}{M}\right)\right) = \lambda^* \qquad (8.13)$$

where U_P' is the first partial of $\bar{U}$ with respect to inflation, and where

$\dot{M} = (M/M^{-1}) - 1$ and λ^* is the increment to W from an extra dollar of revenue.

There are $3n + 8$ independent variables in the system: X_i $(= C_i)$, L_i, P_i $(i = 1, 2, \ldots, n)$, G, M, λ, λ^*, $\bar{U}$, W, T, w. Equations (8.1)–(8.3), (8.4′), (8.5)–(8.9), and (8.11)–(8.13) represent $3n + 8$ independent equations. The system is therefore determined and the solution unique.

What can we say about the model economy? Suppose that we define as "socially optimal" those solutions that maximize $\bar{U}$. Then clearly our economy is not operating optimally.

First, there is underproduction in all markets, including the labor market. All industries are monopolistic; therefore prices are higher than social opportunity costs. Moreover, wages are higher than the household disutility of labor. For both reasons, there is underproduction and underemployment.

Second, government fiscal and monetary policy is not socially optimal. Socially optimal spending would set $U_G' = \lambda$, whereas in our system,

$$U_G' = \frac{\lambda^* - W_G'}{W_U'} = \lambda - \frac{W_G'}{W_U'} \tag{8.14}$$

Since W_G' and W_U' are positive, the system produces overexpenditure on government services. The government chooses taxes so that $-W_T' = \lambda^* + \lambda W_U'$, whereas a socially optimal policy would be to choose taxes so that $-W_T' = \lambda$. Socially optimal fiscal policy would require that

$$-\frac{W_G'}{W_T'} = \frac{U_G'}{\lambda}. \tag{8.15}$$

This, however, is achieved only when $\lambda^* = 0$.

Finally, the economy is "overinflated." It should be noted that the optimal rate of increase in M is zero (assuming households are also deflation averse). In our model, monetary policy is neutral. Consumer demand and labor supply depend only on M/P. Relative prices and real wages are independent of nominal changes in M. When all markets clear, it must be that $dM/dt = dP/dt = dw/dt = dP_i/dt$ $(i = 1, 2, \ldots, n)$. Inflation and monetary policy have no impact on the "real" side of the economy, other than lowering $\bar{U}$ and financing government spending. Optimal monetary creation is thus zero since that would create zero inflation. However, actual monetary creation would be positive and determined by

$$\frac{W'_U U'_P}{M^{-1}} = -\lambda^* \tag{8.16}$$

Inflation is determined indirectly by the same relation.

INSTITUTIONAL REMEDIES

Price and wage determination is Pareto-inferior. Producers and con-sumers-workers may be thought to be playing a version of Prisoner's Dilemma where a Pareto improvement could be achieved if each group agreed to moderate its price-fixing behavior. That is, if the union lowered its nominal wage and if the producers all reduced their nominal prices for given M, output and employment would increase. Since such an eventuality would require agreement and voluntary self-enforcement among the $n+1$ players, Pareto improvements are un-likely without outside intervention. If the government were able to achieve some sort of workable "social contract" among the $n+1$ players, the Prisoner's Dilemma could be escaped. Such a "social contract" would not be self-enforcing, and would not qualify as an "institution."

One form of intervention would be an incomes policy where wage and price increases would be taxed. To illustrate how this would work, let us suppose monetary creation is proceeding at the rate of θ per period. Once all markets are in equilibrium, all nominal prices and wages will continue to rise at θ per year.

Now the government decides to tax all players according to their nominal price increases (perhaps beyond some given nominal in-crease). The tax will work as follows: Producers and workers must pay the government a proportion t of any nominal price or wage in-crease, respectively, in the relevant period. In that case the relevant price for producer i after taxes will be

$$P_i - t(P_i - P_i^{-1}) = P_i(1-t) + tP_i^{-1} \tag{8.17}$$

where P^{-1} is the value of P last period. Note that if the producer were raising his nominal price at the rate of θ per period, his net price (after taxes) would be

$$(1+\theta)P_i^{-1} - t\theta P_i^{-1} = (1 + \theta(1-t))P_i^{-1} \tag{8.18}$$

Nominal wage increases would be similarly taxed, so that the net wage (after taxes) will be[6]

$$w(1-t)+tw^{-1} \tag{8.19}$$

The tax revenue collected will constitute part of T, which will remain, as before, total tax revenue. The difference between T and the revenue from the incomes policy will be collected through a nondistorting Pigovian tax.

The incomes policy, as defined in (8.17) and (8.19), will affect prices and wages through changing the net demand curves that producers and the union face. The incomes policy could (but need not) cause a Pareto improvement in allocation. This can be illustrated for the special case where all price cross-elasticities in the demand functions are zero.

The producer i is now facing a net demand curve with constant elasticity of

$$\eta_{ii}^* = \eta_{ii}\left(1+\frac{t}{(1-t)(1+\dot{P_i})}\right) \tag{8.20}$$

where $\dot{P_i}$ is the nominal rate of increase in P_i, or $P_i/P_i^{-1}-1$. It should be noted that for $0<t<1$, $\eta_{ii}^* > \eta_{ii}$. From equation (8.8) we see that for any w, the incomes policy in the special case noted will cause commodity prices to fall, production to increase, and labor demand to increase.

The impact of the policy on nominal wages is more complex. On the one hand, there is a shift right in the demand curve for labor. On the other, there is an increase in the elasticity of the net demand curve. If ψ were the labor demand elasticity before the incomes policy, and ψ' were the "gross" elasticity after the incomes policy, then the "net" elasticity after the incomes policy is

$$\psi^* = \psi'\left(1+\frac{t}{(1-t)(1+\dot{w})}\right) \tag{8.21}$$

It should be noted that $\psi^* > \psi'$, but it is not clear whether ψ^* is greater than or less than ψ.

The incomes policy will produce new values of w and P_i ($i = 1, 2, \ldots, n$). However, it will not end inflation. Following an adjustment period, nominal prices and wages will continue to rise at the same rate as monetary expansion, or θ. This is because, as before, all supply and demand curves depend on M/P only. In equilibrium, all prices and wages will rise at the same rate that money expands, but along paths different from those existing before the incomes policy.

Figure 8–1.   Goods Market.

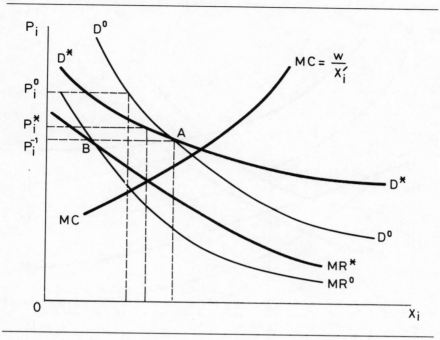

Geometrically, we can show the impact of the policy in Figures 8–1 and 8–2. For our special case with zero cross-elasticities, the incomes policy causes the net demand for good i to pivot counterclockwise around point A. The elasticity of net demand rises by $t/(1-t)(1+\theta)$. The marginal revenue curve also pivots around a point B that lies to the left of A. Note that if $t \to \infty$, the new demand and supply curves would become horizontal at P_i^{-1}.

In the labor market, the "gross" labor demand curve shifts to the right (D^0 to D'). It can be shown that at any gross wage rate, the new curve is $k(w)$ units to the right where

$$\frac{dk(w)}{dt} = \left(\sum_{j=1}^{n} \frac{P_j}{\eta_{jj} MR_j} \left(\frac{X_j'}{X_j} - \frac{\eta_{jj} X_j''}{X_j'} \right)^{-1} \right) \frac{1}{(1+\theta)(1-t)^2} \qquad (8.22)$$

The "net" labor demand curve pivots counterclockwise around point F (Figure 8–2) from D' to D^*. The wage rate is determined by the intersection between the "marginal union revenue" curve (MUR) and the S ($= -U_L'/\lambda$) curve. As a result of the incomes policy, the MUR

Figure 8–2. Labor Market.

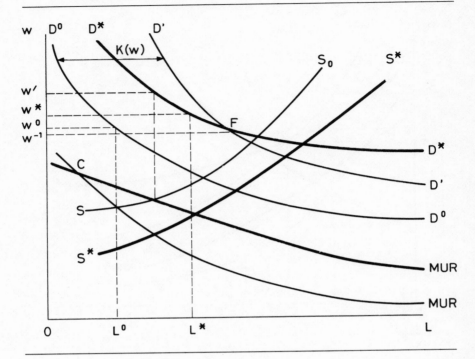

curve shifts, cutting the original S curve to the right, causing the associated net wage rate to increase (w_0 to w'). However, the S curve also shifts right due to the fall in prices caused by the changes in the product markets (*MR* shifting in Figure 8–1). This will serve to lower net wages. The combined wage effect is ambiguous; employment however unambiguously rises from L^0 to L^*. If equilibrium gross *w does* change, the marginal cost curve in Figure 8–1 will have also shifted. Output in product markets will have risen,[7] and commodity prices will generally be lower. Since all markets had exhibited underproduction before the incomes policy, a Pareto improvement results. Once we drop our assumption of zero cross-elasticities, such improvements are possible, but generally one would expect Pareto noncomparable reallocation.

Our conclusion is, ironically, that the incomes policy has no effect on inflation, except in the immediate adjustment to the new price and wage equilibrium paths (which may mean a one-time fall in the price level). Following adjustment, prices and wages will continue to rise at the rate of monetary expansion.

The only "achievement" of the incomes policy would be possibly to produce a Pareto improving reallocation. If such an improvement occurs, the incomes policy would represent a partial solution to the Prisoner's Dilemma of misallocation, but not to the problem of inflation. Moreover, even if the incomes policy did produce a Pareto improvement, it is likely that a straight excise tax-cum-payroll tax would do the job better. The reason is that the commodity demand and labor demand curves would pivot around their X-axis intercepts rather than around internal points (A and F in the figures). Thus the price decrease would likely be more severe and the output expansion more impressive.

In sum, the incomes policy turns out to be useful—at best—as a microeconomic policy instrument for resource allocation, rather than as a macroeconomic policy instrument for inflation suppression. As a microeconomic instrument, it is probably inferior to excise taxes-cum-payroll taxes. Moreover, if applied in competitive goods and labor markets, the policy would cause misallocation and reduce efficiency.

REVERSE INCOMES POLICIES

If the incomes policy does not lead to a reduction in inflation, what does? One possible answer involves what might be called a "reverse incomes policy." Under an incomes policy, the government "indexes" its revenue to wage and price increases in the private sector. Under a reverse incomes policy, the producers and union are committed to indexing their prices to the size of the government deficit.

To see how this would work, let us recall Eq. (8.13), which describes the first order condition for maximizing W through monetary policy:

$$W'_U\left(-\frac{U'_P}{M^{-1}}\frac{\dot{P}}{\dot{M}} + \frac{U'_M}{M^{-1}}\left(1 - \frac{\dot{P}}{\dot{M}}\right)\right) = \lambda^* \qquad (8.13)$$

It has already been noted that in equilibrium, $\dot{M} = \dot{P}$, and so (8.13) would become

$$-\frac{W'_U U'_P}{M^{-1}} = \lambda^* \qquad (8.13')$$

Now suppose that all firms and the union were committed to raising their prices and wages by $\theta(1+\gamma)$ where $\theta = \dot{M} = (G-T)/M^{-1}$. Let us assume $\gamma > 0$. In that case any monetary expansion would cause prices and wages to rise more than proportionately. (The relationship of wages to prices and relative prices would remain constant.) Given the reverse incomes policy and government maximization of W, the new version of (8.13) would be

$$W'_U \left(-\frac{U'_P}{M^{-1}}(1+\gamma) + \frac{U'_M}{M^{-1}}\gamma \right) = \lambda^* \qquad (8.23)$$

In order to maintain the equality, it must be that U'_P is smaller in absolute value in (8.23) than in (8.13) or (8.13′). A smaller U'_P means that monetary expansion and inflation have slowed.

Now the reverse incomes policy noted would produce excess demand for money and therefore excess supply for goods. A slight alteration would cure that. Suppose we were to adopt the reverse incomes policy of setting $\dot{P}_i$ $(i = 1, 2, \ldots, n)$ and $\dot{w}$ equal to

$$\Pi + \theta(1+\gamma) \qquad (8.24)$$

where $\theta = \dot{M}$ and $\gamma > 0$. There exists a unique Π for any γ and any set of W and $\bar{U}$ functions that will cause the expression in (8.24) to be equal to θ at the maximized W. That would be enough to assure market clearing.

The important factor that affects monetary policy is the derivative of the reverse incomes policy,

$$\frac{d\dot{P}_i}{d\dot{M}} = \frac{d\dot{w}}{d\dot{M}} = 1+\gamma \qquad (i = 1, 2, \ldots, n) \qquad (8.25)$$

Therefore judicious selection of Π in (8.24) will avoid disequilibria without affecting the first order condition in (8.23). The higher is γ (which implies a lower Π), the greater is the disincentive for the government to print money. Since relative prices and wages are staying constant, and Π is chosen to cause all markets to clear, the fall in monetary expansion and inflation causes utility $\bar{U}$ to increase (although W will fall). Moreover, the reverse incomes policy does not involve any Prisoner's Dilemma type instability, like "social contract" agreements. Given that the other n players have agreed to the reverse incomes policy, the first-best choice of the $n+1$th player is to agree also. Only if he agrees will his relative price be the same as it would be in the absence of the reverse incomes policy, his utility maximizing relative price. The reverse incomes policy thus qualifies as a "social institution" using Schotter's definition.

The reverse incomes policy leads to an improvement in utility, ironically, by adopting an institutional rule that causes the loss in utility from inflation to rise. In effect, the producers and union agree to a rule that will extract a heavier "toll" from themselves for any monetary expansion. This heavier toll, however, also lowers W. Thus, the reverse incomes policy imposes a cost on the government for monetary expansion. Inflation becomes more "expensive" for the government. The reverse incomes policy is a coordination problem of a private sector coalition used to alter government incentives.

The reverse incomes policy causes utility to rise and reduces inflation in our model. In a more complex model, where wage and price adjustments lag behind monetary expansion, even a reverse incomes policy where $-1 < \gamma \leq 0$ could reduce inflation. This is because adoption of the rule by firms and unions would move up the inflation resulting from monetary policy to earlier periods. If the government's objective function were more strongly affected by inflation and inflation aversion in the immediate future than in later periods, the reverse incomes policy would be even more powerful.

REVERSE INCOMES POLICY VERSUS PRICE INDEXATION

Price indexation agreements have become more common in recent years and are near universal in countries with hyperinflation. The indexation system generally involves automatic increases in a price or wage whenever the overall price index rises. In reality, prices and wages are indexed to lagged inflation.[8]

In our model such price indexation would create a number of problems. If the system began in equilibrium, and if monetary expansion were a constant $\bar{\theta}$, then price indexation to lagged inflation would duplicate the equilibrium price and wage paths that were observed with instantaneous market clearing. However, once in motion, full indexation to lagged inflation would prevent any deviation from the price paths. Even if monetary expansion changed from $\bar{\theta}$ to θ', prices and wages would continue moving up at the old rate of $\bar{\theta}$. Any reduction of the rate of monetary expansion by the government would remain "unrewarded," as inflation would remain constant. On the other hand, there would be no "punishment" for acceleration of monetary expansion, resulting in $\dot{M} \to \infty$. Moreover disequilibrium would result. If $\theta' > \bar{\theta}$ ($\theta' < \bar{\theta}$), there would occur excess supply (excess demand) for money and thus excess demand (excess supply) for goods.

If so, why does price and wage indexation take place at all? Without going into the various theories of indexation,[9] part of the explanation may be that it represents a contingent contract that allows prices and wages to be adjusted without a new negotiation session. Since negotiation is costly, contracts cover several time periods. Without an indexation clause, firms and workers would be "locked in" to a price or price path that could not be altered in response to unanticipated changes in the economy. Rather than wait until the end of a contract's life, the indexation clause allows unanticipated changes (such as inflation) to be incorporated into a price or wage before renegotiation.

That being so, the reverse incomes policy accomplishes essentially the same thing as inflation indexation. Unanticipated monetary changes get translated rapidly into prices through a contingent contract. The difference is that the adjustment of the indexed price to money is direct rather than indirect (waiting for lagged inflation to respond) and immediate. Moreover, the system loses its "inertia"; prices would no longer continue rising at rate $\bar{\theta}$ long after monetary policy had been altered.

An additional advantage to the reverse incomes policy is that it indexes domestic prices to domestic disturbances. If prices of tradable goods change abroad, so will their domestic prices. Now under a system of inflation indexation, it is difficult to change the relative prices of tradables. If their prices rise, so will the domestic price index, and therefore so will all other domestic nominal values indexed to inflation. The more "open" the economy, the more closely will domestic nontradable prices "stick" to tradable prices. Balance of trade changes will be difficult and will necessitate large nominal price changes to achieve small relative price adjustments.

If, however, a reverse incomes policy were followed, changes in the relative price of tradables would have no "echo" in indexed domestic prices. As long as monetary policy remained constant, changes in the relative price of tradables or foreign monetary disturbances would have little effect on domestic prices. This could prove an important advantage for economies with hyperinflation and widespread indexation on the one hand and with large balance-of-trade deficits on the other.

Price indexation has another problem. It is quite plausible that the institution of indexation will lower the inflation-aversion of households. While the model presented here does not allow for risk, any reduction in inflation uncertainty due to indexation would likely lower this aversion. As seen in (8.13), any reduction in inflation aversion $(-U_P')$ must result in an *increase* in inflation. Once households are fully "protected" from inflation uncertainty, the government has no reason to restrain the monetary expansion process. Clearly, the reverse incomes policy provides a form of inflation "protection" while avoiding this problem.

CONCLUSIONS AND SUMMARY

In the model proposed, inflation occurs because the "taste" of the government for spending, taxation, and monetary expansion differs from that of households, resulting in suboptimal policies. Several institutional "remedies" for inflation have been shown to be impotent, because they do not directly alter government incentives. One institutional remedy that could work is the reverse incomes policy, where prices and wages are indexed to the rate of monetary expansion. When judiciously formulated, a reverse incomes policy will maintain market clearing, will increase the "cost" to the government of printing money, and will be self-enforcing for all parties.

APPENDIX 8A
DERIVATION OF EQUATION (8.4')

We know from Eq. (8.8) that the first order condition for maximum profits is

$$P_i\left(1 - \frac{1}{\eta_{ii}}\right)Q_i' = w \quad \text{for } i = 1, 2, 3, \ldots, n \qquad (8A.1)$$

Taking total differentiation and rearranging, we get

$$dL_i = (\hat{w} - \hat{P}_i)\frac{X_i'}{X_i''} \quad \text{for } i = 1, 2, 3, \ldots, n \qquad (8A.2)$$

where $\hat{z} = d \ln Z$.

Noting that $dL = \sum_i dL_i$, we may rewrite (8A.2) as

$$dL = \hat{w} \sum_i \left(\frac{X_i'}{X_i''}\right) - \sum_i \left(\frac{\hat{P}_i X_i'}{X_i''}\right) \qquad (A8.3)$$

where X' and X'' are the first and second partial differentials, respectively.

Next let us totally differentiate the set of demand equations, holding T constant. Written in matrix form, this becomes

$$(\hat{C}_i) = -(\eta_{ji})(\hat{P}_i) + (\eta_i)\hat{w} + (\eta_{mi})\hat{M} \qquad (8A.4)$$

Multiplying through by the inverse of the η_{ji} matrix and rearranging, we get

$$(\hat{P}_i) = -(\eta_{ji})^{-1}(\hat{C}_i) + (\eta_{ji})^{-1}(\eta_i)\hat{w} + (\eta_{ji})^{-1}(\eta_{mi})\hat{M} \qquad (8A.5)$$

Let us write the (j, i) element of the inverse matrix as η^{ji}. Then (A8.3) may be rewritten:

$$dL = \sum_j \left(\frac{X'_j}{X''_j}\left(1 - \sum_i \eta^{ji}\eta_i\right)\right)\hat{w}$$

$$- \left(\sum_j \sum_i \frac{X'_j}{X''_j}\eta^{ji}\eta_{mi}\right)\hat{M} + \sum_j \left(\frac{X'_j}{X''_j}\sum_i (\eta^{ji}\hat{C}_i)\right) \qquad (8A.6)$$

Finally (8A.6) may be transformed into

$$dL = \frac{\left(\sum_j \left(\frac{X'_j}{X''_j}\left(1 - \sum_i \eta^{ji}\eta_i\right)\right)\right)\hat{w}}{1 - \sum_j \left(\frac{X'_j}{X''_j}\sum_i \left(\eta^{ji}\frac{X'_i}{X_i}\beta_i\right)\right)} - \left(\sum_j \sum_i \frac{X'_j}{X''_j}\eta^{ji}\eta_{mi}\right)\hat{M}\right) \qquad (8A.7)$$

where $\beta_i = L_i/L$. This may be written in abbreviated form,

$$dL = -\psi\hat{w} + \delta\hat{M} \qquad (8A.7')$$

Equation (8A.4′) may then be expressed as

$$-\frac{U'_L}{\lambda} = w\left(1 - \frac{1}{\psi}\right) \qquad (8A.8)$$

where ψ is defined in (8A.7) and (8A.7′).

NOTES

1. A more comprehensive survey can be found in Lerner (1980).
2. Our main reason for assuming this is so that we need not keep track of the flow of profits and their uses.

3. That is, the threat of entry of new firms with similar but not identical goods. We will assume, however, throughout the exercise that the total number of firms stays constant.
4. This terminology is proposed by Maital and Benjamini.
5. The specific demand forms are chosen only for ease of exposition and demonstration. No conclusions below owe their legitimacy of birth to the specific functional lineage.
6. We will ignore deflationary monetary policy, but in principle, the incomes policy equations (8.17) and (8.19) may refer to nominal increases *and* decreases in prices and wages. That is, price decreases receive a subsidy of $t(P^{-1} - P)$.
7. If good i is inferior, that is, if $\eta_i < 0$, it is possible that output in that market will fall.
8. If all prices were linked to current inflation, the system would be indeterminate.
9. See Cornell (1978), Fischer (1975), Liviatan and Levhari (1977), McCulloch (1980), and Sarnat (1973).

REFERENCES

Boyes, W.J., and D.E. Schlagenhauf. 1981a. "The Optimal Structure and Length of an Incomes Policy." *Quarterly Review of Economics and Business 21*(4):45–63.

———. 1981b. "Price Controls in an Open Economy." *Journal of Macroeconomics 3*:391–408.

Cornell, Bradford. 1978. "A Note on Capital Asset Pricing and the Theory of Indexed Bonds." *Southern Economic Review 45*:1239–1247.

Dildine, Larry L., and Emit M. Sunley. 1978. "Administrative Problems of Tax-Based Incomes Policies." *Brookings Papers on Economic Activity*, pp.363–401.

Fischer, Stanley. 1975. "The Demand for Index Bonds." *Journal of Political Economy 83*:509–534.

Lerner, Abba P. 1977a. "From Pre-Keynes to Post-Keynes." *Social Research 47*.

———. 1977b. "Stagflation—Its Causes and Cure." *Challenge 20*:14–19.

———. 1978. "A Wage Increase Plan to Stop Inflation." *Brookings Papers on Economic Activity*, pp. 491–506.

Lewis, David. 1969. *Convention: A Philosophical Study*. Cambridge, Mass.: Harvard University Press.

Liviatan, Nissan, and David Levhari. 1977. "Risk and the Theory of Indexed Bonds." *American Economic Review 67*:366–375.

Maital, Shlomo, and Yael Benjamin. 1980. "Inflation as a Prisoner's Dilemma." *Journal of Post Keynesian Economics* 2:459–481.

McCulloch, J. Huston. 1980. "The Ban on Indexed Bonds, 1933–77." *American Economic Review* 70:1018–1021.

Okun, Arthur. 1975. "Inflation: Its Mechanics and Welfare Costs." *Brookings Papers on Economic Activity*, pp. 351–398.

Rees, Albert. 1978. "New Policies to Fight Inflation: Sources of Skepticism." *Brookings Papers on Economic Activity*, pp. 435–490.

Sarnat, Marshall. 1973. "Purchasing Power Risk, Portfolio Analysis and the Case for Index-Linked Bonds." *Journal of Money, Credit and Banking* 5:836–845.

Scott, M.F.G. 1961. "A Tax on Price Increases." *Economic Journal* 71: 350–366.

Seidman, Larry. 1976. "A Payroll Tax-Credit to Restrain Inflation." *National Tax Journal* 29:398–412.

———. 1978a. "Would Tax Shifting Undermine the Tax-Based Incomes Policy?" *Journal of Economic Issues* 12:647–676.

———. 1978b. "Tax-Based Incomes Policies," *Brookings Papers on Economic Activity*, pp. 301–362.

———. 1979. "The Role of a Tax-Based Incomes Policy." *American Economics Association Papers and Proceedings* 69:202–206.

Wallich, Henry, and Sidney Weintraub. 1971. "Tax Based Incomes Policy." *Journal of Economic Issues* 5:1–17.

* *PART IV*

PERCEPTIONS AND POLITICS

Labor and Management Attitudes toward a New Social Contract: A Comparison of Canada and the United States

Shlomo Maital and Noah M. Meltz

Picture a pasture open to all. It is to be expected that each herdsman will try to keep as many cattle as possible on the common pasture. As a rational being, each herdsman seeks to maximize his gain. Explicitly or implicitly, more or less consciously, he asks, "What is the utility to me of adding one more animal to my herd?" The rational herdsman concludes that the only sensible course for him to pursue is to add another animal to his herd. And another, and another.... But this is the conclusion reached by each and every rational herdsman sharing a commons. Therein is the tragedy. Each man is locked into a system that compels him to increase his herd without limits — in a world that is limited. Ruin is the destination toward which all men rush, each pursuing his own best interest in a society that believes in the freedom of the commons. Freedom in a commons brings ruin to all.

> — *Garrett Hardin,*
> "The Tragedy of the Commons"

In the debates over macroeconomic theory and policy, economists divide into three camps. Keynesians believe prices and wages respond slowly to excess demand or supply, that it is easier to stabilize real economic variables by moving aggregate money demand to a given path of money wages than by moving wages relative to a given money demand. Monetarists think past rates of growth of the money stock are the only systematic factors determining the rate of inflation and believe a rise in the rate of monetary expansion temporarily reduces the unemployment rate and permanently raises the inflation rate.

New Classical Economists, who have rational expectations, believe that real variables do not respond to anticipated monetary and fiscal policy (Stein 1983). In none of the three schools does industrial relations play a central role.

A fourth paradigm is taking shape, one in which industrial relations is at the core. The viewpoint of this school, to which only a small minority of economists now subscribe, is best expressed as a syllogism:

1. In individual plants, industries, and whole economies, non-zero-sum games are played by labor, business, and government. In such games, positive increments in output, income, and employment accrue to cooperative behavior. Such increments are very large, and are growing.
2. Western economies have proved unable, in the past decade, to realize those positive increments.
3. Neither business nor labor can gain by moderating their behavior unilaterally.
4. It is therefore necessary to fashion a new social contract, under which labor, business, and government would jointly agree to actions that, if done unilaterally, would prove harmful to each player, but when done together, prove mutually beneficial.

This approach to macroeconomics emphasizes the interdependence of economic players, their power to influence market outcomes, their uncertainty about the actions of other players, the potential for forming coalitions, along with their perceptions about the game structure and trust, or lack of it, toward other players. These concepts win limited space in conventional macroeconomics texts but are the staff of life for industrial relations researchers.

This chapter reports in brief on research undertaken to explore the main underlying propositions of the syllogism just stated, as well as attitudes among corporate and labor leaders in the United States and Canada toward its conclusion: the need to fashion a new social contract. In general, corporate executives in both the United States and Canada were skeptical about the diagnosis and prescription of a social contract, with American executives particularly opposed to it. Labor leaders in Canada were considerably skeptical as well, whereas in the United States our sample of labor leaders would, on balance, support it. The Canadian Minister of Labour, André Ouellet, recently said that "we will have to enter into a social contract with. . . the labour world." (*Toronto Globe and Mail* 1984). Our findings indicate Ouellet will meet with opposition from both labor and management in trying to implement his policy, but there would seem to be more possibility for some type of an understanding in Canada than in the United States, where the parties' views are diametrically opposed. Perhaps in Canada the tragedy of the commons can be averted.

NON-ZERO-SUM GAMES

Some years ago, workers at Alcan tabled wage and benefit demands totaling some $5 million. When management was recalcitrant, workers abandoned hot forges; damage was estimated at $40 million. Whoever was at fault—labor in its intransigence, management in its callousness, or both—it is obvious that society would have been better off had the damage not occurred. Cases like the Alcan strike are widely publicized; the non-zero-sum game losses are visible and tragic. Yet similar damage, greater by many orders of magnitude, and by nature preventable, has been incurred for years, with its true nature unrecognized. The United States plunged itself into a deep two-year recession, with the declared aim of wiping out inflation. Lester Thurow has estimated that close to a trillion dollars in output was wasted in this recession, which dragged Canada and Europe with it, creating thirty million unemployed.

Inflation is not a divine curse; its source is people raising prices and wages. Simulations with a large-scale econometric model, constructed by Professor Ray Fair of Yale University, show that an agreement by labor and business in the United States to hold all wage and price increases to a 3 percent annual rate—close to the rise in output per hour —would virtually eliminate inflation, slash unemployment, create jobs, and obviate the need for recessions induced by tight money. Why, then, is such an agreement not on the agenda for tomorrow?

Theory of games suggests that microeconomic disputes, like Alcan, and macroeconomic conflicts may be modeled in at least three different ways: as Prisoner's Dilemma, Chicken, and Charity (see Table 9-1).[1] Let the players be Row and Column; each chooses one of two behaviors, Cooperation (x) or Competition (y). In Prisoner's Dilemma, y is the dominant strategy for both players, and leads to a strongly stable Pareto-inferior outcome. Each player fears exploita-

Table 9-1.   Three Games (x = wage or price moderation; y = present behavior).

		Business	
		y	x
Labor	y	2, 2	3, 1
	x	1, 3	4, 4

(a) Charity. This game has two Nash equilibria: 2, 2 and 4, 4. At the 2, 2 equilibrium, neither player has any incentive to change to "moderation" unilaterally. For N-person games of this sort, once a "critical mass" of players perceives that others will switch to "moderation," everyone ultimately does.

		Business	
		y	x
Labor	y	2, 2	4, 1
	x	1, 4	3, 3

(b) Prisoner's Dilemma. Each player has y as the dominant strategy, yielding a stable Pareto-inferior equilibrium. Even if a social contract moves society to 4, 4, it will be unstable, since each player has an incentive to "defect" unilaterally.

		Business	
		y	x
Labor	y	1, 1	4, 2
	x	2, 4	3, 3

(c) Chicken. This game has two equilibria. Each player would prefer to yield to an opponent's threat of y by playing x, but misunderstandings and "called bluffs" may lead to 1, 1 outcomes.

tion by other players and at the same time sees opportunities for himself exploiting the others. When everyone acts in this manner, all lose. In Chicken, each player would rather suffer exploitation than suffer mutual annihilation, but wrongly interpreted bluffs and poor communication may result in costly head-on clashes, resulting in the worst outcome for both.

Prisoner's Dilemma and Chicken have found wide use in bargaining settings. Yet, a less well-known game, Charity, may come closer to depicting the facts of macroeconomic life. Suppose the structure of the economy is such that jointly cooperative behavior gives both labor and management their first-best outcome (x for both), while competitive behavior leads to only the third-best outcome for both (y). If trapped in competitive, divisive confrontation (y for both), neither side has any incentive to depart from it unilaterally and shift to x, since that would lead to being exploited. Hence, the "compete-compete" outcome is a Nash equilibrium. So is the cooperate–cooperate equilibrium, x, x; but getting there from y, y will take a social contract. Once society is there, it is self-sustaining.

"Charity" is perhaps the game matrix most likely to emerge. Business may prefer the x, x outcome to x, y, and labor prefers x, x to y, x, because of aversion to unemployment (excess capacity) and inflation. This is a highly psychological game, especially if there are many players, because it is a game of conformity, in that each player tries to do what he or she thinks other players will do. In this sense, it is a game in which perception creates a reality consistent with it. There are two stable equilibria, y, y and x, x. An interpretation of the stagflation of the 1970s is the y, y equilibrium, with neither labor nor business willing to change their behavior unilaterally. This is an optimistic view of society; the sole task of a social contract here is to persuade players to undertake a joint change in behavior. Once done, the new equilibrium is first-best for all, and stable.

Cross-section analysis of inflation and unemployment among the major industrial countries in the 1970s (see Figure 9–1) shows how seventeen nations dealt with these games. The six countries that succeeded in minimizing increases in inflation and in unemployment—

Figure 9–1. Increase in Inflation Rate versus Increase in Unemployment Rate for Seventeen Industrial Countries, 1967–1980.

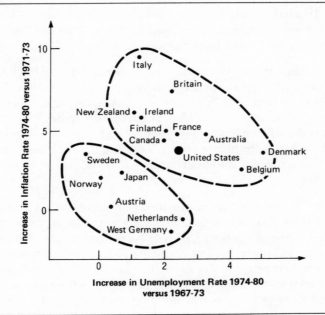

Source: McCallum (1982).

Sweden, Japan, Norway, Austria, the Netherlands, West Germany —
all had some form of incomes-policy social contract in place. Nearly
all the eleven countries with poorer stagflation records lacked such a
policy, though Canada, with the 1976–1978 Anti-Inflation Board, did
substantially better than most.

ATTITUDES TOWARD A SOCIAL CONTRACT

Karl Marx believed that existence determines consciousness. Psychologists tell us that consciousness determines existence, or that perceptions determine reality. With respect to the social contract, this is
clearly true. The perception that fashioning a social contract is not
feasible, or desirable, owing to lack of mutual trust, or to fears that
one player will abrogate the contract and exploit the others, works to
create the reality consistent with such a perception.

We wrote to over 100 corporate and labor leaders in the United
States, and to over 130 similar leaders in Canada, to investigate attitudes toward a social contract. In our letter, we presented our view as
follows:

> Canada [United States] is a free country, and Canadians [Americans]
> have every right to protect their own interests. They can fight to gain
> higher money wages and higher money profits.
>
> Each individual in society can raise his or her standard of living if he or
> she has more money to spend. But there is a catch. When the size of the
> national cake is fixed, one person or group can increase his slice of it only
> at the expense of others. And when *everyone* tries to boost his share, the
> result may actually be less for everyone, as higher wages and prices boost
> costs. So, what is legitimate and rational for the individual, or group,
> may ultimately be to the disadvantage of all of us, as members of a
> community.
>
> Dilemmas of this sort may in principle be resolved by an agreement — a
> social contract — among all parts of society to refrain from harmful, and
> ultimately, futile competitive games to boost their money incomes. (Gov-
> ernment is, of course, an important party to that agreement; govern-
> ments, too, compete for shares of the national cake, along with wage
> earners and stockholders.) Our contention is that without such a plan, we
> are doomed either to persistent inflation, or to intolerable levels of un-
> employment caused by battling that inflation with conventional fiscal
> and monetary tools.

Table 9–2. Summary of Responses to the Questionnaire
Concerning the Role of a Social Contract.

	Canada		United States	
	Labor	Management[a]	Labor	Management
Diagnosis of the problem				
Agree	3	5	5	—
Agree with reservations	1	1	—	1
Total agree	4	6	5	1
Disagree	3	10	3	8
No opinion	2	5	—	1
Total response	9	21	8	10
Solution:				
A social contract				
Approve	2	3	3	—
Approve with reservations	2	5	2	1
Total approve	4	8	5	1
Disapprove	5	13	3	9
Total response	9	21	8	10

Note: Survey was conducted during the fall 1982 in the United States and the
spring 1983 in Canada.

[a] Includes Charles Caccia, Canadian Minister of Labor at the time of the survey,
and Gerald Bouey, Governor of the Bank of Canada.

The survey letters were sent to the United States in the fall of 1982 and
to Canada in the late spring of 1983. We received 18 usable responses
from the United States: 8 from union leaders, and 10 from corporate
executives; and 30 from Canada: 21 from the business sector[2] and 9
from labor. The results are summarized in Tables 9–2 and 9–3.

Opinions on two subjects are tabulated. First, whether the respondents agree or disagree with the analysis of the inflation versus
unemployment dilemma, namely, that if everyone tries to boost their
share of the national cake "then the result may actually be less for
everyone, as higher wages and prices boost costs." The second question is whether they approve or disapprove of a social contract as a
means of resolving the dilemma in which "we are doomed either to
persistent inflation, or to intolerable levels of unemployment."

Table 9-3. Percentage Distribution of the Responses to the Questionnaire Concerning the Role of a Social Contract.

	Canada		United States	
	Labor	Management[a]	Labor	Management
Diagnosis of the problem				
Agree	33	24	63	—
Agree with reservations	11	5	—	10
Total agree	44	29	63	10
Disagree	33	48	38	80
No opinion	22	24	—	10
Total response	100	100	100	100
Solution:				
A social contract				
Approve	22	14	38	—
Approve with reservations	22	24	25	10
Total approve	44	38	63	10
Disapprove	56	62	38	90
Total response	100	100	100	100

[a] Includes Charles Caccia, Canadian Minister of Labor at the time of the survey, and Gerald Bouey, Governor of the Bank of Canada. Some columns do not add to 100 because of rounding.

Before discussing the results of the survey, we should indicate what could be expected from labor and management in each country and from a comparison of labor and management views as between the two countries.

Within each country, organized labor represents a minority of the work force (Meltz 1984). Since labor is thereby likely to perceive itself in a relatively weaker position than management, one would expect that labor would tend to be more favorably disposed toward a social contract than management. As between the two countries, the percentage of paid workers who are organized in Canada is almost double that in the United States, 39 percent versus 23 percent, according to Meltz. For this reason, one would expect Canadian labor to be relatively less favorable to a social contract than labor in the United States. By the same token, the expectation would be that Canadian management (facing a more highly organized labor force) would be more favorable to a social contract than management in the United States.

The respondents include leaders of major trade unions and major corporations in both countries. While we do not pretend that our respondents totally represent labor and management, we think these results are suggestive of views toward a social contract.

The survey results presented in Tables 9–1 and 9–2 conform with both of our expectations. In Canada and the United States, labor is more in agreement with the diagnosis of the problem and with a social contract as a solution. Comparing the two countries, labor leaders in the United States gave much more approval to a social contract (63 percent) than our sample of labor leaders in Canada (44 percent). The reverse is true for management, in which 90 percent in the United States disapproved of a social contract compared with a Canadian management disapproval figure of 62 percent. For those who approved of a social contract but with reservations, the reason most frequently given was a lack of trust. This was the exclusive basis for reservation among labor and management in the United States and among Canadian labor. Canadian managers also cited the problem of fragmented bargaining, that is, the large number of groups involved in bargaining.

Table 9–4 provides the primary reasons given for disapproval. In each country, the dominant reason given by labor leaders is that it is not feasible or enforceable. This same view was expressed by some businessmen, such as Russell E. Harrison of the Canadian Imperial Bank of Commerce, who wrote:

> There is considerable attraction in the notion of a "social contract" whereby each of the major economic players—governments, business and labour—would agree on at least a broad set of societal objectives and to conduct and even limit their own economic demands to support, rather than threaten, the achievement of those objectives. The difficulty is to translate that noble idea into practical reality.

The reason more frequently given by management for disapproval of social contracts was the violation of freedom and of the free market which was implied in a social contract. While a smaller percentage of Canadian management rejected the notion of a social contract (62 percent versus 90 percent), more Canadian managers cited the free market ideal than did those in the United States.

Table 9-4. Reasons for Disapproval of Social Contracts.

| Reasons for Disapproval | Canada | | | | United States | | | |
| | Labor | | Management | | Labor | | Management | |
	No.	%	No.	%	No.	%	No.	%
Violation of freedom, free market	1	20	9	69	1	33	5	56
Not feasible or enforceable	4	80	4	31	2	67	4	44
Total number	5	100	13	100	3	100	9	100
Percentage of total surveyed	56		62		38		90	

Although labor tended to be more favorable in general, there were some interesting differences. U.S. United Auto Workers head Owen Bieber expressed guarded approval, responding to us that "in principle, I believe labor could sit down with government and business, talk through what an anti-inflationary incomes policy would require, reach a consensus, and proceed toward implementation." In contrast, Sam Gindin, Research Director of UAW Canada, pointed to the unfavorable (for labor) controls programs of the mid-1970s, suggesting that unions' surrender of powers under a social contract might threaten their very existence, and noting that "it is not the unions but the capitalist system that stands in the way of consensus."

Some Canadian labor leaders emphasized fears of being exploited under a social contract; indeed, our survey letter itself drew a sharp response from John Eleen, Director of Research for the Ontario Federation of Labour, who suggested the social contract invites labor "to be a junior 'partner' in an elephant and mouse relationship" (Eleen 1983: 20).

On the other hand, Dennis McDermott, president of the two million member Canadian Labour Congress observed:

> It is a matter of historical record that since the AIB [the Anti-Inflation Board] in October 1975, the Congress took the initiative in pushing for a "social contract." We did this for a number of reasons; the most fundamental of which was a recognition that the economic structural changes in the western industrial world were of such a nature that in the future the collective bargaining system would in all likelihood be unable to protect workers' incomes as it had done previously. Also that governments, having once intervened in the economy to such a massive degree, would not hesitate to supplement fiscal and monetary policies with controls policies. Unfortunately, this has proved all too accurate.

PROSPECTS FOR A SOCIAL CONTRACT

The survey results from the two countries suggest that there are greater prospects of achieving a social contract in Canada than in the United States, at least based on views in the early 1980s.

In the United States, while labor is favorable toward a social contract, management appears to be adamantly opposed. The only possible way of changing management's attitudes would be to focus on those who thought a social contract was not feasible or enforceable. This would require the development of specific proposals and a reasonable mechanism before consideration could even begin. The fact that both inflation and unemployment have been reduced in the United States in the past two years may strengthen the views of those who would rely purely on market forces and, at the same time, reduce the incentive even to consider a social contract. On the other hand, as Arnold Weber recently observed in an article on American unions, "we are more likely to see the power of the American labor movement diminished at the bargaining table. Unions will then switch toward increased political action, in closer accord with the European model" (1983). Given the long traditions of not having a continuing national-level labor or social democratic party in the United States, it would seem that a social contract would take a long time to develop.

Canada would seem to offer a greater possibility of introducing a social contract. First, while both labor and management oppose it, they are close to being balanced in their views. Only a small shift is required among those who disapprove (one in the case of labor and three in the case of management in our example) to achieve a favorable view. Second, the Canadian Labour Congress (1976) has already proposed such an approach at its 1976 biennial convention. While the proposal of tripartism was subsequently rejected within the labor movement itself, there does seem to be a basis on which to build support. In the case of management, there is widespread participation with labor on tripartite boards and agencies, including the new government-financed, union and management-run Labour Market and Productivity Centre. Third, there is a long history in Canada of tripartite (government, labor, and management) cooperation as well as governmental involvement in the economy (Meltz 1984). Fourth, the parliamentary system in Canada, in which a labor party exists (the New Democratic party) and is in power in some provinces (currently the province of Manitoba) should also be conducive to a social contract. The bienniel NDP convention, in Regina in 1983, called for an incomes policy within the context of a social contract. While this proposal drew heavy fire from the Canadian Labour Congress, the possibility itself is still clearly one that keeps returning. The fact that the decline in the rate of inflation in Canada has taken place amid record rates of unemployment may provide an incentive for further consideration of a social contract.

CONCLUSION

James Tobin recently wrote,

> Chastened by ten years of stagflation and depression, both business and labor are hungry for sustained resumption of noninflationary prosperity and growth. They should be ready for a social compact in which all would agree to restrain wage and price increases in return for jobs and markets. (1984)

There may be evidence that such an incomes policy would produce Pareto-superior results. But, our survey indicates little readiness among U.S. business to implement such a social contract. Prospects seem to be greater in Canada, but both management and labor have to be convinced that is is feasible and enforceable. Only then can we avoid the tragedy of the commons.

NOTES

1. "Charity" derives its name from the following parable: People donate readily to charity if they think other people are also donating; if they think others are not, they are reluctant. This creates two Nash equilibria, such that expectations about others' behavior are usually self-confirming, if held generally. See Maital (1984), and Maital and Maital (1984).
2. The business sector (management) in the Canadian survey responses includes the then Canadian Minister of Labour, Charles Caccia, and the Governor of the Bank of Canada, Gerald Bouey. Since they expressed opposite views on both the diagnosis of the problem and the solution, they tended to cancel each other out in their impact on the final results.

REFERENCES

Canadian Labour Congress. 1976. *Labour's Manifesto for Canada.* Approved by the 11th Constitutional Convention held in Quebec City, May 17–21, 1976. Ottawa: CLC.

Eleen, John. 1983. "The Social Contract; 'Curbing Labour's Greed'," *Our Times*, November/December, pp. 20–21.

Maital, Shlomo. 1984. "How People Interact." Sloan School Working Paper. Cambridge, Mass.: Massachusetts Institute of Technology.

Maital, Shlomo and Sharone L. Maital. 1984. *Economic Games People Play*. New York: Basic Books.

McCallum, John. 1982. "We Need a Way as Well as the Will." *Financial Post*, November 20.

Meltz, Noah M. 1984. "Labor Movements in Canada and the United States." In *Challenges and Choices for American Labor*, edited by Thomas A. Kochan. Cambridge, Mass.: MIT Press.

Stein, Jerome L. 1983. *Monetarist, Keynesian and New Classical Economics*. London: Basil Blackwood.

Tobin, James. 1984. "A Social Compact for Restraint." *Challenge*, March–April.

Toronto Globe and Mail. 1984. "Social Contract Key to Growth: Ouellet." March 6.

Weber, Arnold. 1983. "Lifeboat Labor Relations." *Across the Board*.

✳ *Chapter 10*

American Politics and Changing Macroeconomic Institutions

Jeffrey B. Miller and Jerrold E. Schneider

The recent past has seen an unusual degree of economic and political instability in the United States. Not long ago many political scientists believed that we had entered an era of one-term presidents. Volatile macroeconomic conditions were seen as a major destabilizing factor. Depending on one's view of the causes of and remedies for inflation, one might conclude that since the beginning of the "Great Monetarist Experiment" in October 1979 we have entered a new phase of stability. Or one might believe only that we are in the eye of the storm. According to one viewpoint, whether or not we are headed toward more economic and political stability may hinge on political tolerance for the present monetary policy regime, or on political tolerance for an even more stringent rule monetarism.

In the first section of this chapter we discuss the political feasibility of a sustained monetarist policy regime, whether of the more or less strict monetarism of the 1979–1982 period, or of the more pragmatic monetarism that has been in place since mid-1982. We focus especially on a widely held misinterpretation of the 1982 election—that political tolerance has increased in the recent past for a tight money policy. We argue, on the contrary, that the political costs to politicians are as serious as ever, and that therefore a sustained reliance on tight money alone to fight inflation is not politically feasible. If our conclusion is true, and if it is faced up to, then greater attention must be paid to accelerating research and development of an incentive anti-inflation policy-*cum*-social contract.

In the second section of our paper we review problems that new incentive anti-inflation policy schemes must face, trace the evolution of recent developments in incentive schemes, and evaluate some aspects of their potential economic feasibility.

In the third section we examine the potential coalition that might support an economically efficient incentive anti-inflation policy tied to policies for controlling inflation in commodities and health. We conclude such a coalition is wider than is generally understood. We describe elements of that coalition and how they would be drawn together. But we assert that a necessary condition of the emergence of a winning non-monetarist anti-inflation policy coalition is that the incentive plan it uses be specified far enough in advance that potential supporters and beneficiaries not be frightened that they will pay the costs of rigid wage and price controls of the past. So the crucial political feasibility problem of such a policy, we claim, is the problem of producing an adequately specified plan in advance of a new anti-inflation policy experiment.

In the fourth and last section, we argue that there is a great need to investigate means for determining a policy development process that would produce an adequately specified plan. In particular we dispute the claim that policy development within a presidential administration would be adequate. That leads us to ponder what new institutional arrangements for accelerated policy development could be formed. We specify six kinds of research expertise that need to be integrated into an adequate R&D effort.

We conclude that all those who believe that the costs of the present monetarist policy regime are oppressive and indeed tragic ought to stop waiting for a change in presidential administrations. Rather, academic statesmen should be encouraged to explore with leaders from other institutions the possibility of initiating some form of a research consortium that would accelerate the development of non-monetarist anti-inflation policies.

THE POLITICS OF THE MONETARIST POLICY REGIME

Fighting inflation continues to be the number one domestic policy priority of American political elites, including both Republicans and most Democrats. This reflects the modal economic priorities of the voting public as well as most political and economic elites (Kiewiet 1983, Peretz 1983). The rate of growth during the recovery of the U.S. economy from the 1980–1982 recession has been greater than had been forecast. Both fiscal and monetary policy vigorously stimulated the economy out of that recession. So much growth and stimulation looked much like a return to the countercyclical stabilization policies of the Keynesian era.[1]

Nonetheless, despite the 1982 monetary stimulation, it is widely believed that there is now a new and fundamentally different policy posture at the Federal Reserve Board. The new policy is thought to promise a more determined anti-inflation posture than had been the case following past recoveries in the United States. Monetary policy is said to be the sea wall against inflation as it was not in the Keynesian era.

In particular, the new policy regime, which we will call here "quasi-monetarism," has the following elements: (1) The Federal Reserve promises that money growth will be reduced over the long run even while it exercises discretion in the short run; (2) Paul Volcker has promised that monetary policy will not accommodate new inflationary surges, which non-accommodation will, of course, be costly to the extent of the inflationary pressures; (3) The Federal Reserve will subordinate the goals of higher production and lower unemployment to the goal of inflation fighting far more than in the past; (4) the Federal Reserve will accept that these objectives will be carried out within constraints imposed by the instability of international and U.S. financial institutions.

The costs of this quasi-monetarist regime, and hence its political sustainability, will depend on the degree of inflationary pressure in the new environment of "quasi-monetarism." Perhaps the dollar will not fall significantly, or if it does, will not cause the inflation rate to ratchet up. Perhaps no major external shocks will occur in the foreseeable future. Perhaps the force of structurally embedded inflationary forces in the fixed-price sector has been substantially vanquished for the near and intermediate term. Then perhaps the change to the new quasi-monetarist policy regime will mark the beginning of a new period of price stability with high employment and growth as the new policy regime matures. This, of course, assumes that the political will to maintain that regime endures. Perhaps all that is needed is the reduction of federal government deficits and of the trade deficit. If so, then discussions of innovative anti-inflation policy schemes will be confined to ivory towers.

Such an optimistic tale may overestimate the capacity of the adjustment mechanism (Gordon 1981) while underestimating the sources of inflationary pressure. If so, then the monetarist story as attached to the credibility hypothesis may underestimate the costs of the present monetarist policy regime and, derivatively, overstate its political feasibility over the long run. Here we explore the possible political problems that may arise if the government fails to take an active position against sustained high unemployment, falls in output, and interest rate volatility. For good or ill, politicians, not economists, will ultimately decide which economic policies are put in place.

The 1982 Election and the Political Feasibility of Monetarism

The 1982 election is the best available test of political tolerance for a monetarist policy regime that produces a severe downturn in the U.S. economy. In 1982 Republican candidates for the U.S. House of Representatives lost support among almost every major voting group. The loss of 26 seats was large but not catastrophic for the Republicans. Yet the election very nearly turned into a much larger loss of seats.[2] Had that larger loss of seats occurred, it might have buried Reaganomics and monetarism. It is important to understand why and how so as to show the limits of tolerance for a monetarist policy regime in the United States.

The month before the election the Republicans' own polls showed them losing at least 45 seats.[3] If that had happened, a shock wave would have hit policy circles that the entire economic policy community would have taken as a reference point for a very long time. What brought the Republican seat loss down from 45+ to only 26 is instructive. The Republicans enjoyed unusual advantages in 1982 in campaign money and organization. They managed coordinated targeting of those resources to the closest races in an unprecedented effort, which political scientists agree made up the difference between the losses that occurred and the losses projected by the Republicans' polls a few weeks earlier (Jacobson and Kernell 1983). However, the *New York Times'* director of polling has observed that "adding just 48,886 Democratic votes in just the right places would have boosted the Democratic gain to 40 seats, an unquestionable landslide" (Clymer 1983: 5).

The fact that so many Republicans won by tiny margins has affected the political climate since 1982. It is reflected, for example, in the refusal in 1983–84 of congressional Republicans to follow Reagan's call for more domestic spending cuts. As Hugh Heclo and Rudolph Penner have pointed out, "the November 1982 congresssional election gave many Republicans a good scare, and did not bode well for continuing cohesion among Republicans such as had existed during 1981" (Heclo and Penner 1983: 42).

Three other points pertaining to the 1982 election indicate the constraints operating on Republicans and on monetarist policies. First, the crucial advantages of money and organization enjoyed by the Republicans, which prevented a landslide, probably peaked in 1982. Although the Republicans will still have a tremendous advantage in subsequent elections, the difference is narrowing and the Democrats are getting closer to the threshold above which differences of money have diminishing returns. The Democrats' technical capacity for professional campaign organization has taken a great leap forward since 1981 under Charles Manatt at the Democratic National Committee.

Second, there is a peculiar pattern to midterm elections. The first midterm election after a change of party control of the presidency, such as 1982, usually sees a much smaller loss of seats in Congress than after the second midterm election. Under Eisenhower the loss was 18 seats in 1954; under Kennedy the loss was 5 seats in 1962; under Nixon 12 seats were lost in 1970; and under Carter 16 seats were lost in 1978. But in the last four elections held six years after a change of party control of the White House the average loss has been 53 seats. So the test of quasi-monetarist policy in 1982 came under conditions that were both highly favorable for those policies and unstable.

Third, the only mandate that can be read from the 1980 election was the mandate to do "something" effective about inflation and unemployment—there was no "swing to the right." In particular the voters did not perceive that Reagan would opt for a policy that entailed trading off more unemployment and lost output for less inflation, as many elites did understand (Hibbs 1982, Markus 1982). Indeed, as we all know, Reagan promised "disinflation without tears," in sharp contrast to Margaret Thatcher's practice. In 1982 the Republican campaign plea to "give the program a chance to work" was used as a centerpiece, and with great effect. Clearly that plea could not be used in subsequent campaigns to defend the effects of another recession. If the relation between the 1980 and 1982 elections is so interpreted, then those two elections will not mistakenly be taken as indicating a new and greater political tolerance of higher costs to fight inflation.

Another factor that may have been large but was not measured by poll data was that the Democrats were repeatedly attacked by the Republicans as lacking an alternate economic policy. Not only was it true that the Democrats lacked an alternative to recession for fighting inflation they were prepared to describe and defend, but many Democrats publicly conceded the point, despite the record inflation levels of recent years. At the height of the campaign Reagan himself repeatedly taunted the Democrats with the question "What is their alternative?" Yet that attack would have been much less persuasive under the same circumstances if Reagan had been in power for a longer time.

This analysis of the 1982 election persuades us that the political constraints on a quasi-monetarist policy regime are severe. If so, no matter how much some economists might believe it desirable to pay the price of a quasi-monetarist policy regime, it does not seem that a monetarist regime that tolerates a permanently and significantly lower ratio of actual output to potential output is politically feasible in the long run, unless the major sources of inflation have been permanently wrung out. The historically high level of real long-term bond rates late into 1984 strongly suggests that markets did not reflect optimism on inflation. If these arguments are correct, then the belief that a change in policy regime has occurred that will prove sustainable is mistaken, *unless* it can be successfully argued that what has happened between 1979 and 1984 has substantially improved the trade-off between inflation and lost output.

It might be asked whether the voters were really all that concerned with the effects of tight money — whether other issues were important also. We believe that the predictive success of the Tufte (1975) model, which depends on changes in real per capital disposable income along with change in presidential popularity, is a sufficient answer. Tufte's model has been claimed to overpredict the Republicans' seat loss in the 1982 election. But that claim has been disputed. In July 1982 Tufte modified his model with an adjustment for redistricting, and the eventual vote percentage was very close to Tufte's forecast (Jacobson and Kernell 1983; Clymer 1983: 5). If Tufte's work does show that changes in real per capital disposable income remains a very powerful predictor of election outcomes, and if the inflation versus unemployment trade-off does not improve, then the electoral risks of a monetarist policy should return to pre-1982 election levels.

Other Political Constraints

But perhaps the costs of monetary contraction have improved under the monetarist policy regime that began in October 1979. If so, decreasing inflation through tight money would bear lower political costs and therefore greater political sustainability. New findings, which are disputed, suggest the trade-off was not improved. George Perry has examined New Classical Economics models that say that a clear policy commitment to disinflation would lead to more prompt and more disinflation relative to the increase in unemployment. He compared those models to ones based on adaptive expectations and Perry's own wage norm model to see if the New Classical models better predict the costs actually occurring in 1979–1983. He concludes that his analyses "lend no support to the view that credible policy has speeded up the disinflation process and made it less costly" (Perry 1983: 601). An analysis by Phillip Cagan and the late William Fellner comes to a different conclusion (1983). But if Perry is right that the economic costs did not improve, then the political costs of fighting inflation with tight money have not improved either.

How politically sustainable the change in the monetary policy regime may turn out to be also depends on the political pressures business and labor put directly on Congress and on the president. Even if elections do not constrain the politicians, and even if the costs are less than they used to be, yet the costs paid by business and labor may not be acceptable to them even if they do not have a clear idea of the alternatives. The fragility of some business balance sheets has weakened tolerance among business for further losses from tight monetary policy. As Paul Volcker testified before Congress in February 1984, "Many thrift institutions and businesses remain in marginal profit positions and with weakened financial structures; lower [interest] rates would repair the damage (Volcker 1984: 8).

A certain euphoria was produced by the strength of the recovery in 1983–84. A new recession may produce swift attitude changes among key elites. What direct evidence is there of elite sentiment in support of a continued monetarist experiment? Press reports of sentiment are highly suggestive. One observer wrote: "Ever since mid-October

[1982], obituaries for monetarism have flowed fast and furiously."
Business Week published an article, "The Failure of Monetarism,"
with the subheading: "Its victory over inflation cost too much—record
interest rates and a deep recession" (April 4, 1983: 64–65). Lindley
H. Clark, the *Wall Street Journal* columnist and a defender of monetarism, titled a January 18, 1983 column, "How We Got into the
Monetarist Mess" (p. 31). A Leonard Silk column in the *New York
Times* bore the heading "The Fading of Monetarism" (July 15, 1983,
p. D2). A Hobart Rowen column in the *Washington Post* was titled
"It Is Time to Delegate Monetarism to a Museum" (March 28, p. G1).
It seems sensible to suppose that these article titles reflect a climate of
opinion and not merely the columnists' own tastes. If so, the political
constraints may be read accordingly.

One other major political constraint needs at least to be mentioned
in passing: the political and economic pressures coming from the
international arena. Many observers have pointed out that the hard-
ships being inflicted on other countries and especially on the Third
World are generating extreme political instability, causing political
situations that it has long been the object of U.S. foreign policy
officials to avoid. Ironically, the preference of conservatives in the
United States for a more stringent rather than a less stringent monetarist policy for economic reasons undermines their own priorities
regarding foreign policy objectives (economic stability as a bulwark
against political instability that might lead to Communist takeovers).
Economically, the fragility of the international financial system seems
to place a rather strict limit on how much the monetary weapon can
be used. The following quotation from the lead story on the front
page of the *Wall Street Journal* that appeared a half year after the
events described is sufficiently suggestive to make the point.

WASHINGTON—It's August 1982, in the midst of the Mexican debt crisis.
The government's top international economic policy makers are cloistered
for the weekend, trying to stave off a default that they fear could trigger
an international financial panic. It is a round-the-clock operation, with
staffers sleeping on couches in their bosses' offices. . . . At one point, a
senior official suggests that one proposed solution—for the U.S. to provide Mexico with cash by buying Mexican oil—would leave Washington
paying too high a price. Mr. Volcker loses patience. "I don't give a. . .
what you pay for oil," he is reported to have shouted. "If you *don't* do it,
the whole thing is going to come crashing down—and it'll be your fault."
(Pine 1983: 1)

Yet there is a more important cause for the apparently undisturbed elite consensus behind the post-1982 discretionary monetarist policy regime. It is widely believed that there is no third alternative to a choice between accelerating inflation and a tight monetary policy. That is why some American elites are presently prepared to inflict further costs on themselves as well as on others to control inflation through tight money. How would elite sentiment change if the present policy regime was seen as generating much more slack in the economy on a permanent basis than the policy regime in place prior to 1979? The crucial question—how much is much more slack—is of course unknown. Nor is it clear what the distribution of attitudes will be if, despite the price that has been paid for a tight money policy, inflation nonetheless accelerates substantially as the economy recovers. These questions provide the real world setting in which the political feasibility of incentive anti-inflation policy, incomes policy, social contracts, and whatever else besides tight money will be considered.

Politics and the Possibility of a "Real" Monetarist Experiment

Many monetarist economists dispute the contention that the policies pursued between 1979 and the present deserve the name "monetarist." We wish to argue that, from a practical point of view, the policies of this period are as monetarist as any that have a reasonable chance of being adopted in practice.

The monetarists claim that what has been termed the Great Monetarist Experiment was no such thing, because money growth was volatile. The standard deviation of M1 growth in 1979–1983 differed little from past periods (Gordon 1984: 513–518). The key question seems to be whether or not the Federal Reserve Board should have altered the money growth rate in order to hold down or bring down extraordinarily high interest rates, if that is what they did. But "ought" implies "can."

There are intense political pressures on policies affecting interest rates. As William Poole points out, "Everyone agrees that interest rate fluctuations perform important allocative functions. It is also true that few other prices are as involved in political disputes." But Poole continues, "These are not issues I want to discuss. My concern is whether something can go wrong in competitive credit markets that argues for temporary abandonment of money stock control and stabilization of interest rates in some sense" (Poole 1982: 587). And he goes on to argue for tolerance of greater interest rate variability by the Federal Reserve than it has so far been willing to tolerate so as to achieve steady money growth.

Yet perhaps that much interest rate volatility entails costs too great for such a policy to be politically feasible. If the monetarists cannot plausibly describe the political circumstances under which the kind of interest rate variability necessary for steady money growth is possible, then their policy proposals are merely scholastic. Their story would have to take account of the range of possible shocks that would cause the monetary authorities to target interest rates. They ought to describe on that basis how the allocation of losses flowing from a constant growth rate rule for money growth would escape political constraints. There does not seem to be any such analysis extant.

If Paul Volcker, Ronald Reagan, and the most conservative Congress in decades cannot bring themselves to tolerate the costs of greater interest rate variability than was the case between 1981 and 1984, we might well wonder if the political conditions for such toleration will ever prevail. We might get into some interesting scenarios regarding a second Reagan term with Reagan pushing *for* and incumbent Republican and Democratic congressmen and senators pushing *against* tighter money, and ponder the relative influence of Congress versus Reagan over the Federal Reserve System, perhaps with a more determined monetarist taking over the Federal Reserve Board chairmanship from Volcker in the summer of 1985.

We might infer from the 1982 election results that the passage of Federal Reserve policy from its declaration of rule monetarism in 1979 to its open and active discretionary monetarism in 1982 should not be viewed as an episodic mistake but as a political inevitability. By discretionary monetarism we mean a policy where the goal is to reduce the long-run growth of the monetary supply, but discretion is used to manage the short-run. If the 1982 elections results gave the Republicans in the House and in the Senate quite a scare, imagine their reactions to the "short-term" effects on the economy of a strict rule monetarist policy. Perhaps, then, the abandonment of rule monetarism cannot be reversed. Then the only sensible question is what are the costs of a quasi-monetarist regime. Rule monetarists have always argued that discretion meant both greater cyclical swings and hence greater cyclical costs, both because of greater expectational instability and because of inevitable policy overreactions. The political costs and the sustainability of the quasi-monetarist regime should be judged accordingly.

What will happen after the 1984 election if policymakers confront a 6 percent inflation rate and an unemployment rate between 7 and 8 percent? They must give considerable weight to the effects of expectations and to the possibility of various larger and smaller inflationary shocks. In particular, a falling dollar could quickly reverse by several points the gains made on inflation so far. Moreover bad grain harvests from bad weather before long could affect the world prices of grains.[4] In this situation what will be the choices available to policymakers absent an incomes policy?

The last recession lasted twelve quarters (ignoring the brief uptick after mid-1980). The previous postwar record was five quarters in 1974–75. All other recessions lasted less than a year. Inflation has come down dramatically. The hope had been that the whole disinflationary job would be done by now. Yet, barring further monetary contraction, inflation will remain or perhaps build from about the 6 percent level. In the future, how much will policymakers engage in further monetary tightening to wring out the remaining inflation or prevent acceleration later? Will this mean a prolonged period of stagnation or a sharp contraction? Political and international financial constraints speak for gradualism, with losses spread over a longer period, as if such "fine tuning" were possible and credibility effects were the same. Or will deficit reduction occur and create room for easier monetary policy despite a falling dollar?

If political and international financial constraints preclude a genuine Great Rule Monetarist Experiment after 1984, then the costs of stop-and-go monetarist policies will continue. But variable rate mortgages and other financial adaptations suggest much higher interest rates than the historically high real rates that obtained in 1984 might be necessary to slow the economy. Even higher rates might be necessary to contain future inflationary pressures if, after all that had occurred between 1979 and 1984, inflation accelerates in the future. And if twelve quarters of recession were not enough, even though inflation starts from a relatively low point, inflationary expectations may accelerate more quickly than in the past, as markets take account of constraints on the monetary weapon. If inflation accelerates in the near-to-intermediate term, then monetary policy by itself may be perceived as too costly or too politically unsupportable to wring out inflation.

And so it is that the path that politics and policy might follow may arrive at some form of experiment with incentive anti-inflation schemes. Sometimes pressures for change cause policy change where the future is only dimly lit. Sometimes the political message is to try something different.

RECENT EVOLUTION OF INCENTIVE ANTI-INFLATION SCHEMES

Prerequisites of a Viable Incentive Scheme

The costs of fighting inflation with recession being so high, a number of economists have suggested alternative institutional arrangements that might make an economy less susceptible to inflationary pressures at high levels of employment. Previous attempts at changes of this kind have generally been one or another form of incomes policy. These policies have not been overwhelmingly successful but as Flanagan, Soskice, and Ulman state:

> It is interesting that the policymakers of Europe should have returned so persistently to an instrument whose record has been spotty and unreliable as the record of incomes policy has been. That record raises the question whether incomes policies are inherently ineffective, even self-defeating, given the nature of the underlying inflationary process, or whether the design and administration of past policies have been inadequate to cope with the institutional forces that they are designed to resist. (1983: 21)

Presented below is a description of some of the basic problems new programs need to confront if they are to succeed. In a number of ways they represent a point of departure from previous efforts in this area. In the next section we shall review some new ideas proposed in response to these challenges.

Any policy scheme that does not allow relative prices and relative wages to change so as to reflect market forces will generate unacceptable inefficiencies, shortages, and inequities and will soon collapse under the combined political pressures of those who suffer the results.

Examples of how problems can arise and cause extensive dislocation throughout the economy occurred during the Nixon controls period. Shortages of logs, fertilizer, and molasses occurred when higher world prices shifted domestic supplies abroad, because domestic producers were prevented from raising their prices in the United States. These shifts affected other firms. For instance, sawmills shut down because of the curtailed supply of lumber (Gordon 1981: 265). Controllers can make exceptions in cases like this. However, in a long-term program the exceptions proliferate to the point where so many economic agents believe they are treated unfairly that the program collapses from political opposition. For these reasons, it is important that prices be allowed to adjust when demand conditions require it.

Second, the institutional changes or the incomes policy should be permanent. There are two reasons for this. First, when the policy is temporary, there can be a "bounce back," in which inflation surges again after the program is terminated. This apparently occurred after Nixon's Phase II, though it did not occur after the Korean War controls were lifted. Second, if inflation is seen as a "structurally embedded" and continuing problem, rather than being the product of an expansionary monetary policy, then there needs to be a permanent program to control it. This structural bias toward inflation can result from managers' needs to satisfy workers who are costly to train and replace, and to maintain morale to maintain or raise productivity. This bias has become worse in recent decades in part because governmental high employment policies make it easier for firms to pass on these costs without seeing a fall in demand. This is an ongoing problem if policy aims at high employment. Hence, it must be handled through a permanent program that will bring pressures to bear to counter these forces.

Third, if the program is to be administratively feasible it probably will have to be focused on a relatively small number of firms. The rest of the economy would only be indirectly affected by the program. This means that a program would have to depend on competition to hold down prices and wages in other sectors of the economy. By narrowing the scope of an incomes policy in this way, the complexity and the potential distortions of incomes policy can be reduced along with administrative costs, but the program does depend on competitive elements for its success.

Fourth, these programs must be tied to a responsible demand management policy. It must not be a temporary shield behind which excess aggregate demand is generated for political purposes, as many people claim President Nixon and Arthur Burns contrived to do for the 1972 election. Under an incomes policy, for example, it should be possible to achieve higher employment levels without setting off a new acceleration of inflation. But there is a limit. If aggregate demand pressure reaches an inflationary level, any incomes policy program will begin to break down. If political pressures to generate excessive demand are resisted, it should be possible to end the radical policy oscillations between stimulus and contraction of the past decade. However, with the higher employment levels possible under an incomes policy, the pressure to stimulate beyond appropriate levels should be greatly reduced.

Fifth, an incomes policy is not an answer to all pricing problems. Some areas where severe pressures are likely to mount will require special attention. For example, prices of raw agricultural products (especially grain) and oil prices are very sensitive to fluctuations in supply. Shortages can arise quickly when prices do not adjust quickly in these kinds of market. Assuming that a political coalition could be worked out to support it, policy should be directed at creating buffer stocks, particularly of grain and oil reserves, which would be released into the market when prices rise, and replenished when prices fall. (See Newbery and Stiglitz 1981, Bosworth and Lawrence 1982.) Other areas, notably health care, with its unique structure in the United States would also have to be singled out for special treatment.

Sixth, there must be broad and sustainable support from both business and labor if there is to be compliance. Such support will come if the policy is demonstrated to be effective and efficient and perceived to be fair. Since wide and deep compliance is a necessary condition of success, a voluntary guidelines program, such as took place under President Carter, is likely to fail. The perception of some degree of noncompliance by some will swiftly unravel compliance by others.

With these notions in mind we turn now to some new programs that have been suggested for relieving our macroeconomic problems.

Some Recent Developments

A number of policies might be used to supplement monetary and fiscal policy. Some of these policies have been tried, while others, such as the ones discussed below, are on the drawing board and represent new ways of thinking about how rapid growth with stable prices can be achieved.

As argued in the previous section, what is needed is a program that will allow relative price flexibility but prevents the overall price level from rising. In other words, what is needed is a program that allows prices to rise only when such a change is necessary to equilibrate supply and demand. For any central administration to determine when a price change is appropriate and when it is not is an enormous task. What some recent authors have suggested is that appropriate price adjustments can be made in a *decentralized* way if the incentives are right. This has led to several new proposals that are designed to permit economic agents to continue to make price and wage decisions but that change the environment under which these decisions are made.

The first of these proposals was one by Weintraub and Wallich (1971) in which corporate profits taxes would be adjusted if the increase in the firm's wage bill exceeded a guideline announced by the government. The idea was that by giving management an additional incentive to keep wages down, inflationary pressures could be better controlled. This original proposal has spawned other ideas for tax-based incomes policies (TIPs). For example, there have been suggestions that price changes, rather than wage changes, be taxed. Other alternatives include the use of subsidies rather than penalites or possibly a mix of tax penalites and rewards. Taxes can be reduced if firms or workers comply with the program. Choosing among these various proposals depends upon both their administrative and political feasibility. It has been suggested, for instance, that using a reward TIP, where payments would be given out for compliance, would not be politically feasible since to monitor it would be extremely costly, and the reward payments might be budget busting for the government. Using increased tax penalties would not need to be applied so broadly, and therefore would be preferred. Researchers have only begun to examine how these different TIP plans could be further specified, and how such extended plans would work under current and projected political conditions. Furthermore, no one seems to have explored how a TIP plan could be coupled with other anti-inflation plans, such as arbitration and profit sharing schemes, to shift incentives more profoundly in an anti-inflationary direction.

Another proposal is Lerner and Colander's (1980) licensing scheme, usually called MAP for "market anti-inflation plan." This proposal essentially amounts to the creation of a market in licenses permitting firms to raise prices. The idea is that firms that are willing to lower prices can sell their government-assigned MAP credits to firms that wish to raise prices. The overall price level will then remain unchanged, and the cost of raising a price will then be determined in the marketplace. A possible advantage of this scheme over a tax-based proposal is that the MAP credit price will adjust as inflationary pressures change, whereas the tax rate, which plays a similar role in a tax-based system, will have to be determined administratively and may not adjust well to fluctuating pressures for price increases in the economy.

One way of thinking about the distinction between MAP and TIP schemes is that TIP is like a pollution tax. The firm can raise prices as long as it is willing to pay the price. MAP on the other hand is like a license to pollute. The government issues so many licenses and firms can buy and sell them as they please. But the government knows how many licenses have been issued and therefore how much overall pollution there will be. In the same way through MAP the government can control the level of inflation.

Much of the recent work on these ideas is the outgrowth of a 1978 Brookings Institution Conference on tax-based incomes policies. At this conference some of the early TIP and MAP proposals were evaluated. As might be expected, given the novelty of these ideas at the time, a number of problems were identified. Since that time the proponents of these proposals have attempted to address the criticisms raised at the conference.

One serious criticism of the early plans presented at the conference was they were unbalanced in the sense that they focused on keeping wages from rising rapidly rather than being directed at both wages and prices (Rees 1978). Since 1978 more work has been done on how prices can be included in the incentive schemes and how measurement problems can be handled. For example, there are "value added" approaches such as Lerner's and Colander's.[5] They argue that using value added can reduce the problems of measurement, and maintain balance by controlling the sum of wages and profits (i.e., net sales minus nonlabor input costs), but not either one separately.

Many of the other criticisms at the conference were directed at how the various plans might be implemented. These problems can vary considerably depending on the nature of plan adopted. Indeed the choice of which plan to use may well be based on these issues.

For instance, Joseph Pechman, one of the more critical conferees, was for these reasons particularly opposed to proposals that involve a subsidy, but agreed that "a penalty on profits based on wage changes is feasible" under certain conditions.[6]

One of Pechman's principal reservations regarding the use of a TIP where the objective is to control wages is the timing problem. He argues that it would be very difficult for the firm to anticipate ahead of time what its situation will be at the end of the period, and, therefore, that the tax should be paid at the end of the period. Paying a subsidy rather than collecting a penalty would be much more difficult under these conditions. To demonstrate this, he posits the following situation: Suppose a union agrees to a small increase in wages in order to comply with the program. But later negotiations between other unions and that firm lead to changes in the overall wage bill which are so large that the firm is no longer in compliance and benefits that the members of the first union anticipated no longer accrue to them. This concern, like some of the others expressed by Pechman, depends upon the implementation of a TIP scheme that specifically rewards workers directly for their willingness to comply with the program. A penalty that focuses on, say, corporate taxes would not suffer from the same problems.

The issue of the administrative burden of a TIP program applied to millions of U.S. firms was also addressed at the conference. This is a problem that is particularly severe for a reward TIP but not necessarily for a penalty TIP. Proponents of the penalty TIP also recognize these problems and suggest that the program be applied only to the largest corporations (Seidman 1981).

Another administrative problem is the identification of an appropriate unit when implementing the program. What do you do about the diversified firm? Actually, the more diversified the firm, the better the program should work. The objective of a tax-based incentive program is to keep the overall price level from rising. Distortions are caused when the program inhibits the movement of relative prices. A diversified firm has more latitude in its individual price decisions, since it is operating in several markets. Allowing the diversified firm, which is sensitive to the trade-offs of pricing decisions among its different products, to make the decisions about price adjustments should actually improve the effectiveness of the incentive scheme. In fact, in a large diversified firm, the pricing decisions might be comparable to an internal licensing scheme à la Lerner. A firm that recognizes limitations on how much it can raise its overall price list will be forced to select carefully when deciding which prices to raise. Indeed the most serious problems are likely to arise in those firms such as automobile manufacturers, where only a few goods are produced and firms have little flexibility. Here TIP incentives must be carefully designed so as not to distort outcomes. These sectors will have to receive greater attention from the administrators of the policies.

A related problem is what to do in situations where the unit being taxed undergoes some fundamental change—a new firm, a merger, a spinoff—so that it is difficult to use past history as a guideline as to what should be done in the next year. For example, Pechman is particularly concerned about the parallels between these kinds of problems and similar problems that have arisen under the excess profits tax where court cases have been common. The most difficult case would be where new firms are created, but if the program is addressed to only the largest firms this is not really an issue. With mergers or spin-offs at least there is some form of a past history upon which to base a judgment as to how the new entity should be treated. Richard Slitor (1979), a tax economist with long experience in the U.S. Department of the Treasury, argued that this ability to identify a past history actually distinguishes TIP from an excess profits tax.

As can be seen from this discussion, the Brookings Conference called attention to some important issues concerning the viability of a tax-based scheme. These issues have formed the basis of a research agenda that is still being worked through.

The effects of tax-based incomes policies have also been explored in a series of papers by Layard, Jackman, and Pissarides. These papers investigate the impact of tax-based policies in models where there is search unemployment and wage determination is specifically modeled. Layard (1982) argues that another force outside of monetary policy should be brought to bear on the inflation-unemployment problem. He feels that incomes policy is the obvious candidate. While monetary policy can be expected to determine the rate of inflation, he sees incomes policy as a means of lowering the natural rate of unemployment. Pissarides (1983) finds that a TIP can affect the inflation versus unemployment trade-off essentially making the long-run Phillips curve negatively sloped. In a more recent paper Jackman, Layard, and Pissarides (1983) explore a number of different wage-setting arrangements and policies. In this paper they find that at least theoretically a tax on wage setting is equivalent to a tax on wage inflation. In each case unemployment is reduced. These papers provide some theoretical support for the notion that a TIP program would improve the long-run unemployment picture and also give the monetary authority the ability to reduce inflation at lower cost.

Still another incomes policy option is an arbitration scheme where labor and management come together to resolve their differences without government intervention. If this fails, then the government imposes some kind of binding arbitration. The incentive to keep settlements within a set of announced government guidelines is the knowledge that if the process goes to arbitration, the arbitrator will follow these guidelines in determining what the settlement should be. There are many possible variations of these proposals. Some have been tried in Australia. Meade (1982) recommends a distinctive approach that is really a full employment policy rather than an incomes policy. He suggests that the arbitrator be told to choose the wage rate which will maximize the level of employment in that particular firm or industry. The advantage of such a program is that the government would only become involved in those cases where agreement could not be reached. This would probably be such a small subset of the whole that those cases can be looked at in detail without large administrative costs. If both the firm and the workers agree that higher wages are appropriate, then wages can be raised by simply agreeing to this without going to arbitration.

Incentives to stay close to the government guideline are twofold. First, if the two parties want to retain control over the situation, they will try to settle any differences between them before an arbitrator is brought into the process. Second, they will be pushed toward settling near the guidelines because the two parties know that if there are disagreements, the position closer to the guideline will be selected by the arbitrator.

Arbitration procedures thus have the advantage of both wage and price flexibility and low administrative costs. A major problem may arise, however, if the incentives to stay within the guidelines are not strong enough. Management must be concerned about labor's contentment, and this can be a strong incentive to provide a generous wage and benefit package. While this is a serious problem, it does not rule out the possibility of using some kind of arbitration procedure; it is just that arbitration alone may not be enough. For this reason the ideal incomes policy may actually be a combination of arbitration and some other program designed to make it more difficult for firms simply to raise prices. For example, a tax-based incomes program directed at preventing price increases might be used to provide the necessary pressure to keep prices and wages from rising as well as provide balance to an arbitration program.

Another problem that may arise with arbitration is that it cannot be applied as widely in the United States, where unionization is much less prevalent than in a country like Great Britain. If such a plan were used in the United States, its impact would depend on the nonunion sector imitating the settlements in the union sector. But any incomes policy would be directly applied to only a limited number of firms. The possible disadvantage is that the firms which come under the program would all have to be unionized ones. Still one would expect a great deal of overlap between the large firms, which would be covered under, say, a tax-based proposal, and the unionized firms, which would come under the jurisdiction of an arbitration procedure.

Recently, two new proposals have been presented which would attack the combined problems of inflation and unemployment on another front. These two proposals are similar in that they both regard the present conventions regarding the payment of labor as an important part of the problem. The earlier of these proposals is a recommendation by Daniel Mitchell that workers be paid on a profit-sharing basis (1981). As Mitchell sees the problem, it is the inflexibility of wages during the business cycle which causes the unemployment rate to rise as business conditions are depressed. Under profit-sharing, wages would move down as profits are squeezed during the downturn in the cycle. Since wages are essentially moving pro-cyclically under these arrangements, there would be fewer layoffs and unemployment would not rise to the same level as it does under the present arrangements.

The other proposal has been put forward by Martin Weitzman (1983). He argues that what he calls a "share economy" would work better than the present set of institutional arrangements. Weitzman defines a share system as any system where the compensation that individual workers receive varies inversely with the number of workers that are hired. Since the wage rate falls as more workers are hired, the owners have a greater incentive to hire more workers than they do under a wage system. Indeed, Weitzman argues that the firm will always have an incentive to hire more workers and will do so until it runs up against a constraint where it can find no more workers to hire. In other words firms will hire more workers until there are no more unemployed workers. The elimination of unemployment in this way means the problem of inflation can then be addressed more directly by monetary and fiscal policy.

As Weitzman admits, there are problems in establishing a share economy. He sees the problem as a public good problem. If there are too few firms that are using a share system, too much of the burden of absorbing the unemployed falls on them. Because of this, there is a tendency for the share economy to be unstable. Government intervention is therefore necessary, and Weitzman suggests that the tax system can be used to encourage participation in the system. How this is to be done is not spelled out in great detail, and this, along with additional analysis of the implications of the proposal, awaits further research.

This survey of recent proposals to improve the trade-off between inflation and unemployment shows that there are a variety of policy options which deserve development. All have their strengths and weaknesses. None of them have reached the point where the problems have really been carefully worked out. The costs of the alternative approach, recession or depressed conditions, highlight the importance of further research in this area.

THE POLITICS OF INCENTIVE ANTI-INFLATION POLICIES

It should be obvious that anyone who can credibly claim to have an economically efficient and equitable plan to control inflation without recession will gain a lot of support. It should also be obvious that if someone makes such a claim but does not have ready at hand a plan that is economically and politically feasible, they will lack political credibility. It is also obvious that any anti-inflation policy will impose some costs on someone.

It is less obvious that, to be credible, the nature and extent of the costs will need to be specified enough to be plain before any incentive scheme is likely to be adopted by Congress. We are reminded of what brought Robespierre to his death. Having instituted a reign of terror, many people had to wonder whether they would be the objects of revolutionary justice. After a while, many people who were not actually targeted by the terror worried that they might be, and they united to bring Robespierre down. Given recent history, that kind of reaction will await an incomes policy that fails to be clear about the allocation of costs it would entail. The burden of proof will fall on those who propose an incomes policy experiment to show what the costs really will be and to whom they will be allocated.

It is not obvious to many potential beneficiaries of an economically efficient and equitable non-monetarist anti-inflation policy that they have a large, even huge, stake in such a policy. True, some will say, but trivially true if in fact there is no such animal as an economically efficient and equitable non-monetarist anti-inflation policy.

But now let us add two more assumptions, and we will see that the assertion is far from trivial. Let us assume, first, as James Meade has pointed out, "There is a great variety of possible schemes" (1982). And let us assume, second, that this great variety of schemes has not been worked on enough to allow us to know whether or not an economically efficient plan can be produced that would also be politically feasible. Now we can assert the proposition in a nontrivial way. Many people who would benefit enormously from the development of (discovery of) such a plan are not aware that a large investment in policy development might be in their best interests. From which it may follow that, if they were made so aware, though they would not press for an incomes policy, they would press for policy development.

From this argument it follows that two propositions are interesting to examine. First, given some political entrepreneurship, the potential beneficiaries of a viable plan would politically overwhelm those for whom the costs would outweigh the benefits. The second point focuses on the policy development process. If we can better understand the institutional processes by which anti-inflation policy development can be accelerated, we will best be able to state the conditions under which a successful incomes policy will occur.

The remainder of this chapter is devoted to a less than conclusive but hopefully illuminating discussion of these two points.

The Potential Coalition for an Incomes Policy

Econometric estimates conclude that it costs at least $1 trillion of forgone output, having a present value of 29 percent of a year's GNP, to achieve a long-run 5 percentage point reduction in the inflation rate by restrictive monetary policy (Gordon and King 1982). In addition there are the human costs not included in that estimate, which are only partially indicated by the 37,000 additional deaths in the United States associated statistically with a 1 percent increase in the unemployment rate (Gordon 1984: 353). (Moreover, disinflationary monetary policy in the United States creates similar conditions abroad, which according to the same estimate, has costs well above that $1 trillion figure.)

Tucked within that estimate is a potential coalition for a less painful way to fight inflation. The costs of disinflation through monetary contraction are unequally distributed. That uneven pattern is an important clue to the politics of the potential coalition for an alternative.

The cyclical industries and industries affected by an overvalued dollar are bound to be available as movers and shakers of a new coalition. Housing, automobiles, consumer durables, capital goods, small business dependent on borrowing to finance inventories, export industries including agriculture, and industries competing in U.S. markets with foreign products—all are potential markets for political entrepreneurs who offer an anti-inflation plan that eschews recession. Not a minor part of the political spectrum!

The Tufte model also tells us that if an incomes policy did work successfully and thereby allowed the economy to be run with less slack, less unemployment, and more growth, that would turn into increases in real disposable income that would increase the electoral margins of incumbent politicians. That indicates further returns to the sort of political entrepreneurship that takes the form of marketing a successful incomes policy program.

Though at present no one has made it clear to them, a large proportion of minorities and women, the young and the old might have the most intense stake in a successful incomes policy. But political entrepreneurs would need to make plain to these groups the connection between incomes policy, high employment, narrowed wage differentials, generally expanded opportunities, and higher living standards from sustained periods of high growth (Okun 1981).

Profits in the aggregate are pro-cyclical. Business pragmatists would be open minded about claims that an incentive anti-inflation plan is more flexible and less costly than rigid wage and price controls. They will be interested in the great profits that go with a high-performance economy. But they will have to be convinced by a plan that is specific enough to be persuasive.

Our preliminary interviewing of labor leaders indicates that labor too may be much more open minded than generally assumed about intervention in wage determination. But they will have to be convinced that the scheme offered for consideration was not just another attempt at wage controls without any substantial quid pro quo. From labor's perspective as well as that of most economists', the role of wages in the aggregate in the inflation of the 1970s was not that of initiating inflation. Labor, along with Keynesian economists, believe wages only transmitted inflationary pressures primarily from exogenous shocks in oil and grains and from the health sector. However, the slowdown in productivity meant that, even as a transmission belt, wages were more inflationary than in the past.

Organized labor must be shown a plan sufficiently specified that its fairness is demonstrated. Labor is familiar with the price equation reasoning that since prices in the aggregate do not outpace wages, wage controls alone will produce price stability. But they also know that the relationship is extrapolated from periods when there were no wage controls, and under wage controls the program could turn into a mechanism to reduce real wages and increase the share going to capital. They weren't born yesterday. The problem has always been and still remains what kind of quid pro quo could be offered that did not produce allocational inefficiencies, distortions, and inequities.

Let us speculate about one package that could be offered to labor as a quid pro quo for an incentive anti-inflation scheme that would put downward pressure on wages. And let us assume a plan were offered which would be symmetrical on wages and prices, such as one that relied on value added on net sales, or a symmetrical TIP scheme.[7]

Although the quid pro quo we describe is only a conjecture, we believe it deserves serious investigation. That the quid pro quo described below has not been offered before may be because it would have been deemed politically infeasible as a matter of congressional realities. We will return to this point. But note well that we are talking about a change in policy regime, and remember the hilarity that would have attended a presentation by a monetarist a few years back that put forward the idea that politicians could tolerate the costs of the Great Monetarist Experiment and live to tell the tale.

Organized labor conceivably would support an anti-inflation policy mix that incorporated direct restraints on wage increases if it also included: (1) regulation of health prices along with extension of health insurance coverage to approximately 25 million Americans now lacking it; (2) greater progressivity in the tax system; (3) increased aid to education and job training; (4) Keynesian high employment policies;

(5) buffer stocks in grains and oil for use in fighting inflationary pressures in those markets that are not linked to long-term changes in supply-demand relationships. The key question is whether a coalition can be led to see food and fuel prices in terms of cost pressures on business directly, or indirectly through wages, in the same way as increased health insurance premiums have only recently been seen as an unacceptable pressure on labor cost.

What is the political feasibility of the package just named? We have just sketched a proposal that would engage the bitter opposition of some of the most powerful lobbies that stalk Congress—the oil lobby, the agribusiness lobby (though not the family farmer), the health lobbies, and the ideological and broad spectrum business lobbies that push for smaller taxes on the wealthy. Congressmen not only seek support but also seek to avoid active opposition that targets their electoral demise. These lobbies would certainly be likely to target for political extinction congressmen who sought such a program, unless there were a well-organized countervailing business-labor coalition that could protect and assure the requisite number of congressmen and senators. From which it follows that a fundamentally new and non-monetarist approach to fighting inflation over the long run will require an unusual exercise of political leadership.

But now consider the political feasibility of the package a bit further. The interest sensitive and dollar sensitive industries and labor are not paper tigers. Nor it is obvious that a wedge could not be driven between the business community in general and those narrow interests—oil, agribusiness, and health in particular—who benefit most from inflation. Our case for the political feasibility of this quid pro quo rests on the possibility that political entrepeneurs could drive in that wedge, and on the likelihood that, after all the pain and grief of the Great Monetarist Experiment, continued inflationary pressures will require still more contractionary monetary policy that may drive many politically influential elites in search of an alternative. A realistic appraisal requires a story of power and of countervailing power and the dynamics thereof.

There is another extremely interesting implication of such a quid pro quo regarding the political feasibility of an incentive anti-inflation policy. Professor Tobin has pointed out recently (Tobin 1984) that incentive schemes cannot contain excess aggregate demand inflation. TIP or MAP schemes cannot fix prices in auction markets such as obtain in commodities. And these schemes cannot evade the direct consequences of shifts in the real terms of international trade. If separate policies to control the inflationary causes or effects of these kinds of problems are packaged with the incentive scheme chosen as optimal, the chances are far greater that such a scheme will be credible and therefore would be adopted. If buffer stocks stabilized grain and oil prices and regulation controlled health care prices, it would be apparent to all that the pressures, real and expectational, on an incentive scheme would be greatly reduced. Incentives to evade or cheat on a TIP or MAP scheme could be reduced a great deal if real and expected inflation were thereby reduced a great deal. The consequent effects on attitudes would make much greater the political feasibility of an incentive scheme experiment.

Let us try to be practical. We will not have grounds for believing that a non-monetarist policy can be institutionalized in the United States unless we can specify the potential bargain that must be struck for legislative action to occur. The program must be politically sustainable amid the inflationary shocks of a turbulent world.

There are two missing ingredients to this tale of a politically feasible quid pro quo or potential bargain. The two ingredients are closely interrelated. The first is political entrepreneurship. The second is the actual production of an economically efficient anti-incentive policy plan that can eliminate Robespierre's problem—that can specify the costs of the program sufficiently in advance to prevent the hostility of potential supporters and beneficiaries. There is little doubt in our minds that political entrepreneurship will be forthcoming in abundance if, and only if, a viable plan is produced.

The Birthing of an Optimal Incentive Anti-inflation Scheme

Before we turn to the task of trying to understand what institutional processes would accelerate the development of a viable plan around which support can be rallied, if in fact a viable plan can be produced, there are prior questions to be dealt with.

First, the perception, correct or not, that past incomes policies have been failures is deeply held. That implies there will be much greater resistance than in the past to proposals for a new incomes policy experiment. As a consequence such proposals may have to be much more explicitly drawn before they will win support or even acquiescence. We do not rule out a crisis that will provide an opening for policy experimentation. But we believe that statutory authority from Congress would be necessary. Even in a crisis it is not clear that the much more ideologically conservative congress we have now and can expect in the near future would easily delegate more than temporary power for any sort of price regulation without a plan of how that power would be used.

Second, we believe that incubating a viable plan within a presidential administration would be far more difficult today than in the past. Barry Bosworth (1981) has made this argument powerfully in relationship to economic policy making in general within the executive branch. His main points along with some of our own are as follows. Economic policy making in the executive branch is much more fragmented today than in the 1960s. Many more agencies are now organized to participate. Consensus is much harder to achieve. A president is faced therefore with many more sources of expert advice, and without a mechanism for achieving consensus must often choose among sharply divergent views from advisors who do not feel personally responsible for the outcomes of decisions. This cacaphony that a president encounters results in some measure from the breakdown of the quality and experience of the bureaucracy. This breakdown has resulted from the vast expansion of the political appointee layer of the bureaucracy under Nixon (Heclo 1977) and Carter and the attack on "neutral competence" by Nixon and Reagan (Nathan 1983). The resulting timidity of many in the career bureaucracy and resignations and retirements of many talented bureaucrats all adds together as a picture of an executive branch much weakened for the task of policy innovation in a controversial area. The greater dispersion of views within the economics profession as compared with the Keynesian period also makes matters more difficult.

Bosworth's argument leads us to the conclusion that, given the intricacy of putting together a viable plan that is truly sustainable, the work may not go well in the future inside a presidential administration. It is possible, however, that a special administration task force of great scope, whose members had no loyalties to other bureaucratic actors, might succeed if given enough time and resources to thoroughly consider fundamental problems. But it would have to be given great and constant support by a president with unusually clear vision. Given the problems raised by Bosworth, we ought to consider other possible sources of policy development.

Third, we believe that some proponents of a social contract approach to generating an incomes policy place too much weight on the value of negotiations, and too little weight on analyses of different policy options that should be the bases of those negotiations. A social contract is part of what is needed. But just as the Congressional Budget Office has made a great difference in congressional deliberations, so an organized analysis of options should serve the negotiations that must take place.

Of course we might merely be satisfied with the present rate of development of incomes policy. A very small group of vanguard academics on both sides of the Atlantic Ocean are carrying on research on incentive schemes. Absent some breakthrough, not yet in sight, that would allow those academics to go to policy makers and announce that they have a new basis for great confidence that an incentive scheme is viable economically and politically, something more is needed. If the costs now paid for quasi-monetarism are oppressive, then the present pace of policy development ought to be accelerated. It should be very clear that the volume of work on anti-inflation policy now carried on is tragically small in proportion to the enormous costs being paid for disinflation through present policies, assuming one believes viable alternatives can be designed.

These reasons lead us to ponder what are better and worse mechanisms for accelerating the development of anti-inflation policies.

What kinds of research are needed to produce a viable plan? By answering that question we will better grasp what would be the scope of an institutional form that would accelerate the policy development process. We think that it will not be clear for some time which if any policy scheme will turn out to be optimal. Therefore our discussion reflects the needs of exploring alternative policy options simultaneously. That alone implies a larger effort. The kinds of research needed to produce a viable plan include research into:

1. theoretical models of the dynamics of different incentive schemes;
2. wage, price, and productivity measurement problems and means of minimizing or avoiding them;
3. legal and accounting problems of different schemes;
4. problems in the behavior of particular markets and industries;
5. cross-national and historical research to increase sensitivity to problems and pressures that need to be anticipated, and to learn of techniques that have failed or improved performance; and

6. the analysis of political feasibility problems viewed analytically and dynamically. (Problems of Type 6 involve discounting present political perceptions in favor of exploring potential bargains as constrained by governmental and private institutional decision-making processes, structures, and forces.)

Integrating these different kinds of research will require institutionally integrating experts from these different research areas — a very tall order even if academics and others participate while remaining primarily at their present posts. In general, since in the past temporary government agencies have always been used and subsequently disbanded, there is an absence in government or in any other place of institutionalized memory of past anti-inflation policy experiences. If all these kinds of research really should be integrated to make the production of a viable plan likely, then an effort limited primarily to a project with any existing government agency as presently constituted looks too narrow. It might be worthwhile, for example, to examine the kind of questions not addressed when the Council of Economic Advisors under Carter tried to hammer out a TIP policy. We suspect that, for example, there was not enough time or resources or the necessary mix of experts to tackle in a systematic and innovative way some of the areas just mentioned, not least the problems of political dynamics.

Outside of a presidential administration's effort, all other attempts at policy development probably look like a cottage industry. But we wonder if that is the end of the matter. We believe that resources exist in this society that could be tapped to bring together on a continuing basis the needed efforts. We believe it falls to those academic and other statesmen whose concerns and convictions lead them to place great value on the further development of incentive anti-inflation policies to systematically explore ways to initiate an accelerated policy development effort. Leading economists should be encouraged to explore with key senators, congressmen, business and labor leaders and heads of foundations and research institutes, both academic and independent, the possibility of a research consortium. The stakes of failure and of success seem proportionate to such an effort. At present there is a bottleneck in the policy development process.

Every Democratic administration since World War II and one Republican administration has adopted some form of an incomes policy. The same forces and pressures that produced these past incomes policy episodes very likely will lead the next Democratic administration to seek an innovative and non-monetarist anti-inflation policy. Our deepest fear is that the next effort will be an execise in ad hocery in response to a crisis, because of inadequate policy development prior to the time when the policy must be used. Those who see the inflation problem as rooted in the structure of advanced industrial economies, and who believe that a monetary ceiling will not keep inflation down at acceptable costs, ought to think hard about how to institutionalize accelerated development of non-monetarist anti-inflation policies.

NOTES

1. For a view that fiscal policy was not as stimulative as many have believed see Eisner and Pieper (1984).
2. Just before the November 1982 election the unemployment rate went over 10 percent, reaching 10.7 percent a few months later. Reversing a secular decline, voter turnout was much greater in 1982 than in the previous midterm election of 1978, and reflected the recession. The Democrats gained 26 seats in the House of Representatives, about twice the average of only 12 seats since World War II for the party out of the White House. An exit poll by NBC News and the Associated Press exit poll demonstrated that President Reagan's program was the major issue. Those who rated inflation as the most important economic issue voted Republican 60–34 percent. Those who put jobs first voted 69 percent Democrat and 25 percent Republican (Schneider 1982). It is also worth noting that 20 percent of the nation's workers suffered at least one spell of unemployment in 1982. A political calculation would add to some part of that number affected family members and those afraid of losing their jobs.
3. According to interviews with senior Republican campaign officials the summer after the November election (Clymer 1983).
4. There is now concern in the Agriculture Department and in the grain trade that the combination of the Reagan Administration's PIK program and the drought has made the balance between supplies of most major commodities and demand too taut. "Bad weather this year could lead to shortages and skyrocketing prices" (Sinclair 1984).
5. Lerner's remarks appear in Okun and Perry (1978: 255–269).
6. Pechman's remarks appear in Okun and Perry (1978: 154–158).
7. For a wide-ranging review of alternative schemes that reflects recent and more advanced work, see Colander and Koford (1983).

REFERENCES

Bosworth, Barry. 1981. "Re-establishing an Economic Consensus: An Impossible Agenda?" *Brookings General Series Reprint 362.* Washington, D.C.: The Brookings Institution.

Bosworth, Barry P., and Robert Z. Lawrence. 1982. *Commodity Prices and the New Inflation.* Washington, D.C.: The Brookings Institution.

Cagan, Phillip, and William Fellner. 1983. "Tentative Lessons for the Recent Disinflationary Effort." *Brookings Papers on Economic Activity* 2:603–608.

Clymer, Adam. 1983. "The Economic Basis For 'Throwing the Bums Out' in the 1980 and 1982 American Elections," Paper presented at the 1983 Annual Meeting of the American Political Science Association, Chicago.

Colander, David C. 1981. U.S. Congress, Joint Economic Committee, *Incentive Anti-Inflation Plans.* May 5.

Colander, David C., and Kenneth J. Koford. 1983. "Tax and Market Incentive Plans to Fight Inflation." In *Economic Perspectives*, edited by Maurice B. Ballabon.

Eisner, Robert, and Paul J. Pieper. 1984. "A New View of the Federal Debt and Budget Deficits." *American Economic Review* 74, no. 1 (March): 11–29.

Flanagan, Robert J.; David W. Soskice; and Lloyd Ulman. *Unionism, Economic Stabilization, and Incomes Policy: European Experience.* Washington, D.C.: The Brookings Institution.

Gordon, Robert. 1981. *Macroeconomics.* Boston: Little, Brown.

———. 1981. "Output Fluctuations and Gradual Price Adjustment." *Journal of Economic Literature*, 29 (June):493–530.

———. 1984. *Macroeconomics*, 3rd ed. Boston: Little, Brown.

Gordon, Robert J., and Stephen R. King. 1982. "The Output Cost of Disinflation in Traditional and Autoregressive Models." *Brookings Papers on Economic Activity 1.*

Heclo, Hugh. 1977. *A Government of Strangers.* Washington, D.C.: The Brookings Institution.

Heclo, Hugh, and Rudolph G. Penner. 1983. "Fiscal and Political Strategy in the Reagan Administration." In *The Reagan Presidency: An Early Assessment*, edited by Fred I. Greenstein. Baltimore: Johns Hopkins University Press.

Hibbs, Douglas A., Jr. 1982. "President Reagan's Mandate from the 1980 Elections: A Shift to the Right?" *American Politics Quarterly 10* (4), October:387–420.

Jackman, R.; R. Layard; and C. Pissarides. 1983. "Policies for Reducing the Natural Rate of Unemployment." Centre for Labour Economics, London School of Economics, Discussion Paper No. 587.

Jacobson, Gary C., and Samuel Kernell. 1983. *Strategy and Choice in Congressional Elections*, 2nd ed. New Haven, Conn.: Yale University Press.

Kiewiet, D. Roderick. 1983. *Macroeconomics and Micropolitics: The Electoral Effects of Economic Issues.* Chicago: University of Chicago Press.

Layard, R. 1982. "Is Incomes Policy the Answer to Unemployment?" *Economica 49*:219–240.

Lerner, Abba, and David Colander. 1980. *MAP: A Market Anti-Inflation Plan.* New York: Harcourt Brace Jovanovich.

Markus, Gregory B. "Political Attitudes during an Election Year: A Report on the 1980 NES Panel Study." *American Political Science Review 76* (3), September:538–560.

Meade, James. 1981. "Fiscal Devices for the Control of Inflation." *Atlantic Economic Journal 9* (4), December:2.

———. 1982. *Wage-Fixing.* London: George Allen and Unwin.

Mitchell, Daniel J.B. 1981. "Alternatives to Current Anti-Inflation Policy: A Look at Previous Suggestions and a Not-So-Modest Proposal." In *Controlling Inflation: Studies in Wage/Price Policy.* Washington, D.C.: Center for Democratic Policy.

Nathan, Richard P. 1983. "The Reagan Presidency in Domestic Affairs." In *The Reagan Presidency: An Early Assessment*, edited by Fred I. Greenstein. Baltimore: Johns Hopkins University Press.

Newbery, David M.G., and Joseph E. Stiglitz. 1981. *The Theory of Commodity Price Stabilization: A Study in the Economics of Risk.* New York: Oxford University Press.

Okun, Arthur M. 1981. *Prices and Quantities.* Washington, D.C.: The Brookings Institution.

Okun, Arthur M., and George L. Perry. 1978. *Curing Chronic Inflation.* Washington, D.C.: The Brookings Institution.

Peretz, Paul. 1983. *The Political Economy of Inflation in the United States.* Chicago: University of Chicago Press.

Perry, George L. 1983. "What Have We Learned about Disinflation?" *Brookings Papers on Economic Activity 2.*

Pine, Art. 1983. "Fed's Chief Took on Big Role in Attacking World's Financial Ills." *Wall Street Journal*, March 14, p. 1.

Pissarides, Christopher. 1983. "Tax-Based Incomes Policies and the Long-Run Inflation-Unemployment Trade-Off." Centre for Labour Economics, London School of Economics, Discussion Paper No. 146.

Poole, William. 1982. "Federal Reserve Operating Procedures: A Survey and Evaluation of the Historical Record since October 1979." *Journal of Money, Credit, and Banking 14* (4), November, Part 2.

Rees, Albert. 1978. "New Policies to Fight Inflation: Sources of Skepticism." In *Curing Chronic Inflation*, edited by Arthur M. Okun and George L. Perry. Washington, C.C.: The Brookings Institution, pp. 217–241.

Schneider, William. 1982. "Reaganomics Was on the Voters' Minds but Their Verdict Was Far from Clear." *National Journal*, November 6, pp. 1892–1893.

Seidman, Laurence S. 1981. "A Tax-Based Incomes Policy to Reduce Inflation without Recession (and Other Alternatives of Reaganomics)." In *Controlling Inflation: Studies in Wage/Price Policy*. Washington, D.C.: Center for Democratic Policy.

Sinclair, Ward. 1984. "It's Quittin' Time for Costly, Controversial PIK Farm Program." *Washington Post*, January 8, p. A3.

Slitor, Richard E. 1979. "Implementation and Design of Tax-Based Incomes Policies." *American Economic Review 69,* May:212–215.

Tobin, James. 1984. "A Social Compact for Restraint." *Challenge*, March-April.

Tufte, Edward R. 1975. "Determinants of the Outcomes of Midterm Congressional Elections." *American Political Science Review 69*(3), September:812–826.

Volcker, Paul A. 1984. "Facing Up to the Twin Deficits." *Challenge*, March/April. (Excerpted from congressional testimony of February 7, 1984.

Wallich, Henry C., and Sidney Weintraub. 1971. "A Tax-Based Incomes Policy." *Journal of Economic Issues 5*, June:1–19.

Weitzman, Martin. 1983. "Some Macroeconomic Implications of Alternative Compensation Systems." *Economic Journal 93*:763–783.

Index

About the Contributors

Benjamin Bental is Senior Lecturer in the Faculty of Industrial Engineering and Management, Technion-Israel Institute of Technology. He received his Ph.D. from the University of Manitoba and his research interests include the intergenerational distribution of wealth and the microfoundations of macroeconomics.

Clive Bull is Associate Professor of Economics at New York University. He received his Ph.D. from UCLA, and his research interests are in the economics of information and game theory.

David Colander is currently the Christian A. Johnson Professor of Economics at Middlebury College. He is the coauthor (with Abba Lerner) of *MAP: A Market Anti-Inflation Plan*, and editor of *Neoclassical Political Economy: The Analysis of Rent-Seeking and DUP Activities*.

Paul Davidson is Professor of Economics at Rutgers University. He received his Ph.D. from the University of Pennsylvania and is the author of several books on macroeconomics and money. He is currently editor of the *Journal of Post-Keynesian Economics*.

Kenneth Koford is Assistant Professor of Economics at the University of Delaware. He holds degrees from Yale and UCLA and has done research on efficient vote-trading in legislatures and on incentive policies to reduce inflation.

247

Noah M. Meltz is Professor of Economics at the University of Toronto and Director of its Centre for Industrial Relations. He received his Ph.D. from Princeton University.

Jeffrey B. Miller is Associate Professor of Economics at the University of Delaware.

Steven Plaut is Lecturer in the Faculty of Industrial Engineering and Management at Technion-Israel Institute of Technology. He received his Ph.D. from Princeton University and his research interests include the economics of inflation.

Jerrold E. Schneider is Associate Professor of Political Science at the University of Delaware. He is author of *Ideological Coalitions in Congress* and has been a Research Fellow at the The Brookings Institution. He was a National Endowment for the Humanities Fellow in 1976.

Andrew Schotter is Professor of Economics at New York University and Associate Director of NYU's C.V. Starr Center for Applied Economics. He is the author of *The Economic Theory of Social Institutions*.

About the Editors

Shlomo Maital is Associate Professor of Economics in the Faculty of Industrial Engineering at Technion-Israel Institute of Technology. He has been Visiting Lecturer at the Woodrow Wilson School of Public and International Affairs, Princeton University, and Visiting Professor of Applied Economics at the Sloan School of Management, MIT. He is the author of *Minds, Markets, & Money*, coeditor of *Lagging Productivity Growth*, and coauthor of *Economic Games People Play*. He is a founder of the Society for the Advancement of Behavioral Economics.

Irwin Lipnowski is Associate Professor of Economics at the University of Manitoba. He received his Ph.D. from the London School of Economics and was the Lady Davis Post-Doctoral Fellow at the Hebrew University of Jerusalem and Visiting Senior Fellow at Princeton University. His chief research interest is on the application of game theory to social and industrial conflict. He is also an international chess master and has represented Canada on its Olympic Chess Team.